The Enduring Effects of Education

Herbert H. Hyman,
Charles R. Wright, and
John Shelton Reed

D0001615

The University of Chicago Press / Chicago and London

HERBERT H. HYMAN is professor of sociology at Wesleyan University. He is the author of numerous books, including *Survey Design and Analysis, Political Socialization*, and *Interviewing in Social Research* (University of Chicago Press).
CHARLES R. WRIGHT is professor of communications and sociology at the University of Pennsylvania. He is the author of *Mass Communication: A Sociological Perspective* and co-author with Herbert H. Hyman of *Inducing Social Change in Developing Communities*.
JOHN SHELTON REED is associate professor of sociology at the University of North Carolina at Chapel Hill. His previous book is called *The Enduring South*.

Manufacture of this book was supported by a generous grant from the Spencer Foundation.

The University of Chicago Press, Chicago 60637
The University of Chicago Press, Ltd., London

Library of Congress Cataloging in Publication Data
Hyman, Herbert Hiram, 1918–
    The enduring effects of education.

    Includes index.
    1. Education—United States. 2. Academic achievement.
3. Learning and scholarship. I. Wright, Charles Robert, 1927–
II. Reed, John Shelton. III. Title.
LA217.H86   370'.973   75–9860
ISBN 0–226–36549–2

In Memory of I. L. Kandel
Whose Influence on Education Endures

Contents

Acknowledgments

Secondary analysis of existing sample surveys is a most economical form of research, when compared with the cost of undertaking new surveys. Nevertheless, it is a costly enterprise when conducted on a large scale. The dimensions of our study far exceeded our own resources. We express our appreciation to the Spencer Foundation and to its president, Dr. H. Thomas James, for generous support and encouragement.

The surveys, now conveniently available in archives, were the scientific wealth we tapped, and we thank the Inter-University Consortium for Political Research, the National Opinion Research Center and its librarian, Patrick Bova, and the Roper Public Opinion Research Center and its director, Philip K. Hastings, for their cooperation and help in making their data available.

The volume of data processing seemed almost insurmountable to us at times, and this phase would not have been brought to completion so economically and efficiently without the fine services provided by the Institute for Research in Social Science, University of North Carolina, Chapel Hill. We thank the staff, particularly Richard Rockwell and Sue Dodd, for their contribution, and express a special debt to Thomas Sloan, who rendered careful and continuing services as programmer during this phase of our study.

For excellent research assistance at various stages of our inquiry we thank Carolyn Arnold, Sally Healey, March Kessler, Linda Park, Deanne Shapiro Diesenhaus, and Mary Tanner.

For expert advice on special technical matters, we acknowledge the guidance of Lawrence Cremin and Richard Link; and for carrying the burden of typing a lengthy manuscript, we thank Irene Spinnler.

1 Introduction

That education imparts knowledge and creates receptivity to further knowledge has been the universal hope. Reasonable men have differed about other goals of education, the best instructional means for achieving such ends, and the pace at which learning should proceed, but surely all share Emerson's view that "the child shall be taught . . . the rudiments of knowledge and, at last, the ripest results of art and science."[1] Indeed, the justification, to quote Emerson again, for having the learners "taken up by the state, and taught at the public cost" is that they and ultimately society will reap the benefits of knowledge.

The measurement of the harvest is the critical question. Whenever studies of students in some schools, in some places, at some time, have found it to be small, complaints have mounted and debate has begun on the accuracy, meaning, and generalizability of the findings. What may be surprising is how little unambiguous and generalizable evidence exists. Jencks and his associates, in their recent reexamination and reanalysis of studies, remark on the effects of schooling per se on pupils: "Perhaps the most astonishing feature of this whole inquiry is that virtually no research has been done on these issues, either by defenders of schools or by their critics. As a result, our conclusions are all based on problematic inferences of uncertain validity. The most we can claim is that such evidence is better than nothing."[2]

Others may regard that judgment as too sweeping and severe. They may point with pride to monumental inquiries begun in the 1960s that now provide a wide variety of achievement test scores on hundreds of thousands of children. However good such research may be and however better it becomes in the future in the quality and generalizability of the sampling, the accuracy and breadth of measurements, and the power of the design to isolate the net effects of schooling, it is bound to have one severe limitation. Because only the *young* are incorporated into most such research, it never can trace how long and how much the effects of education endure in the *adult* years. It is *relatively* easy to measure individuals while they are still in school or college

1

or at the point of leaving. They are captive subjects. Once they have left, they become fugitives. Tracking them down is difficult and expensive and few attempt it. Research on the effects of education is beset by many problems. The prime requirement, however, in any study of long-term effects is to catch the adult population.

Inquiries, almost without exception, have lowered their sights to a young target group that is easier to hit and sample and have thereby limited their findings to immediate or short-term rather than enduring effects. Thus in 1969, when Feldman and Newcomb had completed their encyclopedic review of 1,500 studies on *The Impact of College on Students*, they remarked: "College is supposed to do something to students, and that something refers primarily to consequences that make a difference *in later years*. There is, therefore, a very special irony in the fact that few studies of *post-college* persistence of such effects, especially those justifying confident conclusions, have been reported."[3] The few studies they cite may permit confident conclusions but hardly broad generalizations, since they refer to samples from particular colleges or, on very rare occasions, some ad hoc set of colleges.

Occasional studies that are exceptions to the rule only prove the point. The tests routinely administered by the military services to screen recruits have provided large-scale data for various analyses of the effects of education. Although adults are included, once again, these investigations turn out to be studies of *captive* groups, and the results perforce refer mainly to males, young and close in time to their educational experiences.[4]

One current, huge, and lavishly funded inquiry, *The National Assessment of Educational Progress*, has departed from the usual target and aimed much higher. The study makes a final compelling case for our argument, and its scope therefore deserves brief review. It "is the first description on a nation-wide basis of various educational attainments of groups of Americans," showing "what information people have, and also what misinformation people have."[5] Yet, here again, "people" generally must be read to mean *children*, since the bulk of the inquiry, about 90,000 tested individuals, involved three discrete age-groups, those who were nine years old, thirteen years old, and seventeen years old in 1969. By incorporating a fourth nationwide sample of about 10,000 young adults—more specifically, members of the cohort aged from twenty-six to thirty-five in 1969—the study averted the common fate.

We have finally escaped from our previous confinement to children, but we are far from being free to generalize about all American adults. At best, the conclusions refer to educational effects that have endured for about fifteen years into adult life, but there is a less obvious limitation as well. Those conclusions are limited to one particular cohort, those between twenty-six and thirty-five in 1969, who began their education in the 1940s and who therefore may reflect only the schools of that one historical period. Fully aware of these limitations and concerned to describe the "progress of learning" over time, the National Assessment staff has planned for future periodic measurements that "will take more than a decade." It is not clear whether all the cohorts in the first study will be traced and measured again, thus revealing their progress up to a point when they have matured a bit longer, or whether new cohorts, the next generations of youth, will be measured at those same four stages of life. In any case, such findings on effects that endure into the early or middle years of maturity and that are generalizable at best to adjacent generations who are products of the schools of the present and recent past will demand, as noted in the Foreword to the first report, "continuous operation, continuous funding and—patience" (p. x).

Must we really wait so long and so patiently, hoping that the millions necessary for continuous funding will be provided? What uncertainty surrounds the entire enterprise![6] The only certainty—if it all should come to pass—is that we will know nothing about older adults and earlier generations. Is there no way of measuring the harvest from the seeds of knowledge implanted long ago by the schools of the distant past? There is. The approach through "secondary analysis" is circuitous and all the aspects of the complex design involved will unfold slowly only as we go along. Although imperfect, the justification is not simply Jencks's canon, that it is a bit better than nothing, but that it is far better. Since this is one of the first large-scale attempts to apply the general approach to the study of enduring effects of education, improvements can be anticipated, and we ourselves shall have some recommendations to make. Thus it should get even better in the future.

MEASURING ENDURING EFFECTS AMONG ADULTS BY SECONDARY ANALYSIS OF NATIONAL SAMPLE SURVEYS

In the United States, surveys of large and representative samples of the *adult*, noninstitutionalized population of the nation have been a continuing enterprise for almost forty years. If we limit ourselves to the period beginning about 1950, by which point the major agencies already were using improved sampling designs based on probability models, we span over twenty years during which thousands of surveys measuring millions of individuals were conducted. This period also coincides with the emergence and growth of sample surveying in other countries that by now has also produced thousands of surveys.

These studies, of course, deal with an endless variety of topics, often trivial in character, and many of them do not incorporate measures of knowledge plus the other kinds of measures required to illuminate our problem. But out of the thousands of surveys, even the small fraction that meet the specifications will yield, as we shall see, a very large data base.

The possibility of secondary analysis—of extracting findings on topics other than those that were the primary focus of the original inquiries—had long appealed to scholars familiar with the omnibus character of many surveys. They were aware that even a survey focused on a trivial topic could well contain as an incidental by-product other data valuable for the study of fundamental problems or that the very data at the focus of inquiry, seemingly of transient importance, could, from another vantage point, be of strategic importance later. Consequently, in recent years an archival movement has begun, and the surveys and background documents have been deposited in various data banks, organized for easy retrieval of materials. Many secondary analyses have already been accomplished and establish the merits of the general approach, but only a few have dealt with knowledge or the enduring effects of education. Investigations by Glenn, Schramm and Wade, Stember, and Withey and his colleagues are the main examples. These pioneers have inspired us, but our inquiry has explored somewhat special problems by new paths.[7]

Sampling the Adult Populations from Different Times

From the files of the Gallup Poll, of the National Opinion Research Center, University of Chicago, and of the Survey Research Center, University of Michigan, we have drawn fifty-four surveys, each designed to approach the ideal of an unbiased sample of the adult population at large at the time of the original inquiry. In the aggregate, this yielded a pool of about 80,000 individuals on whom measurements of various relevant variables had already been obtained. All these surveys were conducted during 1949–71. They were chosen, as best we could, to provide big enough clumps of surveys around four points in time so as to assess the patterns of several historical periods and to document uniformities and changes. For example, a pool of about 25,000 cases from fifteen surveys provides the estimates of the knowledge of the adult population of the late 1960s. The smallest pool, of about 11,000 cases drawn from nine surveys, describes the population of the late 1950s. (The exact sizes of the various groups are presented in table 7 in Appendix A.)

Since the dependent variables that are indicative of the effects of education are not spread equally through all the surveys of a period— some are richer than others—a more precise way to date the findings is by reference to the temporal distribution of measures. In the first period, the central point around which the measures spread is 1951. For the second period, it is 1956; the measures are almost equally and exclusively in the years 1955 and 1957. In the third period, the center falls in the year 1963; and in the last period, in the year 1968.

Inevitably, all sampling of human populations departs in practice from the ideal. One can never achieve the perfection of the original design, but only approximate it. The surveys of very long ago were neither operated nor designed so well as the more recent ones. For the period we have chosen, however, there is no reason to assume that a new and specially conducted survey necessarily involves better sampling than one already conducted; and there is every reason to feel that nine or fifteen surveys provide a much greater margin of safety than one survey. Some misfortune may fall upon the most well designed survey, some insidious error may creep in, and by chance alone an unbiased and well-executed survey may just be that one in a hundred that produces a result that is very far from the truth. It is most unlikely that anyone will have a run of bad luck nine times in a row, or that anyone would be so perverse or foolish as to choose only the worst surveys. Our fifty-odd surveys, like all others, are subject to some biases and errors in sampling, but we have hedged against the risk. The magnitude of error and, more important, how we have contained it so that it does not distort the conclusions, remain to be considered. For the moment, let us assume that we have taken the first step necessary for generalizing about the enduring effects of education by obtaining large and satisfactory samples of the adult populations over a considerable span of time.

Locating Educational Strata

Consider the next step to be taken toward assessing the enduring effects of education. The amount of formal schooling the adult has had is a routine datum enumerated with considerable refinement in every one of our surveys. Indeed, American survey agencies, sensing its explanatory power, have enumerated education on almost every single survey. Ironically, survey agencies in some other countries have eliminated measurement of the variable from almost all their inquiries, and this has severely limited the choice of a country for the comparative study we shall present on the enduring effects of other educational systems.

By referring to these data, we have isolated within the total pool unbiased samples of the respective subpopulations (again recognizing this as only an approximation to the ideal) who have completed various levels of education in all the schools and colleges of the country. We can thus make generalizations about these several groups. If their members are still alive and at large, they must fall into the samples of the adults of the nation. To be sure, in any one sample by chance we may not have obtained the correct number of those who came from a particular type of school, for example, parochial school in Louisiana; and the size of the cell representing some rare type of individual, for example, those who went to college in 1910, might be too small for special analysis. However, we have, again, hedged against these risks by using many surveys. Thus, our fifty or so surveys, taken together, yield about 8,000 college graduates for analysis, and the surveys of the late 1950s, the smallest pool on which we have to draw, yield almost 1,000 college graduates. The other educational strata are, of course, much larger; the exact figures are presented in table 7.

Locating Alumni from Specific Classes

Consider the next stage along the way toward a solution of the problem. In every one of the surveys, age is enumerated and coded to the exact year. (By contrast, in many other American surveys, age is only requested or recorded in gross categories, and in some foreign surveys it is only guessed at by the interviewer in gross terms.) As our first step, we have eliminated from all analyses individuals under age twenty-five, thereby ensuring that most if not all the adults studied have completed their formal education. It would hardly be fair to include among "enduring" effects those which stem from continuing, present exposure to school. Equally important, this exclusion solves a problem implicit in the fact that our surveys, like most others, perforce limit themselves to sampling the noninstitutionalized population. Since a fairly large and perhaps distinctive segment of adults in their early twenties may be members of the military or in residential colleges, any generalization about all young adults—more precisely, about all young adults with given levels of education—made on the basis of samples of the noninstitutionalized could be in error.

Similarly, we have eliminated all individuals over age seventy-two. In part, the same reasoning dictated this decision. Since a considerable portion of the very old are in institutions, one would not want to venture generalizations about all the oldest adults on the basis of the kind of sampling designs employed in the surveys. It is also important that some unknown portion of those oldest adults who are living in ordinary homes and are therefore approached in the course of the survey may excuse themselves or have to be excluded from the sample because of illness, deafness, blindness, or infirmity, or who, if interviewed, may not function at their best or normal capacities.[8] Findings obtained from them might not be a fair sample or fair test.

Alternatively, some may argue that those well enough to be at home and interviewed despite their longevity are a peculiar and hardy breed and hardly a sample from which to generalize.

Seventy-two is not a magic age that provides absolute justification for the cutoff point in our studies. We could have set the limit lower. By not setting it higher, we have not pursued the question of enduring effects out to the farthest reaches of time but out to as far as we dared. Findings on the "oldest" adults pertain essentially to individuals in their sixties and never older than seventy-two. (The size of the various groups used in our analyses, as mentioned earlier and throughout the report, refer only to those aged between twenty-five and seventy-two. The pools of cases prior to the exclusions were considerably larger.)

Reference to the age of those included provides the key to the solution of much of our problem. The comparisons made between educational strata are always *age-specific* and thus can be "dated" historically. For example, when we compare those with contrasted schooling, all of whom were sixty-one to seventy-two (one of the age-groups employed) in the surveys conducted in the *early 1950s*, we are tracing the effects of the schooling they had had forty years ago or more, specifically in individuals who are the products of the colleges around 1910 and of the schools around the turn of the century. Similarly, when we compare those with contrasted schooling, all of whom were sixty-one to seventy-two in the surveys conducted *in the late 1960s*, we have located individuals who also are removed from their education by forty years—but we are tracing the products of the schools and colleges circa 1930. Thus, either one of these comparisons by itself would not permit a *generalization* about the effects of different amounts of education that have endured for forty years or more. The findings may only reflect the particular character of the schools and environing conditions of the period in which that birth cohort developed, learned, matured, and grew old. But, since there are *four* such cohorts, each of whose members reached the age sixty-one to seventy-two at a different point corresponding to the dates of the four clumps of surveys, we can establish both the uniformities that endure to that advanced stage of life and the variations that represent special circumstances in the schooling and life course of a cohort.

Four age-groups or life stages have been examined in each of the sets of surveys clumped at the four points between 1949 and 1971. In addition to the oldest adults, the "young adults" are represented by those aged twenty-five to thirty-six, and two intermediate stages along life's course are represented by those aged thirty-seven to forty-eight and forty-nine to sixty. In each one of these age-specific comparisons, the individuals are equated in the life stage reached and the temporal distance from their education but are contrasted in the level of schooling, the effects of which have then been traced out that far into maturity. Again, the uniformities and variations can be observed by examining the pattern across the four sets of surveys, in the four cohorts that have reached a common age at different historical times.

Within a *single* survey or a single set of surveys from the same point in time, for example, 1970, a comparison across the four age-groups of those with a given level of education, for example, college, is a synthetic, quasi-developmental picture. The wearing away, persistence, or consolidation of the effects of education with aging seems under scrutiny, but there is some obscurity in any *one* such comparison. The groups have reached successively advanced stages of life, but the same birth cohort is not being tracked as it moves through time. The youngest adults in 1970 are the products of the colleges of the 1960s and represent the World War II generation. The oldest adults represent the World War I generation and the colleges of the 1930s. However, repeating such comparisons within the four different sets of surveys widely spaced in time helps resolve the obscurity. If one were to find that the pattern of "change" was uniform, no matter what historical period of education was implicated in the experiences of a given age-group, it would suggest that the process revealed was genuine and fundamental. The obscurity in such comparisons can never be completely resolved, especially for one reason still to be presented, but the conclusions from a series of such analyses are far from flimsy.

There is a way, however, to eliminate the obscurity in the picture of change in the effect of education with aging obtained when age categories are juxtaposed. The four sets of surveys fortunately are spaced in time so that the *same* birth cohort can be tracked down again at a later stage in life. The surveys of the early 1950s and the early 1960s are about twelve years apart, as are the surveys of the late 1950s and late 1960s. Thus the adults who were twenty-five to thirty-six in the first set and those who were thirty-seven to forty-eight in the third set are members of the very same cohort, caught at those two points in their growth. Those who were twenty-five to thirty-six in the second set are located, when they have reached thirty-seven to forty-eight in the fourth set of surveys. In this fashion we have obtained *two independent tests*, based on two different birth cohorts, of whether the effects of earlier education endure through the dozen years of aging in that phase of life. Similarly, we obtain two tests of what happens to a cohort as it ages over the segment of life bounded by the age categories thirty-seven to forty-eight and forty-nine to sixty, or the categories forty-nine to sixty and sixty-one to seventy-two.

Our surveys are not a nationwide longitudinal study of the *same individuals* measured at several points in time, but they yield something almost as good—equivalent national samples of a given birth cohort with a given level of education, representative of it at two stages of life. As the group moves further and further away from its earlier exposure to education, the process can be described—and for more than one birth cohort. To extend the evidence, a small amount of space was purchased on a 1974 national survey. Some of the instruments that had been used to measure effects in the old surveys made around 1956 were piggybacked on the new survey. Thus some cohorts could be reexamined, after almost twenty years had passed, to determine whether the effects of education endured after that longer interval and up to a point when some had reached very old ages.

All sorts of subtle problems boggle the mind as one ponders such comparisons. Since only adults are caught in the net of our surveys many years after graduation, of course, all we have are samples of the survivors of those classes who have remained alive and at large. The image of an alumni reunion of the remnants of the High School Class of 1903 or the College Class of 1907 is appropriate. There is no way the cohorts, and in turn our samples, can escape the ravages of time. The further out we go to trace the enduring effects, the greater the attrition in the original populations and in the original samples left to be surveyed. Not venturing beyond age seventy-two, the general practice we followed, surely reduces the errors in generalizing from the group that survives.[9] However, there are other ways to reduce the errors and protect the conclusions.

The race and sex of the respondent are enumerated on every one of our fifty surveys, as is done in almost all American surveys. Because whites and women live longer, the older age-groups in the total population and in *unrestricted*, representative samples are likely to differ in these respects from the younger age-groups. Then any differences observed in a cohort as it ages, or in the comparisons of young and old age-groups, could reflect changes in the social composition rather than the sheer fact of aging. However, since these two characteristics were measured, they could be controlled in various ways in the comparisons, and thus the major sources of attrition cannot confound the conclusions.

All nonwhite respondents in our original samples were excluded before any analyses were begun, just as those under twenty-five and over seventy-two were excluded. As a consequence, all the generalizations refer only to the *white* population—a limitation, to be sure, but eliminating once and for all the danger that any of the comparisons reflect "racial" differences rather than age or educational differences. (Throughout the period under study, blacks were far less likely than whites to have attended college, and whites have had greater longevity. Thus, racial composition is not equated in any gross comparisons of age or educational groups and this leads to ambiguous findings. The "racial" differences in knowledge that may be implicated, needless to say, reflect the many handicaps blacks experienced in the pursuit of knowledge.) There were many other advantages stemming from this decision, to be reviewed later.

The loss in generalizability was the price we were willing to pay, for the time being, to simplify these first, novel and difficult, secondary analyses of the problem. Thus we have not assessed the effects produced by that part of the American educational system that perhaps has been the most glaringly deficient. However, all sorts of schools, good and bad, that have served whites are incorporated in the study. Nor have we tested the effects of education that endure through the worst deprivations and hazards that alumni may experience in the course of their later lives. The nonwhites would have provided such a test, since their life chances have been such as to dampen and depreciate the outcomes that might normally follow upon being educated. But here again, our white samples incorporate individuals in all walks of life, advantaged and disadvantaged. Some of our refined analyses will test the effects of education when various handicaps are introduced and provide tests of its staying power under such conditions.

The size of the various groups mentioned earlier and throughout the analyses refers to the samples after the exclusion of nonwhites. Although the fifty samples yield a large pool of about 80,000 white adults, the nonwhites in the aggregate would have numbered only about 8,000. Within this group, the refined subgroups of nonwhites needed for all the analyses would have been too small for us to venture confident conclusions. Among the whites, the total pool of individuals aged sixty-one to seventy-two is about 13,000. Just within the set of surveys in the late 1950s, the smallest pool, the oldest adults number close to 2,000. Since the educational attainment of the old is relatively very low, there are only about eighty college graduates within that age-group in those surveys (the smallest cell in the inquiry). The shrinkage factor of about a thousand—from 80,000 to 80—shows that some of the cells among nonwhites would have been truly microscopic, and indicates why an initial supersample must be so extravagant in size in order to yield the various subsamples required for the analysis. (In principle, it might be possible to build up a supersample large enough to permit a separate analysis for some of the cells in the black stratum.) The size of the various age and educational groupings from all the time periods are included in table 7. Most groups are substantial, and in those that are not safety lies in the fact that the results are replicated over many independent, albeit very small, samples.

There was no need to eliminate either men or women from our analyses, and to have done so would have resulted in the terrible loss of about half the sample. Instead, the influence of sex was examined by controlling it in a large series of tests wherever necessary. Thus the conclusions drawn from the various comparisons about the effect of education cannot have been distorted by the initial differences in the sex composition of age and educational groups.

The basic mode of analysis used throughout automatically solves much of the problem of the confounding of the conclusions. In gross comparisons of educational strata among adults, the differences may simply reflect age, since the old have less education. By the same token, when age-groups are grossly compared, the differences may simply reflect education. Since our basic comparisons always involve specific educational strata of a specified age, the influence of each variable is controlled in the examination of the other one.

In theory, the comparisons of educational strata and age-groups in a given time and across periods, and the findings as a cohort is traced over time in successive sets of surveys, may also be distorted to some minor degree by the past waves of immigration into the United States. The ethnic composition of the different groups may vary, as immigrants are added to or subtracted from a cohort over time, depending on the date of the surveys and the age of the members. The weight of this factor and its equivalence in the various comparisons must be considered. An obvious concern is the possibility that many of the immigrants were educated prior to their arrival in the United States. The effects implicitly attributed to *American* education thus may represent the contribution of another nation's education, and there is the further confusion that the less educated from the schools of other nations may be compared with the better educated from American colleges. However, immigration into the United States became a trickle after 1930, and the majority of those involved were already in their teens upon entry. Thus the younger adults in the surveys of the early 1960s, and all but the oldest adults in the surveys of the late 1960s, are almost all native-born. Even between 1910 and 1930, immigrants entering the United States constituted a small fraction of the total population, well under 10 percent, and thus are a small component of the samples studied in the 1950s and mainly add that small weight into the two older age-groups studied.

The problem is no cause for worry, but there is a way to isolate its effect in our comparisons. Enough of our surveys enumerated place of birth for us to make a series of tests of educational effects among only the native-born.

All of the surveys provided information on the current socio-economic position of the individual, and a substantial number also included measures of social origins, the occupation and education of parents, and religion. The exact function of such variables in the analysis will be presented later. We shall not burden the reader now with any more technical details. The basic design should already be clear. Within each of sixteen groups—four groups of adults widely contrasted in age in each of four time periods—comparisons by level of education have been made. The reader should be able to see the avenues, opened through secondary analysis, to generalizable evidence on the enduring effects of education by the multiple comparisons among these groups, all drawn from good samples of the national population. The reader can sense how time-consuming and costly it would be to create anew the long string of large national samples that would permit safe generalizations about the universes of adults who are the products of the universe of schools from more than one historical period. But the reader should also entertain the thought that there is a benefit that far outweighs the savings. One has, so to speak, turned back the calendar with the measurements from surveys conducted long ago, thereby describing populations and states of affairs that would be completely unknowable to investigators beginning new long-term studies now.

There is nothing sacred about the four age-groups and four periods examined. In secondary analysis, one has to settle for what one can find, and the four periods provided the richest clumps of high-quality surveys, spaced as widely as possible after 1950, each set of sufficient size. Given the refinement with which age was coded, we were free, in principle, to cut the continuum of age anywhere along the line and at as many points as we wished, creating few or many groups, each less or more homogeneous in life stage and experience. It was not difficult to make the reasonable decision to begin with age twenty-five and to end with age seventy-two, but the other cutting points and the restriction to four groups were a compromise that had to serve various ends. Although finer grouping would have dated the experiences better and permitted charting more points along the course, it would have reduced the numbers in each group. More groups would have increased tabulating costs and would have meant more comparisons to digest and interpret, to condense and present. As the reader will soon see, the present design yields about a thousand basic comparisons between educational levels, and each additional age-group adds another 250 to the load.

The continuum of age also should have been cut in such a way that, within the limits already set by technical constraints, the cohorts obtained were representative of contrasted types of schools and environments during their formative years. Otherwise, the four tests of enduring effects up to some life stage are really replications of one another—not that that should be discounted—rather than tests under widely varied conditions. The nature of the schools and learning environment for each of the sixteen cohorts cannot be described with exactitude, nor would it have been possible to make an exact separation between two adjacent cohorts whose experiences have been sharply different. In part, any global description is bound to be in error for some of the thousands of schools and communities across the nation: some schools and places are ahead of their time; some lag far behind. Periods shade into one another rather than beginning and ending in a given calendar year. The single portrait of any period, like Francis Galton's quaint and classic experiment in "composite photography," is a blend of many actual portraits. His composites, as he put it, produced "idealized features." Similarly, any attempt to provide a global statement about the functioning of the schools and the nature of the larger learning environment across the nation in a given period is an abstraction. Nevertheless, it is certainly true that the four birth cohorts examined at each life stage, on the average separated by a span of seventeen years, implicate wide contrasts in schooling and experiences in the formative years.

When the high school or college graduates of a given age are examined, as many as four full cycles when innovations could have occurred in the operation of these institutions can come under study. No fewer than two full cycles in elementary schools are implicated. Across all sixteen cohorts and all the years of the surveys, we have brought under observation individuals born as early as 1877 and as late as 1946. Some learned the three Rs by rigid discipline, and some are the products of the rise and vicissitudes of progressive education. Some grew up long before television and even radio ever came on the scene, and many grew up without access to these media. Only the youngest cohorts may be described as products of the age of television.[10]

Theorists who speculate about the critical experiences of a generation may fasten on all sorts of variables—some fastening on such dramatic experiences as wars, depression, etc. Whatever importance should be attached to such happenings, they impinged on some studied cohorts during their growth but not on others. One striking contrast among our cohorts that it is important to consider derives from the expansion of educational opportunity in the period under study. In the population from which our oldest cohort was drawn—those who were already around age sixty-five in 1950—only about 8 percent had gone to college, and about 3 percent had graduated. Indeed, only a minority—about 20 percent—had been fortunate enough to have *any* high school training; about half of these graduated. The equivalent age-group surveyed around 1970, simply by virtue of being born twenty years later (although still around the turn of the century), had double the opportunities. About 15 percent of that population had gone to college and about 8 percent had graduated, and some exposure to the high school characterized about one-third of them, in contrast with the one-fifth in the earlier cohort. Even among our youngest cohorts, the same pattern occurs. Among the young adults surveyed in the 1950s, about 18 percent had gone to college and a little over half had gone to high school. For those born about twenty years later, who had reached the ages of twenty-five to thirty-six around 1970, again opportunity had about doubled. Around 30 percent had gone to college, almost two-thirds had gone to high school.[11]

When we examine the effects of education across the four different birth cohorts who have reached the same given life stage, the implicit contrast is between a select group who had experienced the education of the past, available to a small elite, and a group who come progressively closer to being representative of mass secondary and higher education. To anticipate our later findings, it will be difficult to argue away the enduring effects of education as simply the knowledge that highly selected individuals already had on entrance into schools, if we find the effects to be uniform and dramatic in magnitude over a period when selective recruitment had declined radically.

Although the declining selectivity works to sharpen the meaning of the comparisons of a life stage across the four sets of surveys, it unfortunately introduces one constant element of obscurity into all the quasi-developmental comparisons of different life stages within the *same* set of surveys. The older age-groups are further away from their education, but they represent the more selective recruitment of past eras. Thus any wearing away of effects among them may be offset to some extent by the fact that they started with a greater advantage. The net result could be that changes with aging are somewhat obscured. This is why the earlier caution was urged, even though the many such comparisons do average out the variety of contents implicated in the education of the different cohorts.

The general implications of the design, involving many age-specific and "dated" comparisons among groups contrasted in educational attainment, have been reviewed in sufficient detail for now, but one last point may be pondered. When college and elementary school graduates at any given age—for example, among the youngest adults —are compared, one must realize that both groups have reached the same stage of maturity but are not the same distance from their schooling. Some of the college group graduated only yesterday, but in the elementary school group what is measured are the traces of the education from which they were removed ten years or more ago. One may even entertain the perverse thought that college graduates know more not because of what they have learned but only because they have learned it so recently. Perhaps if we enrolled individuals in elementary school only when they had reached fourteen, they'd be as good as college graduates! The plain fact is that higher education is not just higher but *later*. The two facets may be inextricable in the effect; and certainly, among the youngest adults studied, higher education is very recent experience. But surely *recency* cannot be a potent factor in the patterns observed among the better-educated oldsters. Those college graduates may be only forty years away from their education, whereas the high school graduates are forty-four years away. Surely one cannot weigh that variable heavily. It hardly varies. Safety, again, lies in the fortunate fact that mature and old adults can be brought under study by secondary analysis.

So much for the design superimposed on the old surveys: the selection and arrangement of groups to represent the *independent* variables, exposure to different amounts of schooling of the contrasted types provided by the institutions of several historical periods, at differing years earlier in the lives of adult individuals. The ways in which samples of these groups have been drawn to permit generalizations and some of the controls on other sources of error in the comparisons have also been described. Now consider the next stage, the coverage of the *dependent* variables, the enduring effects that follow from the varieties of exposure.

Measurement of Knowledge and Receptivity to Knowledge

The present studies have been confined to measures of knowledge and receptivity to further knowledge. Effects in these two spheres are central to assessing the effectiveness of education. The amount of data and analysis required to treat only these two problems on an extended time scale and to incorporate some comparative evidence from another country already has reached almost unmanageable proportions. The present pool of surveys contains measures of other dependent variables—for example, tolerance, civic attitudes, and conduct—that could be employed as criteria of the effectiveness of education, and many past surveys could be drawn upon for studies in such realms.[12] Batteries of questions measuring other relevant variables—logical reasoning, problem solving, aesthetic standards, etc.—that existing surveys rarely contain could even be piggybacked, attached as periodic supplements to ongoing national surveys to build up new data for wider studies of enduring effects. These are all extensions into the future toward which the present studies may lead us.

Fifty-one surveys in our pool included one or more questions on specific knowledge. The total number of discrete tests made of the *knowledge* of various educational groups, across all the surveys and the four periods, by happenstance, was exactly 250. Since the knowledge revealed by each of these tests is examined separately for each of four age-groups, the basic findings involve, as noted earlier, a thousand comparisons between educational levels.[13] Over half the measures of knowledge are also *indirect* indicators of the individual's *receptivity* to further knowledge after his formal education has ceased, since they could not have been learned before that time. However, in addition to these measures, exactly fifty more tests from surveys spanning the total time period provide evidence about the individual's *seeking out* of new information. These tests were based mainly on questions included in the fifty-one surveys already in the general pool, but three additional surveys especially rich in such data served exclusively for such tests. The total data base is therefore fifty-four surveys and 300 discrete measures for 1949–71. If we include in the count the 1974 piggyback and one other survey employed for a supplementary analysis of American and Canadian education, the final data base is fifty-six surveys and 305 measures.

Some surveys were much richer than others and contained long batteries of knowledge questions, while others only contained one or two questions. Indeed, so many surveys had to be included both to build up the pool of cases so that one could have confidence in the various subsamples and to build up the pool of questions so that one could have confidence in the breadth and quality of the measurements of knowledge for each of the sixteen groups in the design.

A single survey, on the average, contained only four to five items of knowledge, and the testing situation is one in which discrete measures are spaced out over many surveys involving different individuals.[14] At the level of the *individual* respondent, such a brief test of knowledge is far from comprehensive or reliable, but this level of description is not our concern. Our aim is to describe a *category* of individuals; and the consolidation of measures bearing on such a unit from different surveys is sufficient for our purposes and not without advantage. If a long battery of questions were administered in a single survey, they would all be vulnerable to the constant errors of that inquiry at that time. In the combined data, the weight of any single survey and the errors peculiar to it are attenuated. We can still obtain a profile of knowledge of each *category* or type of individual, based on a great many measures.

The *reliability* of the descriptions of the knowledge of groups contrasted in education and life stage reached should not worry us, and evidence on the quality of the measures will be presented. In the early 1950s, for which the data are most plentiful, the combined test is based on about 90 items of knowledge; and in the early 1960s, when the data were least plentiful, about 35 items constitute the test. However, the domain of knowledge is not so wide as one would like, especially in the 1960s, or so lofty as some might like. Comprehensiveness of measurement is a problem, but the secondary analyst, like everyone else, must accept the universe. Despite extensive searching, we find that the 250 items of knowledge almost exhaust the universe of questions in the twenty-two years under study.[15] That universe can, of course, be expanded in size and extended in time by piggybacking the same or new questions onto future surveys. The detailed nature of the domain of knowledge will be reviewed in later chapters along with the findings, but a brief summary will convey its character.

Eleven of the two hundred and fifty tests are drawn from surveys widely spaced in time and form a distinctive cluster that tests knowledge of popular culture. How much the various groups know about the heroes of the sport world, the movie idols, the conquerors of space, the writers of best-selling fiction, the beautiful people, is anything but highbrow knowledge. Yet it is knowledge of a sort, accessible to all, and it may be expected to be of special interest to the young, the vigorous and manly types, the romantic, and those whose tastes have not been trained in rarefied, refined directions. Thus the findings provide compelling and, as it turns out, unexpected evidence about the kinds of knowledge to which groups may become receptive or hostile with age and education.

One hundred and forty tests, well distributed over the four periods, fall in the domain of knowledge of *public affairs*, both foreign and domestic, and of notable persons in that sphere. This is information current in the environment at the times of the surveys. The reasonable assumption is that it is easily accessible to all. It relates to the big happenings of the day, and that is why political polls and surveys are always loaded with such questions. This information could not have been learned in school. It hadn't happened yet! Seemingly, the only way earlier education could have been associated with such patterns of knowledge would have been by inculcating special skills and orientations that would work in later life; and these variables thus test the effects of education in creating an enduring receptivity to knowledge. Some may argue, however, that any chain of effect in which the initial link is forged in the schools and colleges includes some different connecting links. Perhaps it is simply that the educated end up in more fortunate circumstances, with a life style that provides greater opportunities to learn. Whether the chain of effect is dependent on these links can be tested by controlling current socioeconomic status in the comparisons. We have gone beyond that and tested what happens when the educated are handicapped in their pursuit of knowledge by having fallen into lowly circumstances and when the uneducated have the advantage of a better station in life.

Such knowledge could not have been taught in the schools. In another sense of the term, it is also *not academic* knowledge. It deals with the world in which the person is living, and knowing more might make a difference to him. By contrast, eighty-eight of the tests fall into a different domain, labeled "academic knowledge." Unfortunately, only about a dozen of these items date from the 1960s. This important area had fallen into neglect in more recent survey research and strong evidence based on many measures in this domain was available only for the two earlier periods. But, by including four of those early items in the instrument piggybacked in 1974, we obtained some evidence for a fifth, very recent period, built up the number of measures for more recent times to a total of sixteen, and ensured that the cohort analysis of change was based on identical measuring instruments.[16]

Most of the questions relate to simple matters of fact in geography, history, the humanities, and the sciences that probably were taught in the schools when the adults in our samples were doing their studying. And, if they were not, they certainly are of the kind that could have been taught. The knowledge may well be academic in the other sense of the term, that knowing it does not make any difference in adult life.

These tests examine effects that could have been fully formed during schooling and that have then endured through all the years. To be sure, they could be re-created or reinforced along the way as a result of receptivity, the adult's desiring to relearn history or geography or some other discipline.

There is an occasional and inevitable anachronism built into our system of classification. An item is classified once for all age-groups. An "academic" item, although in the curriculum of the young in that period, may not belong in that class for the very old. In any case, the two major spheres of knowledge are strikingly contrasted in content, and many measures cover the fairly heterogeneous realm. The specific dimensions along which the measures fall are conveyed by the refined classifications presented in chapter 2.

A last cluster of eleven items, although drawn from only one survey, can serve a special purpose somewhat like the one served by the cluster dealing with popular culture. It deals with knowledge of the tools and duties in four occupations, two industrial and two white-collar. For the higher and better-educated classes, the former pair pose "academic" questions, outside of daily experience and perhaps known only through books and intellectual processes. For the lower and less-educated classes, the questions present concrete, meaningful matters closer to home, about which there has been much opportunity to learn. The educated thus are handicapped by their status and milieu on the first pair of items. The pair of white-collar occupations reverse the odds. Now it is the uneducated who are handicapped by dealing with what for them are academic matters. The patterns of effects over this special battery may again be compelling evidence.

In the aggregate, the domain of knowledge is fairly wide and has sufficient variety that it permits some very pointed tests of the effects of education. Upon inspection, however, all the items may appear too simple and easy, hardly testing the ceiling of knowledge that could or should be reached by those who have been educated. Worse yet, the items may seem so close to the floor of knowledge on which everyone stands that whatever extra knowledgeability the educated truly have could not be registered by such crude instruments. But this would be to prejudge the matter.

Given the ignorance that national surveys have often documented, we find plenty of room for gains to be registered. Perhaps the very judgment "simple or easy" is unwarranted in light of the empirical national norms the surveys provide. Of course, the perverse may then suggest that the educated look good only in the light of the low standard against which they are compared. They may not look so good when measured against some ideal standard. To be sure, these items are not way up near the ceiling of human knowledge, but if they were, there would be the alternative technical problem—practically no one but an expert would score high. Then differences in the knowledgeability of ordinary men could not be measured. The reader will judge for himself. What our empirical norms suggest is that the items range over many levels, from easy to hard.

In comparing the effects of education across periods or in tracing changes in a particular cohort over time, we must deal with the critical problem of the equivalence of the tests. Hardly any of the items in the sphere of public affairs are repeated, since they represent topical matters that have faded out or emerged over time. But the identical question at different times would not have ensured equivalence. Consider an apparently very simple item from 1957, when the individual was asked if he had *heard* of George Meany and is scored as knowledgeable however little he knows. If this same question had been asked again in a survey in 1973, George Meany having risen to new heights of national politics, the "yes" answer would hardly have the same meaning it had sixteen years before. That it was a "difficult" item in 1957 is suggested by the fact that fewer than a third of those with elementary education claimed even to have heard of the man. Consider another one of our items where time has reversed the fortunes of a man. In 1952, those who could correctly identify Harold Stassen, then a perennial candidate for the presidency, numbered 14 percent among the least educated. The figure may appear surprisingly low, but surely the question would be much more difficult if asked now, years after he has faded from national prominence. The equivalence of the items in terms of content area and level of difficulty, and not their nominal identity, is the problem in comparisons across time. A refined classification of content and an index of difficulty computed from our empirical norms will be employed to treat the problem. The difficulty of items must also be considered in evaluating any discrete finding or the overall conclusions about effects, since, for the reasons already illustrated, the absolute magnitude of the differences that can be demonstrated is dependent on the location of items—near the floor or ceiling. That problem is clarified by the computation of an "index of effectiveness," which is a relative or standardized measure and will be presented along with the absolute scores on knowledge. It will be reviewed in chapters 2 and 4. Basically, the difference found between groups is expressed in ratio to the maximum difference that would be possible, given the difficulty of the item.[17]

The eighty-eight items of academic knowledge would not present the same vexatious problem of equivalence across time periods, since by and large these are staple matters unaffected by the stream of information flowing to adults. Ideally, the same items should have been repeated in the surveys over the four periods studied. Unfortunately, they were not, and we faced the more critical problem that the supply of such measures was ample only in the first two periods. Our findings for the last two periods are therefore tentative. The piggybacked battery ameliorated the situation to some extent; and some of the academic items in different periods, although not identical, were equivalent in difficulty and similar in content.

There are specific limitations, but in general we have a very large number of measures—three hundred—at varying levels of difficulty covering several broad domains of knowledge and receptivity to further knowledge over a number of periods, including particular classes of items that can provide compelling evidence. These will surely provide ample tests of the knowledge that accompanies various amounts of education. But will such evidence really establish the *effects* of education?

Establishing the Effects of Education

The various steps outlined so far will soon lead to the findings that the better educated do have wider and deeper knowledge not merely of bookish facts but also of the contemporary world, and that they are more likely to seek out knowledge and be attuned to sources of information. The differences will be found to be substantial in magnitude in national samples of adults who are the products of the universe of schools in several historical periods. These differences are found to have endured despite aging and many years of removal from school or college and to be manifold rather than limited in character.

If these thousands of individuals had been assigned at random in something like a continuing national lottery or giant experiment, some by chance receiving the prize of more education and others losing the chance—beyond that, if they all had been made to stand by the luck of the initial drawing, never reversing their fates by dropping out of the course or squeezing into it—then there could be no doubt that our findings in full measure represented the effects of education. The findings, however, are not derived from such an ideal experimental design.

Some categories and classes of individuals have been recruited by educational institutions and other groups have not. Some types have applied and been welcome; others, not. Particular individuals with strong inclinations and large resources have entered upon long courses of education and have had the staying power, while those with other inclinations and meager resources have not tried or not persisted. Opportunity in the past has been far from equalized and then maintained, as in an experiment. The statistics cited earlier on the distribution of educational attainment in the population suggest how extreme social and self-selection has been at certain times.

A critic may argue, therefore, that the gross findings incorporate the greater knowledge or propensity to knowledge that the better-educated groups brought with them upon their entrance into school as well as the effects that followed from their schooling. It is reasonable for him to request that we take some additional steps to purify the gross findings and make more precise tests of the net effects of education. But it would be unreasonable to demand that the findings be as pure as they would be if a true experiment had been conducted on a grand national scale. That demand has never yet been met, and

probably never will be. Even on a *small* scale, that type of evidence
has been out of reach. As Feldman and Newcomb remark in reviewing the effects of higher education: "The perfect design for an answer
would consist of comparable information from individuals in, say,
their thirties, forties, and fifties, half of whom had graduated from
college while the other half had never attended, both groups having
been selected as 'identical' at the age of seventeen. No such study has
ever been made, nor perhaps could it be."[18] Reasonable men must
settle for what is possible. If they really want empirical studies of the
long-term effects of education, they must place their reliance on imperfect and inferential, rather than definitive experimental, evidence.[19]

The first step in the direction of purifying the data has already
been accomplished automatically by the inclusion of sets of cohorts
from four different points in the past. As earlier noted, educational
opportunity has greatly expanded over the time span studied. Consequently, the more recent findings are derived from a situation moving progressively closer to the ideal experimental design, in which
the groups contrasted in education have tended to become equated in
other respects. To be sure, that ideal has not yet been realized, but
most selective factors, in combination, enter in greater degree into
our earlier findings. If the gross effects observed are seriously inflated
by such uncontrolled variables, the effects should be of much greater
magnitude in our earlier sets of data.[20]

In a way, an invisible but powerful set of controls has been introduced over the sources of selectivity, whatever they may have been.
But controls on specific major sources of selective educational attainment can also be introduced in a direct and visible way. We have
already taken the first step in that direction automatically by limiting
all analyses to *whites*. The likelihood of a long education as well as a
long life has been lower for nonwhites. Apart from sheer schooling,
nonwhites also may have been deprived in other ways of an equal
chance to become knowledgeable. However, since all of our gross
comparisons are confined to whites, none of the differences found by
education (as well as by age) can reflect the concomitants of race.

Apart from race, the sex, religion, and class origins of individuals
have been found to be major social correlates of educational attainment. All four factors (counting race) have been introduced into the
refined analyses in various ways, and their influence on the results
brought under substantial control. In addition, ethnicity, certainly a
determinant of the kind of education a person obtained and *where* he
received it, and to some degree also of the amount, has been brought
under scrutiny. And various controls, not so refined or precise as
would be ideal, have been imposed on a sixth social correlate of educational attainment, rural origins.

There are two other factors which could not be measured and which therefore we were powerless to control directly. Early intelligence and propensities to learn may have determined subsequent educational attainment as well as knowledgeability in later life and thus could distort our conclusions. Their influence, however, is controlled *indirectly* to some extent by the imposition of the other controls. Their weight can also be gauged by evidence in the literature. And whether they have really damaged our conclusions can be determined by examination of the detailed patterning of our findings in different cohorts and periods, among subgroups, and among those who dropped out at various points along the educational course. Our obtained findings do not conform to the patterns that would be expected if such distorting factors were really at work. The detailed findings will be presented in chapters 2 and 3; only a brief review will be presented here.

Women in the United States in the past generally have not obtained so much education as men. If women, for reasons other than schooling, were to be less knowledgeable in some respects, then some of the gross differences by educational attainment might simply reflect the uncontrolled factor of sex. In every instance where there was ground for such a control, additional comparisons of educational groups were made separately for men and for women. In fact, as will be reported, there were many instances where no such control was necessary. Women were often as knowledgeable as men and, in occasional surveys, the samples showed no significant differences in the total *distribution* of education by sex. This source of obscurity both in the tests of knowledge of various educational groups and in tests of aging (given the longevity of women) is thus no cause for concern.

In the past, Protestants, providing they were white, have been more likely than Catholics to have attained higher education. Jews have tended to have unusually high educational attainment. If, apart from their subsequent schooling, members of different religious groups were likely to differ in knowledgeability, some of the gross differences might simply reflect religion. Although not enumerated in all our surveys, religion was included in a sufficient number to introduce this control in about 100 tests, when found necessary.[21] In these refined tests, comparisons by education were made separately for Catholics and Protestants. Although Jews are included in the initial gross tests, they are such a tiny proportion of the population that their weight is negligible in the findings. Subgroups of Jews varying in education are almost microscopic, and those tests are too insubstantial to be reported.

Ethnicity has also been a factor influencing, in various ways, individuals' educational opportunities and attainments. Anglo-Saxons, for example, have been advantaged educationally in the United States in contrast with groups of other ethnic origins. Perhaps for reasons other than schooling—money and language may suffice—immigrant groups would be handicapped in the pursuit of knowledge. As earlier noted, a control on this factor was desirable simply to resolve the ambiguity of having our findings refer to the effects of the education received in *another* country by the immigrants contained within some of our cohorts. Although nativity and ethnicity are not enumerated in many surveys, it was possible to examine their influence on about forty of the items of knowledge. Then, when found necessary, the influence of education on knowledge of those items was examined for all native-born individuals. This ensured that *American* education was under examination and at the same time controlled to some degree ethnicity and its concomitant liabilities, although national origins of the individuals—once removed—still could vary. Refined comparisons by education for the various immigrant nationality groups are not reported. The groups are so diverse and many are so small that it is difficult to impose any sensible and feasible arrangement for analysis on the data.

Individuals from families of higher socioeconomic status have attained more education, and merely growing up in a milieu with an educated father and/or mother and with the advantages that money can buy, apart from schooling, may have increased their knowledge. Multiple indicators of social origins were available on enough surveys to make over forty refined tests in which the influence of education on knowledge was examined when controls on father's status and mother's status—sometimes one measure, sometimes a combination— were introduced by various statistical means.

To anticipate the later findings, let us state that the superiority in knowledge of the better educated persists after these major sources of educational attainment have been controlled. Despite such evidence, a critic may still argue that the case is not proved. He may discount the effects of education and allude to other unknowns that could lead to knowledgeability and also to educational attainment. To be sure, the evidence is not proof positive, but to see such a critic in a proper light, one may summon from the pages of R. A. Fisher's classic work, *The Design of Experiments*, the "heavyweight *authority*." Fisher tells us that "the authoritative assertion 'his *controls* are *totally* inadequate' must have temporarily discredited many a promising line of work."[22]

The moral is clear. Surely controls on six factors, including those which have been repeatedly demonstrated to determine selective educational attainment, cannot be "totally inadequate." If the gross findings were illusory, the apparent effects spurious, certainly they should be radically diminished by controlling such *weighty* factors, even if some other potent factor could still contribute to the effects. That our factors are truly weighty can be conveyed by some of the findings from the large-scale, long-term program of research by Sewell and his associates on the factors governing the attainment of *higher* education. They remark: "Whatever measure of socio-economic status we use—parental income, father or mother's education, father's occupation or any combination of them—we find enormous differences in the educational attainments of the socio-economic groups." They find that these differences persist even when academic *ability*, as measured by a standard test of "Mental Maturity" administered in the senior year in high school, is controlled. For example, in a group equated in that respect, all located in the *lowest* quarter of that distribution, "a student from the high socioeconomic category enjoys a 4 to 1 advantage in attending college and a 9 to 1 advantage in graduating from college."[23] To elevate other *unknown* factors to greater importance than our six seems captious. There have to be better grounds if the substantial evidence is to be discredited.

Legitimate questions may be raised about the specific modes employed to refine the analysis and control particular variables. These will be examined later, but the methodological debates in the literature will suggest that the right decision is in no sense obvious, nor is it readily implemented since circumstances often compel departures from ideal practice. It is also legitimate to suggest that intelligence in childhood, whose influence was beyond our powers of direct control, may account for some of the gross effects. Within any of the social groups examined, it may be that some individuals became more knowledgeable simply through the exercise of their greater intelligence, and, for the same reason, initially gained entrance to more advanced education and were capable of completing the course.

It is possible to administer brief intelligence tests in sample surveys, but this cannot extricate us from the difficulty. Indeed, one of our surveys did contain a classic vocabulary test of "intelligence."[24] The educated *adult* scored higher, but this may simply prove the effect of education in increasing his vocabulary and verbal comprehension. That is how we construed the measures. However, because of their special dual character, the findings from the six discrete tests made are reported separately and not incorporated into the summary tables. The variable one wishes one could control is intelligence, measured during *childhood*, before the scores could be much influenced by the past education obtained. Such measurements, needed for *direct* control over the variable for many national samples of adults, are beyond our or anyone else's reach, since surveys catch the individuals only when they are adult—at the right point for measuring the enduring effects of education but too late to measure early intelligence prior to education's having had any influence on it. How ironic! Studies among children catch the population at the right point for measuring intelligence but too early to measure education's enduring effects.[25]

We cannot rely on the possibility that childhood intelligence has been indirectly and automatically brought under better and better control as we study cohorts from more recent historical periods. Some may argue on logical grounds that, as social and biological characteristics have declined as criteria for educational selection and attainment, inevitably, merit—intelligence—has come to play a larger role. Others may reasonably argue that earlier, stringent standards of academic performance have become progressively relaxed and that members of recent generations have been allowed to pursue education and have persisted in school even though they have had little intellectual promise. The question is moot. But whether one argues one way or the other, the advocates of *both* formulations are asserting that the contribution of intelligence must have *changed* over time. Consequently, if we find that the effects of education do not vary as we move across time periods and cohorts, it will suggest that ability is not the explanation. Admittedly, Beverly Duncan, a knowledgeable investigator whose study of the problem is one of the few yielding substantial data, concludes: "Unfortunately, there is no prospect that better estimates of the relations among ultimate educational attainment, social background, and intelligence measured early in life will become available in this century, let alone that it will be possible to determine whether the importance of background relative to intelligence has been changing over time."[26] But her remarks are addressed to the problem of *empirical* evidence about the relative weights of class and ability and cannot be taken to contradict the logic of our argument.

The relevant data in the literature are scanty, as noted by us and lamented by her, but they can help us ponder the weight that intelligence may have in our results. It should be stressed that the *simple* correlation between early ability and later educational attainment would lead to an exaggerated and maximal estimate of its influence on our findings. The controls imposed on social origins eliminate considerable variation in intelligence that would otherwise be present in comparisons of educational groups, because of the substantial correlation between class and intelligence. But within homogeneous social classes, there would still be some variation in intelligence which could be confounded with educational attainment. It is only this *residual* amount that could distort our refined measures of the effects of education and should be estimated.

In the program of research on Wisconsin high school seniors by Sewell and his associates, we find appropriate information for appraising the contribution intelligence makes, apart from social class, to entry and completion of *college*. In one formulation of their findings, they note that, by adding measured intelligence to their prior analysis of socioeconomic background, "the explained variance in *higher* educational attainment is increased from 18% to 30%."[27] In another of these analyses, multiple indicators of family background *plus* child's intelligence all together explain "less than . . . one-fourth of the variance . . . in college attendance, and college graduation." In this light, the contribution of intelligence can be seen more clearly. It is a factor confounding the effects of education, but not of such overwhelming potency. For reasons which will become clear in chapter 2, the contribution of intelligence to college *graduation* is more critical for us than its contribution to *entrance*. The additional variance in graduation explained by intelligence is about 11% for boys, but only about 6% for girls.[28] Perhaps one should not underrate the importance of the variable in determining *college* attainment. Its contribution to the attainment of high school education, however, is likely to be less, since secondary education has become so widespread. Findings that graduating from high school increased knowledge thus seem less vulnerable to the criticism that intelligence has not been controlled in the comparisons.

Apart from estimating that the *general* influence of intelligence is modest and suggesting that its relationship to educational attainment is not linear—an increment of intelligence does not produce the same gain in attainment all along the educational ladder—Sewell clearly documents that intelligence does not have equal importance for the educational attainment of men and that of women. A recent longitudinal study by Alexander and Eckland of a national sample of the cohort of youth who were high school sophomores in 1955 also finds differential effects of intelligence on educational attainment for men and women that are dramatic in magnitude.[29] Sewell's finding, quoted earlier, that the chances that a dull child of the rich will graduate from college are nine times better than those that a dull child of the poor will is an even more dramatic demonstration that intelligence would have differential significance depending on the group involved. Trent and Medsker computed the odds for 10,000 youths enrolled in the senior year of high school in 1959. Their independent finding is as dramatic: "Of the graduates at the high socioeconomic level . . . nearly 60 percent in the lowest 40 percent of the sample's ability distribution matriculated, but of the graduates at the low socioeconomic level . . . only about 40 percent in the upper 40 percent of the ability distribution went on to college."[30]

Only the naive or the elitist would believe that equal intelligence would produce the same educational chances for all kinds of people—those in favored positions and those discriminated against or with meager resources. No one else would hold to such a belief in the face of such vivid evidence or would assert that the effects of intelligence have been uniform in the long period spanned by our surveys and cohorts—from the 1880s on through the next seventy years, during which time educational opportunity expanded greatly.

The few old studies of the influence of childhood intelligence on subsequent educational attainment are based on small, often biased, samples of specialized universes (incidentally, suggesting that past generalizations about the problem may have weak foundations) but, at least, they suggest that its influence has been small and varies between groups and periods. Lorge reports the *simple* correlation between intelligence measured in eighth grade and subsequent schooling for a sample of the cohort of boys enrolled in the eighth grade in New York City schools in 1922 and concludes that the "correlation of .36 would not permit very reliable predictions of how much schooling a person would complete."[31] Obviously, the partial correlation, after social class is controlled, would be even lower, and the figure would still be inflated, since intelligence measured in eighth grade already to some extent reflects prior schooling. Bradway and Thompson followed a small sample of the cohort of children of preschool age in San Francisco in 1931 and found that there was *no* difference in the intelligence (measured at about age fourteen) of those who went on to college and those who did not. Benson studied a sample of children in the sixth grade in Minneapolis in 1923 and reported a simple correlation of .57 (the recomputed value reported by the Duncans and Featherman is .54) between intelligence at that point and later educational attainment.[32]

The invariant patterning of the effects of education on knowledge over our groups and periods, to anticipate our findings, does not conform to the pattern that would be required if intelligence (whose influence is not uniform) were the explanation.

What about early propensities to learning (rather than abilities) that also were not directly controlled? To some extent they were *indirectly* controlled. Differences in general, intellectual value orientations have been amply documented for class and religious groups.[33] Sex roles, surely in the development of some of our earlier cohorts, were rigidly prescribed, and men and women were guided toward different intellectual pursuits. The consequences have been well documented in the classic findings of differential psychology on sex differences in achievement in various cognitive spheres. In addition, the usual imagery of propensities toward learning understandably has a schoolbookish, intellectual flavor. Such early propensities would help a person through school and perhaps account for his higher learning as an adult but would hardly incline him to learn about baseball or movies. Indeed, they could disincline him toward such vulgar knowledge, and an early taste for such knowledge could hinder him in school. So when we find—as we shall—that education has positive effects in spheres of pop culture, it does not seem tenable to regard this as the product of intellectual propensities. And when we find that dropouts from school, who may lack resources but who also lack tenacity or propensity for learning, nevertheless show education's enduring effects, it seems illogical to invoke propensities as the explanation of the findings.

Most major factors *predating* education that could account both for selective attainment and for knowledge and receptivity have been brought under control or scrutiny. There are, of course, endless experiences, *postdating* education, over the long lives of these adults that may have modified their knowledge. The influence of most of these variables need not be controlled. The unique feature of our study is the measurement of *enduring* effects of education. What one truly wants to know is whether the seeds of knowledge implanted long ago will wither with time or endure throughout the vicissitudes of experience and into old age. The variables that time carries, however destructive their force or beneficent their influence, generally should not be controlled or eliminated in reckoning the effects of education, although it would be informative to unravel some of the complexities of the long process.

In contrast, chains of *distinctive* experience that represent only the perpetuation (albeit in new forms) of the original advantages or handicaps that particular social groups had prior to their education should be controlled. But this has been accomplished automatically by the controls on the major social factors that determine selective educational attainment. Whatever later experiences are distinctive to whites, or women, or the offspring of the poor, for example, have been equated when refined comparisons by education are made within groups homogeneous in such respects. Furthermore, differentials in the power of education to endure under various conditions—for example, when one functions throughout life in the role of a woman—can be revealed.

In contrast with such distinctive experiences predetermined long ago, there are other, later chains of experience that begin to be forged simply as a result of education, whatever the person's initial status. These, too, need not be controlled. After all, education can do its work only indirectly, once individuals have left school, through creating the links that join together a long causal process. It seems reasonable, for example, to regard adult information seeking as a propensity that is itself affected by education and one that in turn leads to further acquisitions of knowledge. This hypothesized effect of education, indeed, has been tested many times over, as indicated earlier.

An obvious link in the long chain of effect from early education to late knowledge is the life style that the educated can achieve. Educational credentials facilitate entry into privileged occupations and/or into marriages with the more privileged, thus in turn easing the acquisition and buying of knowledge. Whether this link is essential to the process has been tested, as noted, by introducing controls on current socioeconomic status. Such tests also incorporate and control whatever privileged position individuals may simply have "inherited" from their families, and thus are dramatic evidence about the power of education. Some of the tests, as mentioned, have been set up in ways that make the evidence most compelling.

We have outlined the steps taken to control variables that could distort conclusions about the enduring effects of education and to clarify the process underlying the effects. These are subtle matters and the model that has guided our steps has been summarized. One last step must be taken. The accuracy and generalizability of the conclusions could also be distorted by errors in the sampling and measurement procedures used in the original surveys and by errors subsequently introduced in the course of secondary analysis. What kinds of quality controls have been instituted to protect the conclusions from such flagrant sources of error?

Control of Error

It would be ideal if *all* fifty-four surveys had employed procedures that created little or no measurement error and minimal sampling errors and bias. Absolute perfection cannot be achieved, even though we have tried to move in its direction by choosing surveys made by good, long-established agencies at times when they had already reached a stable and competent level of functioning. But impeccable standards are not required. Occasional errors peculiar to a single survey or to the circumstances surrounding inquiries in a particular week or season or in the work of one agency are attenuated by the fact that our conclusions are based on many surveys and on the work of three agencies.

Errors of considerable magnitude present in *many* of our original surveys—whether they be random in direction, reducing reliability, or biases resulting from some systematic factor distorting results in some constant direction—are, indeed, a problem not to be ignored, but we shall soon present evidence that should allay concern. Sometimes, such errors seriously distort survey findings, but whether and exactly in what way each kind of error jeopardizes particular types of analysis is a subtle question not yet definitively answered.[34] But it should be stressed that these errors may be present in the body of *raw* data and be inconsequential, because seriously damaged portions of the total data are eliminated prior to the secondary analysis or because the errors are controlled by the analytical procedures employed. Moreover, some of these errors, even if left freely operating on the final data, sometimes may not distort the conclusions one bit. For example, a systematic error which results in the inflation or deflation of the true knowledge of our respondents and which is of the same magnitude and direction over all our surveys and all our comparison groups would not change our conclusions at all. If some knowledge should be added to or subtracted from everyone's score, the differences would still be the same. This implies that constant errors or biases that affect some of our comparison groups and some of our periods more than others are a special source of worry. But in such instances, the biasing error may even work to make our findings on the effects of education *conservative* or have been so controlled that it does not distort the conclusions at all.

One subtle type of constant error, however, could be insidious. It could have been introduced at the point of secondary analysis when all of our surveys were selected, if we were not protected against the danger. We decided to make the selection *blindly*, choosing the surveys before inspecting any of the tables on the relation between knowledge and education. If we had not so blinded ourselves, we might have prejudiced the general conclusions, rationalizing or inventing some apparently good reason for excluding surveys and questions on knowledge where the results did not conform to our original hypothesis. In fact, the straits in which we found ourselves gave us double protection. We needed practically every survey from the period and agencies involved that we could obtain in order to build up the pools of cases and knowledge items.[35] The only relevant surveys excluded were those that had become fugitive or those containing such meager data that investment in them was not warranted. Occasional tests of knowledge omitted from our analysis, although available in our surveys, mainly represent oversight in searching rather than deliberate exclusion, although some items were omitted in an attempt not to overweight the general conclusions with too many items of homogeneous content or with indicators that prima facie were dubious instruments. In none of these instances was the exclusion based on inspection of the tables.

Now consider the major steps that have been taken toward ensuring that the sampling and measurement procedures have yielded us good data and that whatever errors remain are contained in such a way that they do not distort our conclusions. The very oldest and very youngest adults have been excluded from the original samples. It is among these age-groups that sampling biases can be extreme, even when the sampling is designed and executed so as to be effective for most of the population. There is also evidence that response error may be higher among the very old. Indeed, they are prone to misstate their age and to forget simple background facts out of their very distant past that are essential if they are to be classified accurately in the experimental design imposed on our data.[36]

Recall also that the nonwhite stratum in the original samples has been excluded. Here again, although the sampling generally may be of high quality, there is some evidence of special difficulties and consequent biases in the sampling of the black population. There is also reason to worry that the sampling of that stratum may have changed in character, in the years under study, in obscure ways that would be difficult to determine. Equally important is the possibility that response errors may be present and *not* constant over our period, as a result of assigning white interviewers to interview some black respondents in the earliest years but not in the later years. The facts are lost in the chronicles of some of these old surveys, but the danger is best avoided. In one classic study done in the South years ago, black interviewers obtained more reports of higher educational attainment from black respondents than did white interviewers, and the information-seeking behavior differed significantly by the race of the interviewer.[37]

The sampling all three agencies have followed is a highly sophisticated form of a probability-model design, relatively elaborate in character.[38] In the work of the Survey Research Center and the National Opinion Research Center, the designs have been stabilized for many years. Major improvements were made in the Gallup Poll, around 1949 to 1952, and the sampling procedures have remained relatively stable since. The major sampling bias that seems to have been present in the surveys—especially in the earliest Gallup Polls, but declining in more recent ones—has been some tendency to over-represent the *better*-educated class in the population. Here we face a situation that may seem to create havoc in light of our introductory remarks: a bias is present and it is not constant in magnitude over the clumps of surveys. Yet this error is automatically contained by the basic mode of analysis employed for all of our major comparisons. Since we first subdivide the sample and then examine the knowledge of separate educational groups for our comparisons, it does not matter whether we have too few of the one group and too many of the other. Whatever improper weight they may have in the aggregate makes no difference. By contrast, the summary statistical measures of the association between education and knowledge computed over the entire sample we used as supplementary evidence could be moderately distorted by any improper weights the educational strata have, and some caution should be exercised with those findings.[39]

A crude sense of how small the bias is in the sampling of educational strata in our better surveys—not that it is consequential for us—can be conveyed by tables from the published accounts of two of the NORC surveys. These compare the educational attainment of the national population (over the full age range) as estimated in our small sample surveys and as reported by the U.S. Bureau of the Census from its giant samplings. These findings do not prove the absolute accuracy of the surveys, since any *constant* errors in *reporting* level of education to both agencies would not be revealed. Census inquiries, like all surveys, are not infallible in this respect. Indeed, the census has published data on such errors in enumerating education that indicate that there may be an overestimation of education in about 6% of the population twenty-five years old and over during the period we were studying, but the error essentially tends to be reporting completion of a level rather than some education at that level.[40] This suggests, incidentally, that such a bias is small and of no consequence for our comparisons between three grouped levels of education. It seems reasonable that the errors in our surveys would be no higher and perhaps lower, since only a small crew of interviewers are used in contrast with the army of interviewers that the census must recruit, train, and supervise. Since we shall regard the response errors as about equal in magnitude, the census data may serve as a convenient criterion to give the reader some confidence that our bias in *sampling* educational strata is small. Only the three gross levels of education are presented in table 1. More refined levels of education show equally close agreement. (The tables appear in the appendixes.) Similar findings for an SRC survey we used, the 1964 election study, are reported in the literature but will not be presented.[41]

The fact that the samples incorporate a few too many well-educated respondents is not consequential for our method of analysis, but what about the constant errors in *response* to which we have just alluded? If there is a consistent, if small, tendency for American adults to claim more education than they have, we will be classifying some of them as if they had been affected by an education they never really experienced. This is one of the special instances where a constant error over all surveys does distort the conclusions. But brief reflection will suggest that this can only make the findings more *conservative*. What is treated as evidence of the failure of education to inculcate knowledge are cases that are not failures at all. Education never got the chance to do its work on them.

In addition, there are random errors or unreliability in the measurement of education in our surveys. Special analyses of particular surveys have found them to be small, and there is no reason to regard our batch of surveys as worse than the ones examined. Evidence about unreliability in *individual* reports is provided by studies where the same respondent is reinterviewed after an interval and is asked about his educational attainment both times. In an early NORC study of this type, the responses after a six-month interval were "identical" (using the levels employed for our comparisons of educational groups) in about 80% of the cases. In a more recent study by other investigators, where the interval between interviews was briefer, the reliability was considerably higher. An examination of such error based on special reinterviews with a great many cases from the 1960 census, obtained a reliability coefficient of .93, and the census, after all, is simply a giant survey. The reliability of a measure of socioeconomic status also is high (.87 over all individuals), although not quite so high as that obtained for education. The investigators note that the reliability is slightly lower for *nonwhites*, suggesting that the reliability of our data (since we have restricted ourselves to the samples of whites) would be even higher. The reliability of the estimate for the aggregate population (the relevant statistic for us, since our concern is various subgroups or aggregates) is suggested by the agreement between the census figure and that obtained from the special interview of higher quality. Since the latter measure may be taken as a relatively accurate criterion, the discrepancy may be treated as unreliability plus bias. The estimates of years of schooling completed are close: the medians are 9.97 in the census and 9.84 in the check interview.[42]

To round out the picture of the problem of error in the measurement of educational attainment, we should note that some crudeness characterizes our measurement of *higher* education. Although some of the surveys distinguish "graduate" and "professional" education from undergraduate college, the Gallup surveys do not. In estimating the effects of college graduation, we eliminated where possible those with still higher education. However, in the other instances, the effects of "college" graduation may indeed represent the additional years of training some of those respondents had received. Those who have falsely inflated themselves and those who are deflated in this fashion by the crudity of the classification may have about balanced each other out, but in any case the latter numbers involved are small and the error in the estimates not grave.

There is one other feature of the measures of educational experience which should be noted. The surveys almost never enumerate exposure to *adult education* outside of and beyond the time of formal schooling. A considerable portion of the better-educated groups in the United States have been enrolled in adult education classes. Some of the differences in the comparisons involving these groups thus may represent the effects of later educational experiences rather than of formal college. Enrollment in adult education, in our view, should be regarded as an effect of formal education, a link in the growth of knowledge. Thus it need not be controlled or eliminated from our comparisons. The evidence is presented in chapter 4, along with other measures of information seeking.

Thus far, we have given some general indication of the quality of sampling and measurement and some data specifically on the accuracy of the measurement of educational attainment. But another independent variable, *age*, is as crucial to our analysis. The mythology suggests that people tend to understate their true age, and such a bias, even one of constant magnitude throughout, would be consequential. When we find that those who are "old" and those who are not quite so old do not differ much, this bias would understate the true difference if, in fact, a considerable number of old individuals had declared themselves younger.

What are the facts, rather than the myth? In a classic, large-scale study of the validity of respondents' reports obtained in an NORC survey, individual answers were checked against various criterion records. Reports of age agreed with driver's license records in 92 percent of the cases; for the other 8 percent, the discrepancies were random and exaggeration and understatement were equal in magnitude. To anticipate the question of bias in the reporting of socioeconomic status—this same study validated such indicators of status as telephone ownership, home ownership, and automobile ownership against official records in 94 to 98 percent of the cases.[43]

We may anticipate that the other *independent* variables figuring in our analysis would be subject to no greater biasing or random errors than those we have already examined. Surely, sex would be enumerated with almost 100 percent accuracy. In fact, one of the studies already cited as supporting evidence on reliability of measurement indicates that most factual characteristics were subject to little unreliability.[44] The reliability of the estimates of distribution of religious affiliation in the population is very high, as indicated by the agreement between different surveys of the same organization and surveys by different organizations, and agreement with the one instance when the census enumerated the variable. It should, however, be noted that the surveys measure *current* religious affiliation rather than religion in childhood. The latter is the critical factor to consider in the educational selection process and in the stages when knowledge may have developed. However, the evidence is that conversion to and apostasy from one of the three *major* religions between childhood and adult life are very small, and there is little error in substituting the one measure for the other.[45]

It is essential to raise the problem of error in the measurement of our *dependent* variables, knowledge and information seeking. It is very difficult to conceive of a bias that operates on most such questions so as to distort the conclusions. Since Americans often like to appear informed, such inclinations would not push many of them in the direction of understating any knowledge they have. If those few who engaged in that practice were equally distributed throughout the strata, our conclusions would not be distorted. If the educated, higher-status groups were more inclined to pose as ignorant, that would work only to make the conclusions conservative. The conclusions about the effects of education would be exaggerated only if the *less* educated were more inclined to pose as ignorant, and the data soon to be presented suggest the opposite. However much individuals desire to appear informed, it would be impossible for them to fake knowledgeability, since they have to produce the correct answers to most of our test questions.

In contrast, the specific questions on information seeking, which accept the respondent's answer at face value, or questions asking about simple acquaintance with or awareness of an event, which do not use any follow-up questions to probe the knowledge involved, could be subject to a bias, because of the "social desirability" attached to such patterns. One must entertain the possibility that such a bias is of greater magnitude among the better educated, if they, more than other groups, like to appear knowledgeable. This would overstate the effects of education, but this pattern is not probable. Indeed, in the validity study already mentioned, lower-status respondents were more likely to overstate status characteristics that added to their social desirability. And, if we may extrapolate from these findings, the less educated may even wish more than others to appear knowledgeable and thirsty for information; thus any differences between our groups would be conservative.

Consider some rather dramatic data about the problem. In each of two Gallup surveys, conducted in 1950 and 1952, the respondent was asked two questions about the Hoover Commission. The first simply asked if he had "heard or read" about it, and the second asked him to define its nature. It is perfectly reasonable to assume that some persons may have some vague "acquaintanceship" but that their knowledge is too rudimentary for them to answer the second question correctly. However, to produce a correct answer to question 2 certainly substantiates the claim to acquaintanceship. Table 2 presents the levels of acquaintanceship and knowledge for the age-specific educational levels used throughout our later basic comparisons. In both surveys, a very large proportion of those who claim acquaintanceship do in fact exhibit knowledge on the more rigorous test item. Yet it is among the *least*-educated group that we are more likely to find acquaintanceship without knowledge. The column headed "ratio 2:1" documents, for both surveys and every cohort, that the better educated are more likely to know something about the matters they are acquainted with. We may construe this as indicative of the shallower character of knowledge among the uneducated. However, if one regards the phenomenon as indicative of a "social desirability bias," then it is the least educated who are more prone to making false claims. This, as noted, can only make our general findings more compelling. The sensible way in which many of these acquaintanceship measures behave can be observed in the later tables. Inspection of the data should allay the reader's skepticism. Why, for example, do so few individuals claim to be acquainted with some of the more esoteric items—sometimes as few as one person in ten? If they were so eager to wrap themselves in a false cloak of knowledge, would the figures not run much higher?

There is another possible source of error in measurements of knowledge based on acquaintanceship—the honest confusion of individuals about the notabilities and happenings in the world. Public figures, laws, events come in such abundance that some may be duplicates of each other. When one is in doubt about whether he has heard or read about something, it is nicer to appear informed than not. After all, that is not a flagrant lie that could prick one's conscience. The two sources of response error may thus converge. The findings of table 2 tell us that respondents generally are not all that confused—at least when it comes to the Hoover Commission, which could well have mixed them up between J. Edgar Hoover and Herbert Hoover. If they had been, they would not have answered the second question correctly so frequently. But there is another type of evidence we can present. An estimate of the net effect of such response errors, plus still one other source of error, is provided by introducing "fictitious" public figures, whose names have verisimilitude, into the battery of acquaintanceship measures. Although a person with such a name may exist among the millions of ordinary people, no such *public figure* exists, and reports of acquaintanceship by definition are in error. By special manipulations, such erroneous reports may also serve as "cheater traps" to catch interviewers who fabricate the errors themselves. In any case, the device is a net measure of the three sources of error.

The data are presented in table 3. The particular name involved probably provides a *maximum* estimate of the usual error, since it is very similar to that of a New York notable of the period. There is no evidence that the error is more characteristic of one educational level than another, although there is some suggestion that it is not a constant by age, since the old, especially the less educated among them, for one or more reasons show a higher incidence.

Random error or unreliability in the measurement of knowledge is controlled by using so many items from so many different surveys. It is also comforting that evidence from intercorrelational analyses and from panel studies where the knowledge of the individual respondent is measured at several points in time shows how stable and solid a phenomenon measured ignorance or knowledge is. Moreover, our analysis does not require that each individual be measured with a high degree of reliability, but only that groups and categories of people be accurately measured. Table 4 is relevant to this level of measurement. It presents estimates of knowledge for equivalent half-samples in each of two 1949 Gallup "split-ballot" surveys. Later surveys rarely employ the device, but one may reasonably assume that variability would be better controlled as a result of improved procedures.

The variation in the estimates, representing the net effect of sampling variance and random measurement error, is small. It never exceeds five percentage points and is much smaller in most of the eight tests presented. Six of the items represent "acquaintanceship" measures where the respondent is not actually tested on knowledge, and these estimates are also stable.[46] It should be noted that the least stable item, awareness of NATO, was asked in the two surveys separated by a three-month interval. The variation between surveys is much larger, but this should not be interpreted as unreliability. A change in knowledge of topical items can easily occur as a result of exposure to stimuli in the period around the surveys. When the item is measured in the simultaneous half-surveys, the variation is much less.

In light of all the evidence about the small amount of sampling and measurement errors and of the fact that the errors often cannot operate in such a way as to distort our findings, we feel safe in suggesting that we can assess with high accuracy the differences in the knowledge of educational groups. It is difficult to believe that anyone

who inspects comparisons that often reveal differences of fifty percentage points in the prevalence of knowledge could evaluate these
as simply error. Having reviewed all the steps in our inquiry, let us
now turn to our findings.

2 Enduring Effects on Knowledge

The domain of knowledge we have been able to examine by secondary analysis contained 250 discrete items of information requested in American national surveys between 1949 and 1971. Since the influence of education on each item (with a few exceptions) is examined separately for each of four age cohorts, our fundamental findings involve about a thousand sets of comparisons of knowledge among several educational levels. How to present such massive evidence creates a severe problem. Compression and condensation are essential if the reader is not to become submerged and finally drown in the ocean of data. In a letter to the *New York Times*, one poor soul who had waded through the Coleman report, survived then to read Jencks's work, only finally to confront the recent multivolume report of the International Association for the Evaluation of Educational Achievement, put the problem poignantly: "The voice of reason is overwhelmed by the vast array of codified data" (9 June, 1973, p. 32).

We are alerted to rescue our reader from the vasty deep of our data. But if we condense too much and too quickly, we shall prevent his drowning only to leave him on the surface or in the shallows, barred from exploring our basic findings in depth. The compromise we have adopted is to present the detailed findings in lengthy tables that may appear formidable but provide, for the interested reader, a substantial portion, but *not all*, of the specific results from the analysis of each item of knowledge. These tables, however, are presented only in Appendix B rather than in the text in order not to burden readers who need only a summary of the detailed findings or who would feel "overwhelmed by the vast array" of the many thousands of numbers presented. In Appendix B, the two domains, knowledge of "public affairs" and "academic" knowledge, are treated in separate tables, and within each table the items have been grouped into more homogeneous categories of content. From the multiple findings for all items in each category, summary measures have been computed and also incorporated into the tables. Thus some order and simplification have been provided to encourage and help the reader to inspect and comprehend the many pages of details. Tables containing only summary measures are presented in Appendix A and present the basic findings for all readers in a compressed, but still quantitative, form. The findings and conclusions we have drawn from the detailed analyses are also summarized in the lengthy, but simpler and qualitative, text of this chapter. And the text also describes the nature and purpose of the various indexes and statistics employed to assess the effects of education, thus serving as a guide to the tables.

FUNDAMENTAL FINDINGS IN THE DETAILED TABLES

The set of tables numbered 1.1 through 1.8 in Appendix B present the detailed data for the first period, the early 1950s. The sets prefixed by 2., 3., and 4. present the data for the late 1950s, early 1960s, and late 1960s, respectively. Within each of these periods, separate tables are presented for each of the four age cohorts. Thus tables 1.1 through 1.4 show the knowledge of public affairs of the four cohorts reaching the specified ages in the year each survey from the early 1950s was conducted, and tables 1.5 through 1.8 provide data on academic knowledge. Tables 2.1 through 2.8 present equivalent findings for the second period, and the remaining sets contain equivalent data for later periods. In the two periods in the 1960s, as earlier noted, there were unfortunately very few measures of "*academic* knowledge." Thus it was possible to consolidate the findings for the four age cohorts into one table for each time, tables 3.5 and 4.5, respectively. Tables 1.1–4.5 in Appendix B, taken together, thus present the detailed fundamental findings for the four periods between the early 1950s and the late 1960s. Detailed results for the four cohorts on each of the four items piggybacked on a 1974 survey to enlarge the number of tests of academic knowledge for a fifth—most recent—period are presented in table 5.1.

The clusters of items representing two specialized content areas mentioned earlier, knowledge of vocabulary and knowledge of tools and duties of occupations, are presented in separate tables in Appendix A, as are the cluster of eleven items dealing with "popular culture," in a set of four tables, one for each cohort.

Various indexes could be employed to show the extent of the influence of education on each item. Any single index, by its unique properties, would provide some special perspective on the question of effects, but it could also have some special limitation. To prevent arbitrariness, we have used various ways of gauging effects that are incorporated in the tables. In assessing the problem, the reader can follow any or all of the avenues opened for him, but the basic data presented also permit him to construct other preferred indexes of his own. As essential background for understanding the various approaches chosen and for interpreting the general findings, we must make some brief prefatory remarks about the measurement of the two variables, education and knowledge, in the surveys.

Educational attainment is measured in the surveys in a series of fairly fine step intervals—generally six, but never fewer than five or more than nine, levels. Those who completed high school or college are always distinguished from those who did not complete the stage, and those whose education terminated *no later than* elementary school graduation are always distinguished from those who went on to secondary education. Except for occasional surveys—too few to cause worry—those who reported "no schooling" whatsoever are separated from those who had any schooling at all. It should be stressed that the most disadvantaged group have been so small a component of the white population of the United States during the periods studied that mixing them with those who had elementary schooling (in the "cruder" surveys, where this practice perforce was followed in the analysis) adds very little error to estimates of knowledge for the elementary school group. Although those who had no schooling could be and were isolated in the analysis of most surveys, no separate estimates of the level of knowledge of such individuals are presented because the size of the group in our samples is too small.[1] These are the usual six levels of educational attainment distinguished.

Sometimes, but not often enough for that refinement to be routinely applied to the analysis, those who did not complete elementary school are distinguished from those who graduated. Thus the knowledge attributed to the group labeled "elementary school" in our tables may be taken safely to reflect the influence of at least some quantum of school but represents the effects of from one to eight years of education.[2] At the higher levels of education, sometimes those who had some vocational or trade school in addition to regular high school are coded in a separate category, and, as noted earlier, sometimes those who had professional or graduate training in addition to college are also coded separately. In a considerable number of instances, when it was possible to make the distinction, the estimates of knowledge for the high school and college graduates apply to the purified categories of those who stopped at those points, but more of the time these two groups may in fact be reflecting the effects of some additional training that cannot be eliminated.

In contrast with the relatively refined measurement of educational attainment, the dependent variables, knowledge of discrete items, were generally measured by single questions which classified the individual as either having "correct knowledge" or not. Sometimes a more refined score was obtained: individuals were classified at more than two points along an ordinal scale, as having "completely correct" knowledge, having "partially correct" or "vague" knowledge, or being incorrect or having no knowledge at all. Occasionally, an even more refined measurement was obtained. The discrete "item" was itself an index or scale based on a battery of related questions or on a complex question with subparts. In such cases, the scores sometimes could be construed as reflecting an interval scale—individuals having zero knowledge or having double, triple, etc., the knowledge of some multiplicity of facts—or the scores could be treated simply on an ordinal scale of lesser or greater knowledge rather than as precise quantities of knowledge. Many of the indexes could be treated certainly only in terms of ordinal measurement, with individuals being coded only into such categories as "high," "medium," or "low" in knowledge.

In the first approach to the data, in tables 1.1–4.5 in Appendix B, using the maximum refinement permitted by the particular instruments in each survey, we examined the relationship between education and each item of knowledge over the full range of the two variables. The results from this approach to gauging effects are summarized by two statistics in the last two columns of the detailed tables. A chi-square test indicates that the relationships are almost always, over the hundreds of discrete tests, significant. In most instances, the null hypothesis can be rejected. The simple symbols used to convey the findings in these and later tables are: "NS" when the chi-square value does not reach the .05 level, one asterisk when it reaches .05 but not .01, two asterisks when it is between .01 and .001, and three asterisks when it reaches or exceeds the .001 level.[3] To be sure, in making a thousand tests, an investigation is bound to find *one* where the differences are so big that they would occur by chance only once in a thousand times. But what we have found are several *hundred* tests where differences so great would occur only once in a thousand times. Running his eye down the column of symbols, the reader will observe that the findings are uniform. Significant differences occur equally frequently in both realms, public affairs and academic knowledge, and in all subareas of content. They are characteristic not only of youngish adults but of adults up to age *fifty*. The occasional tests where no significant relationship is observed have no special content, although items so easy that everyone knows the answer, or so esoteric or difficult that no one knows the answer, often fall in this grouping.

The 250 items may all be construed as referring to the same most general hypothesis, that education affects knowledge. Of course, all the items in one domain or particular content area do refer to a less general, but common, broad hypothesis. Thus the different tests may be treated as replications. Since batches of items (on the average, 4–5 per survey) were carried on the same survey and asked of the same individuals, not all the tests are independent of one another. But a great many are. Obviously, findings from the respective surveys of the four periods are independent and each period also contains many separate surveys. For example, seventeen surveys are drawn upon for the tests in the early 1950s, and the smallest number implicated in any time period is nine in the late 1950s. Because of the additive property of chi-square, it should be stressed that the likelihood of obtaining a *sum* so high as would be yielded by adding chi-squares from nine or seventeen independent tests (most of them very large to start with, but including the occasional low values) would not be one in a thousand by chance alone but far, far less than that.

In contrast with the consistent run of findings for the two cohorts up to about age fifty, within the cohort aged forty-nine to sixty, a few more of the tests turn out to be nonsignificant. Table 5 in Appendix A summarizes the number of tests that did not reach the .05 level within each age-group, across all *four* periods. There is a suggestion that the effects occasionally wash out among the older individuals who have passed fifty. The change in pattern is perhaps too slight to mention. The overwhelming number of highly significant chi-square tests argue that the effects of education endure right up to age sixty. And if an overall test had been made by combining the few nonsignificant tests with the many significant ones, it would have been highly significant.

Among the oldest age-group, those sixty-one to seventy-two— whatever time period and specific generation they represent—there are enough nonsignificant tests to make one pause. The change in the pattern at that point is rather sharp. We must consider that effects of education are sometimes washed out by old age and whatever vicissitudes it has brought to the individual (put picturesquely, the senility hypothesis) or that the added years of experience have made up for the initial deficit of the uneducated (the "wisdom of age" hypothesis), or that the educational system has been *steadily* improving. (We shall examine these hypotheses with the aid of more rigorous data in the next chapter.) But changes in the pattern of the findings are not that frequent, and we should not take these ideas too seriously yet. Even among the very old, the great majority of tests are significant, many of them at the .001 level. Again, if one were to employ the additive property of chi-square, the many large chi-squares and the modest number of low chi-squares taken together would certainly yield a highly significant combined chi-square. And the negative findings may reflect the facts that the oldest are the smallest stratum in our samples and that the size of particular cells, e.g., the highly educated old, is very tiny. Perhaps the most striking thing is how many of the educational differences remain intact, despite the afflictions that accompany old age.

The data presented in table 5.1 about the items of academic knowledge piggybacked on a 1974 survey are consistent with the findings for earlier periods. The differences in knowledge are highly significant on all four items for the three cohorts up to age sixty. With one exception, the chi-square tests reach the .001 level. For the oldest cohort, three tests are significant at the .001 level and one test is not significant.

The chi-square test by itself gives no indication of the magnitude or the direction of the differences across all the educational levels. This information is provided in the last column of the tables, where the gamma (a coefficient of association developed especially for ordinal variables) obtained for each item appears. As we shall review in detail later and as the reader can see for himself from other columns in the tables, the relationship between education and knowledge, although often not linear, is almost always monotonic. Every step upward over the whole range of education is accompanied by an increment in knowledge. The gammas also convey this. There are only a negligible number of instances where the sign is negative or the value hovers near zero. The magnitude of the coefficients rarely drops below .3; it often runs as high as .6 or .7 and occasionally higher yet. To summarize these hundreds of gammas, we computed the average value over all the items in a content area separately for each age cohort and period. They are presented in table 6.

Table 6 confirms some of the conclusions already presented. There is no indication that the average relationship declines in magnitude up to age sixty, no matter what generation is involved. The pattern is uniform across all the different spheres of content and the two domains of knowledge, although the effects of education do appear strongest in the tests on the humanities. (It should be noted, however, that the test items are much more difficult in the humanities area, and the level of difficulty as well as the content may contribute to the special finding.) Again, there is the suggestion of a decline in effect in old age. The mean coefficients suddenly drop in magnitude, in rare instances, in a few content areas among the oldest cohort in some periods. Again, we should take note but reserve our judgment.

A summary of the many findings on the effects of education with two such statistics certainly extracts important information from the more elaborate distributions and compresses it into a convenient form for the reader. But it robs him of much of the richness and informative value of the descriptive findings. It gives no picture of the actual extent of knowledge prevalent among adults from particular educational levels and does not convey some of the complexities and curvilinearities of the relationships.[4] However, if we had presented the descriptive findings on each item for *all the levels* of education distinguished in the surveys, we would truly have confronted the reader with an enormous task. Our compromise has been to present, in the first three columns of the basic tables, detailed findings for the three levels that appear most strategic to examine. This is a second approach to gauging the effects.

Those who have *graduated* from high school or college have had the full benefit of those institutions. If one must choose, it would seem more important to describe the levels of knowledge among such individuals rather than among those who have not finished the course provided at the given level. The prevalence of knowledge—the percentage of each of the two groups informed on each item—is provided in the second and third columns of the tables for the four periods and age cohorts. The first column of the tables shows the prevalence of knowledge among those who have not gone beyond elementary school, although, as previously noted, some portion of the group may not have completed that level. The elementary school group provides a base line for assessing the gains from secondary and higher education. By using only graduates, the comparative findings address the question of the *maximum* enduring benefits yielded by such educational experiences when one has been exposed to the *complete* treatment.

The figures in parentheses are the bases or the number of cases used for the computation of each of the percentages. The reader, of course, will note that the base for estimating the prevalence of knowledge of a discrete item in particular groups is small; this is especially true of the better educated in the oldest cohort. The many replications, however, safeguard the conclusions. In totality, if one aggregates the cases in any particular cell over all the surveys from which tests were derived, the base is a most impressive number. Table 7 summarizes these aggregated sizes for the elementary school and college graduate groups within each cohort and period and the grand totals at each of these educational levels across all age-groups and time periods. The table may be interpreted in the following fashion. *At least one* estimate of knowledge about a discrete item is available for a sample of the size indicated of the specified group. For example, among those between twenty-five and thirty-six in the early 1950s who had not gone beyond elementary school, there is some evidence about the prevalence of knowledge for as many as 1,269 cases. (To simplify the table, the aggregated sample sizes for the high school graduates within the various periods and age cohorts are not presented, since one may realize without such detail that these numbers would be considerably larger than the corresponding cells presented.) The final column provides background relevant to the earlier findings of the effects of education based on the analysis of *all levels* of the variable. Naturally, these aggregated sizes are much larger, since they also include the dropouts. It should be noted that the aggregated figures reported in table 7 include the surveys used to estimate knowledge in the several specialized areas mentioned earlier—e.g., about popular culture, about tools and duties of occupations—the findings from which are not incorporated in tables 1.1 through 4.5 but reported in separate tables. Table 7 was intended to provide definitive counts of the total samples drawn upon for the complete analysis.

We return to the general findings presented in the sets of basic tables 1.1 through 4.5. As one runs down the two columns that compare high school and college graduates, one sees that the benefits of *higher* education indeed seem substantial in magnitude, pervasive over all content areas, and persistent among the oldest cohorts, whatever time period and corresponding generation they represent. When one juxtaposes the knowledge of the elementary school group, presented in the first column, one finds the benefits of high school also to be substantial (though smaller), pervasive, and enduring into old age. To simplify the inspection of the hundreds of discrete comparisons, the reader may examine the *mean* percentage informed for the set of items in each content area, which is also entered into the basic tables. Table 8 consolidates all the means for the different areas and periods and cohorts.

Whether one inspects the means or the long array of findings on the discrete items, one reaches much the same basic conclusions. In general, knowledge is about 40 to 50 percent more prevalent among college graduates than among those adults who did not go beyond elementary school. The differences *frequently* run as low as 30 percent and/or as high as 70 percent. On very rare occasions, a difference may be as small as 10 percent, but there are counterbalancing instances, also very rare, where the difference is as large as 75 percent. Inspecting the means, which naturally iron out irregularities and unusual departures from the general run of findings, suggests that the differences are of about the same magnitude in all areas, except for academic knowledge—especially in the humanities—where the differences are most dramatic and much the same for the three age cohorts up to about age sixty, no matter what periods and corresponding generations they represent. There are a modest number of instances where the means suggest that the advantage of higher education has diminished by old age, whatever generation from whatever period the cohort represents. But the differences between educational groups hold up amazingly well, despite age, in the majority of such comparisons.

When one compares all the means in table 8—by sheer accident, there are exactly 100 means for all the cohorts at *each* of the three specified levels of education—one finds not a single instance where the college graduates are not the most informed group, nor a single instance where the high school graduates do not fall between the two polar groups—being more informed than the elementary school group but less knowledgeable than the collegiate group. When we consider only these three levels of education and the pattern revealed by the *mean* scores, the relationship is without exception monotonic. There is an increment of every kind of knowledge with each step up the educational ladder that is preserved, no matter how old the individuals and no matter which of the four periods is examined. The mean scores for the four cohorts examined in 1974 (see table 5.1 in Appendix B) also show no exception to the rule. In this light, the previous observation that the difference in *magnitude* between the means is sometimes less among the *oldest* cohort should continue to be noted, but its importance should not be exaggerated. Any waning of the effect of education in old age that may occur never goes so far as to reverse or even equalize the superiority in knowledge of the better-educated groups.

Although the means convey a reliable picture of the general pattern, they do submerge the irregularities and deviations. Naturally, it is difficult for any reader to juggle mentally hundreds of comparisons of the knowledge about each discrete item prevalent at the three educational levels and then to sort out the pattern by cohorts. There is, however, a clear avenue elsewhere in the detailed tables leading the reader to such insight, although it sacrifices some of the detailed information.

The second set of three columns in tables 1.1 through 4.5, headed "index of effectiveness," are intended to serve a larger purpose which we shall review shortly. But they also incorporate a simple device which reveals the pattern of variation in knowledge among the three educational groups. A minus sign (or dash) in any of these columns indicates some reversal or decline in knowledge when a better educated group is compared with a lesser educated group. The sign in the *first* column denotes a drop when elementary and high school are compared; in the second column, a drop when high school and college are compared; in the third column, a drop when college and elementary school are compared. If there are *no* such signs, the pattern for the discrete item is monotonic with an increment of knowledge at each of these steps up in education. If there are three such signs, the relationship is negative with the slope such that the college educated end with a lower level of knowledge than even the elementary school group. Other combinations of signs denote curvilinear patterns of different types depending on the columns in which they appear; all, however, involve a reversal that produces a *"doubling back"* of the curve rather than a curvilinearity which is merely a change in the *rate* at which knowledge is enlarged by education. The reader can scan these columns quickly for the presence and location of such signs. He will note that, even when the several hundred discrete items are examined, departures from the monotonic pattern revealed by the comparisons of the means are very rare. Such departures are most characteristic in the oldest cohort; they are most likely to follow a particular curvilinear pattern with the sign appearing in the middle column: the high school educated are most knowledgeable, superior to the elementary school group and the college group, but the college group rarely fall below the elementary group. These patterns are summarized in table 9. As tallied there, such reversals or declines occur in far fewer than 10% of the tests except among the oldest cohort, where they are more frequent but still rare. Most of those reversals show the collegiate group among the oldest who fall below the high school group but still remain superior to the elementary school group in knowledge. The average magnitude of the decline, as there noted, is small. Since the many gains in knowledge accompanying education average forty to fifty percentage points, the two to thirteen percentage point drops on the average are properly seen as not only rare but also relatively small.[5] The evidence in table 5.1 from the four items in the 1974 piggyback agrees with these general findings. In the cohort aged forty-nine to sixty, one of the tests shows a departure from the monotonic pattern. Knowledge declines four percentage points between the high school and college levels. But in the other fifteen tests made, knowledge increases with each step up in education—the gain often exceeding fifty percentage points.

We have dwelt on what may be the most striking feature of the general findings, the degree to which the advantages of education endure into *old* age. Whether individuals are sixty-five or twenty-five, they seem to have learned and not forgotten the kinds of bookish facts taught during their schooling, and the skills and inclinations that help them to master current knowledge of the world have also persisted through long years. These conclusions seem borne out by the two different modes of analysis thus far presented. We shall have additional types of evidence to present that will make the case stronger yet, but we should now underscore other more subtle, but equally important, features of the basic findings that have been noted only briefly.

If one turns one's attention away from the *oldest* cohort and focuses instead on the variations in effects of education by *time periods* for adults at any given age stage, one observes another dramatic uniformity. The individuals, although of constant age, represent different generations who experienced distinctive types of schooling and whose lives unfolded in distinctive environments. These factors seem to make little difference. It is as if the sheer benefit from more education—no matter what kind prevailed and no matter what had surrounded it in life—is so substantial that these other factors do not blunt it. The least schooled, even when their schooling may have been of higher quality and even when they lived in a more stimulating and enriching environment, do not seem to make up for their lack of education. The more educated—even if their high schools and colleges deteriorated in quality—still have a big advantage.

One can observe this pattern if one juxtaposes, for any given age stage, the differences in knowledge between educational levels for each of *two* time periods, or if one juxtaposes the prevalence of knowledge among the lesser educated from one time period with the knowledge of the better educated from another time period, again holding age constant. No matter what pairs of comparisons one examines, the pattern is the same (with minor exceptions, noted below). To be sure, it is assumed, when such comparisons across periods are made, that the tests of knowledge have been equally reliable and no more or less demanding in the two periods. Let us extract, from the basic tables, some sets of data that reasonably satisfy this assumption. We shall use the norms obtained from the aggregate national samples, aged twenty-five to seventy-two, for the stratum of individuals who did not go beyond *elementary school*, as an index of the difficulty of the battery of test items in some homogeneous content area.[6] If we restrict ourselves to areas where the battery is fairly lengthy, we can still find a number of spheres where the combined tests administered to two age cohorts born at least a dozen years apart are of equal difficulty.

Two content areas in the domain of public affairs satisfy the requirements nicely. The reader could locate the findings within the detailed tables, but a major feature of them is extracted and presented in table 10. In the domain of academic knowledge, as noted, there are very few items in the surveys of the last two periods. However, we can make a similar analysis in this domain for cohorts born about *seven* years apart by comparing the findings from batteries of equal difficulty asked in the early and late 1950s. These findings are also included in table 10.

To simplify the table, in the five sets of comparisons of the effect of education on equivalent knowledge in two periods, we show only the *difference* between the mean percent informed among *college* and *elementary school* adults. It is, of course, possible for knowledge to be inflated or deflated by some constant amount among individuals from a given period, no matter what their educational attainment. Such a historical change would not be revealed in the *difference* between means. The table also docs not include any comparisons of *high school* graduates and does not provide any evidence on the extreme possibility, mentioned earlier, that the lesser-educated generation from one period might surpass the better educated from another. On such matters, the actual means in table 8 for the three educational levels must be examined, and the reader can inspect the detailed relevant entries corresponding to the time periods and five content areas to be examined in the tiers A-E of table 10. There is no indication of any marked lowering or heightening of knowledge in all members of one or another period. There are but two minor exceptions to the generalization that the lesser educated from one period and the schools of that time *never* surpass the knowledge of a better-educated group from another period. In the academic area of "geography," the *high school* graduates who were *forty-nine or older* in the late 1950s are on a par with the college graduates who had reached the same ages by the early 1950s. We shall not attempt any interpretation of these minor exceptions at this point. Some clarification will be contributed by the analysis to be reported in chapter 5, and we should not make too much of the finding. Certainly there is no indication that the elementary school pupils of any of the periods brought under scrutiny ever come near in knowledge to any of the high school groups, or that the college educated ever decline to the level of the elementary school groups or fall below the high school groups.

The four items of academic knowledge asked in 1955–57 that were repeated in the 1974 piggyback yield the set of comparisons presented in tier F of table 10. At each of four stages of aging, the effects of education on a pair of generations born twenty years apart provide a sixth, dramatic documentation that the education provided in widely separated times, however distinctive, generally produced similar effects.

All of the findings we have been reviewing, following the *second* approach to the basic data, are drawn from comparisons limited to *graduates* of high school and college. It may be argued that this is a serious limitation in drawing conclusions about the effects of education. Individuals who completed the course of instruction at either level, in contrast with those who dropped out along the way, may have had some unusual blend of tenacity, resources, and passion for learning and social pressures which led them to continue in their education. That blend of factors as well as the instruction they received may contribute to the substantial differences in knowledge that have been demonstrated. The critic who argues this way with respect to *our data* should realize how heavy a burden he is taking upon himself, what potency he is assigning to that constellation of factors. It is plausible to argue that way when one examines individuals who are eighteen or twenty-two or even twenty-five, who are fresh out of school and college and still carrying the tenacity, passion, and pressures they presumably brought into the experience of being educated. It is not so easy to make the same argument about individuals of fifty or sixty, whose pressuring parents have long since departed, whose youthful passions for learning have cooled, whose resources may have dwindled through the misfortunes that some of them inevitably encountered. They would have to have the tenacity of bulldogs to have maintained throughout the years their earlier tenacious attachment to knowledge. We do not intend simply to rule the argument out, but it must be seen in the special light of our unusual kind of data. If it were truly the explanation of the results, that would be a serendipitous finding from the secondary analysis of surveys among *mature* adults—one to be treasured as an unusual large-scale demonstration of social psychological processes enduring over a lifetime.

We can confront the question, however, not only with logic but also with empirical evidence. Recall that the first approach to gauging the effects of education examined the complete distribution of knowledge over the *full range* of education. The high school and college dropouts thus were incorporated into that assessment. As we noted, the signs and the magnitudes of the coefficients, gamma, suggested that the relationships were monotonic. Knowledge tended to rise with each step up in the educational ladder, including the steps up to *some* secondary and *some* higher education. If the positive conclusions drawn from the second approach stemmed from the exclusion of those groups who were "turned off" by the institutions and the inclusion of only those who were "tuned in" to start with and especially "turned on" by the experience, the findings from the first approach would not have been in agreement.

Since those coefficients provide only an approximate picture of the pattern, the distributions of all 222 items of knowledge (in the public affairs and academic domains) were examined to determine exactly how many departures there were from a monotonic relationship over the *five* steps involved along the dimension of education.

(Given the laboriousness of the procedure, we examined only the aggregate distribution for all age groups rather than the separate distributions for all cohorts.) In 82% of the items, there was no departure at all from a perfect monotonic pattern created by the inclusion of those with some high school and those with some college.[7] They exhibited some superiority in knowledge over the group on the rung of the educational ladder below them but were inferior to the group on the next-higher rung.

Seven of the items that deviated from the monotonic pattern were peculiar or special in character. Some were so easy that practically everyone knew the answer, and any deficiency in knowledge reflected, so to speak, some strange quirk, e.g., not knowing the number of inches in a yard. Others involved some very difficult or exotic item where hardly anyone knew the answer unless he had some special interest, e.g., knowing the size of the Chinese army or the identity of Sam Lubell or of the county clerk. (For items so extreme that hardly anyone or almost everyone knows the answer, very small percentage differences that could arise simply from sampling error could produce departures from a monotonic pattern. These would not be a dependable source of evidence about the problem.) If we eliminate the seven items that conservatively would be diagnosed as offbeat or undependable, in only 15 percent of the tests was there any departure from a monotonic pattern across the five steps involved.

If we inspect the findings over the same five steps of the educational ladder for the four items in the 1974 piggyback, we find no departure whatsoever from a complete monotonic pattern. Adding these few later findings in with those for the many items in the earlier periods strengthens the overall conclusion. There is a gain in knowledge with each little increment of education for almost 90% of the items.

In light of all of this evidence, we see that the graduates do not appear to be *qualitatively* different in character from the dropouts, although they may have more of that undefined blend of factors that helps them to complete their course.[8] If the dropouts are diagnosed as utterly lacking in that unknown blend, then the findings can only mean that some fragmentary education can produce gains in knowledge even among those who are unreceptive.

These analyses do not answer a more fundamental question. Those who *begin* secondary or higher education, whether or not they complete the course, may still be a select group in contrast with those who never enter that next stage. We have to confront that big question. As suggested in our introduction, we shall control many of the factors that have been found to account for such selection in order to assess the net effects of education. These controls will automatically function to equate individuals at all levels of education, the *dropouts*

as well as the graduates, in many respects that would affect any constellation of resources and inner states and social pressures that could
be hypothesized as a determinant of knowledge. Those analyses
therefore will provide additional incisive evidence, but will be postponed until chapter 3 so that we may consider the third approach to
gauging the general effects of education presented in the basic tables.

In the second set of three columns in the detailed tables 1.1–4.5,
a special index of the "effectiveness" of education in increasing knowledge about each of the items is presented. This index, computed
from the findings on the prevalence of knowledge among the elementary school group, high school graduates, and college graduates
(already presented in the first set of columns), was intended to solve
a number of problems.

As we reviewed in some detail in chapter 1, the various findings
and inferences about the effects of education are dependent on the
level of difficulty of the test items. If a great many of our items had
been so easy that most adults, including the least educated, knew the
correct answers, it would have been impossible for our tests to register
the superiority in knowledge that the better-educated groups truly
might have had. Fortunately, the test items are distributed over a
fairly wide range of difficulty. Most of them are not easy for ordinary
adults to answer, judging by the national norms the surveys provide.
There is plenty of room for large gains to be registered. Using the
empirical norms as our standard of difficulty, we find that the gain
expressed in *absolute* percentage points among the higher groups is
a meaningful index of effect. When an item has been found to be
difficult, that number can become big and impressive and have much
weight in the computation of means. That, from one point of view,
provides a fair picture. If an item is difficult, a gain should be given
much weight in our assessment. If it is very easy, why regard a gain
in the kind of knowledge involved as worthy of much weight in our
assessment? From this vantage point, the previous approach employed was meaningful.

From a technical point of view, however, a problem is presented
by those particular items that turned out to be very easy. It is almost impossible for any gain to be registered. And as we have noted
at various points in our discussion, comparisons across periods or
between contrasted age-groups within a period also implicate the
problems that different items are not equally difficult and that the
same item may not be equally difficult at two time points or for two
age groups. Such problems are reduced in the third approach we have
taken to the data—the computation of an index of "effectiveness."
Each gain in absolute percentage points when expressed in terms of
its ratio to the *maximum* gain that is possible over the level of

knowledge exhibited by the less-educated group yields the index of effectiveness and translates the absolute gain into a relative or standardized measure. The index also helps in comparing the effects of high school and college. If knowledge is widely prevalent among most high school graduates, it is almost impossible for the college graduates to show any gain. In using this device, one should realize that a very *small* gain in absolute percentage points, for an item that is already widely known among the less educated, can become a very large index number. A gain in knowledge from 90 percent in one group to 98 percent in the next group yields an index of 80, but quite properly it means that the gain was 80 percent of the maximum gain that was possible.

Reckoning the effects of education by reference to such indexes gives a big weight to items that have been very easy for the least educated or for the high school educated. If the reader keeps this in mind, he will not be misled. In one way it is not misleading at all, since it overcomes the technical problem that the more educated are handicapped in such instances and cannot exhibit whatever superiority in knowledge they may truly have.

The first of these indexes in the second set of columns in the detailed tables express the gains in knowledge high school graduates make over the elementary school group; those in the second column express the gains college graduates make over high school graduates; those in the third column express the gains college graduates make over the elementary school group. Where there was no gain at all, but rather a decline in knowledge, the index need not and cannot be computed, and a minus sign is entered. These signs serve to indicate a complete lack of effectiveness. In addition, each set of them provides, as earlier noted, a convenient device to gauge the pattern of change. The means presented for each content area are not an average of the indexes for the discrete items. Since the items carrying a minus sign could not be entered into such a computation, such a mean would not be an accurate representation of the general effectiveness for that content area. Instead, it is the index of effectiveness computed from the *mean percent informed* on the set of items for each of the three educational groups, those means being presented at the bottom of the first set of columns.

The reader can inspect these summary indexes of the average effectiveness of various levels of education for various content areas and periods and age cohorts or inspect the long arrays of discrete indexes. Following this third approach to gauging the effects of education, the reader will see that occasionally college has 100 percent effectiveness or close to it, but most of the time it is only 30 to 60 percent effective. Its lasting accomplishments are only 30 to 60 per-

cent of what they might have been, given the gains that could have
been registered over the ignorance that prevailed among the high
school group. The indexes of effectiveness of high school or of college,
relative to the level of ignorance among the elementary school educated, have a similar import. Although such an index may give undue
weight to a small gain in absolute percentage points, it clearly con-
veys that education does not function at maximum effectiveness. The
indexes of average effectiveness are presented for convenience in
summary table 11.

The three approaches establish that high school education, even a
fragmentary amount, has considerable effect in increasing knowledge;
college education, even a fragmentary amount, is effective in increasing knowledge still further. These findings came from the basic data
on the 222 test items in the two domains of "public affairs" and
"academic" knowledge and in the various subareas of content. The
findings can be broadened and strengthened and the limits upon the
generalizability of the present conclusions tested by some additional
evidence and analysis.

Table 12 presents additional data based on the special battery of
vocabulary items asked in a 1966 survey. The six items used are
chosen from various points along a larger steeply graded classic test,
Thorndike's CAVD. The findings are often treated as a measure of
verbal intelligence and therefore were not incorporated in the detailed
tables, although they surely belong in the domain of academic knowledge.[9] These questions were put only to individuals up to age forty-
five in the original survey. The findings therefore apply only to the
two younger cohorts but are consistent with earlier conclusions about
the substantial effects of education.

In table 13, parts 1–4, findings from the battery, mentioned in the
introduction, on knowledge of the tools and duties of four occupations are presented for each of the four age cohorts.[10] Since the two
occupations in the top half—boilermaker and metal caster—are industrial, the questions asked would be "academic," their answers
known perhaps only vaguely and remotely, to the educated whose
daily lives rarely bring them into close contact with blue-collar work.
Thus, in these tests, the educated would be handicapped compared
to the less educated for whom, as members of the working classes,
these are concrete matters close to home about which they have much
opportunity to learn. For the two occupations in the bottom half of
the tables—personnel director and proofreader—the situation is reversed. Here the uneducated, by virtue of their usual class position,
would be handicapped in learning about such white-collar and professional occupations. It turns out that the better educated are markedly more knowledgeable on the five questions relating to these occu-

pations, by all the indexes used to gauge the effects of education. The critic may simply say that this is to be expected and that the tests are unfair, because the respective classes have not had equal opportunity to learn the facts. But then, by the same argument, the uneducated should show a marked superiority on the first six tests, where they have been given an unfair advantage. Clearly this is not the finding. The differences between educational groups are generally nonsignificant and even a bit more likely to show a slight edge in knowledge for the *better educated*. The tables provide quite compelling evidence of the power of formal education, in contrast to what may be called the school of life. They suggest that our earlier findings are not limited to items that could putatively be labeled as loaded in the direction of middle-class culture.

The findings from the cluster of eleven items measuring knowledge of "popular culture" presented in table 14, parts 1–4, provide even more compelling evidence for the generalizability of our previous findings and for the powerful effects of formal education. In contrast with the tests of occupational knowledge drawn from a single survey in 1965, these are derived from half a dozen different surveys spread over a fifteen-year period. Thus any single age-group examined is not drawn from one homogeneous birth cohort or generation but represents several cohorts. These items clearly do not give the educated any unfair advantage. They do not tap high culture or highbrow knowledge. If anything, they deal with highly publicized matters that presumably have great appeal to the common man. They deal with sports, romance, popular heroes, and movie stars, and ought therefore to be of special interest to the young and the vigorous. Thus by examining the pattern among the old they should provide compelling evidence not only on sweeping but also on enduring effects of education.

Two of the items turned out to be terribly difficult. Bob Hope's and Loretta Young's newest movies in 1950 were *so* new that hardly a soul knew about them. In his essay on the "Vicissitude of Things," Francis Bacon stated correctly that "all novelty is but oblivion." Thus, these items can legitimately be set aside as insensitive and incapable of providing any information on our hypothesis. If we ignore them, the evidence, by any of our three approaches, documents the power of education. The gammas almost without exception are positive in sign and of considerable magnitude. Knowledge on the average is about 20 percent more prevalent among the most educated. The chi-square tests (leaving the two insensitive items aside) are for the most part highly significant. The findings are not limited to the young.

The items dealt with in tables 13 and 14 lent themselves to a kind of contest or race between the several groups that had a natural "handicap" built into it. From our total pool of 250 items and from collateral measures in the surveys, we can set up some more races in which we can handicap the better-educated group to provide compelling tests of the power of education.

The first two columns of table 15 present comparisons of nine items, drawn from three surveys, that test knowledge relevant to organized labor, for college graduates and the elementary school group. By reference to other data in the survey, the college group is restricted to those individuals (both men and women) who are not members of union households and who therefore have less interest or opportunity to learn the answers. By contrast, the elementary school group has been restricted to members of union households, who therefore have been given an advantage in the race. The two groups have been raced nine times, and the handicapped college group has come out the winner every time, and by more than a nose.

Some spectators may not regard this as all that dramatic a contest. To be sure, the college graduates labored under a handicap; their advantage, however, in education was so large as perhaps to have evened the odds. The results of more dramatic races are presented to the spectator in column 3 and 1 of the table. A group with only a *moderate* level of education, high school graduates, have now been handicapped by being members of nonunion households and entered against the elementary school members of union households. The races are closer, but the handicapped group still wins seven out of nine times.

In table 16, three items from a 1955 survey dealing with knowledge of "manly" sports permit us to race the college and elementary school groups once more, under conditions where we have handicapped the better educated. By examining the pairs of columns comparing men and women of *equal* education, we see clearly that men are advantaged in learning such matters. Therefore, if we compare women who are educated with men who are uneducated (columns 2 and 3), we can test the power of education in broadening knowledge of this sphere of popular culture under handicapped conditions. Here we evidently have gone too far in creating an unequal match. Education does not override the obstacle introduced, but it does counterbalance it. If one now makes it a fair or equal race, comparing educated groups matched in sex (columns 1 and 3 or 2 and 4), one does replicate the earlier findings of table 14, under more precise and fair controls. The educated members of each sex are considerably more knowledgeable about these popular matters.

These many basic findings establish that the better educated have wider and deeper knowledge not only of bookish facts but also of many aspects of the contemporary world; that the differences override obstructions and endure despite aging, and characterize individuals who represent several generations and several historical periods in the functioning of the schools. But, of course, we have only documented the differences and not proved that education is the cause of it all. We turn to this phase of the secondary analysis, following the steps outlined in our introduction.

3 The Influence of Other Variables

The prime concern of this chapter is to establish that the large, pervasive, and enduring differences in knowledge demonstrated for groups contrasted in educational level really represent the effects of education. Chapter 1 reviewed at some length the severe difficulties of drawing conclusions about effects and outlined the variety of steps that would be taken toward a solution of the problem. We shall not repeat that earlier formulation but do stress that in more than one way most of the major factors that have been found to affect educational attainment and which also may influence knowledge have been controlled, discretely and in combination, in the comparisons between educational groups. The differences by educational level are hardy. They withstand the massive barrage of controls. Thus the conclusions seem safeguarded by strong, if not definitive, measures. Reasonable men, recognizing the impossibility of exercising complete control over every conceivable factor that may contribute to both knowledge and educational attainment, of designing on a grand scale a perfect experimental test of the enduring effects of education, should find the evidence persuasive.

We shall move quickly to review the findings from comparisons of groups contrasted in education but equated in sex, religion, ethnicity, social class origins, and residential origins. As earlier noted, in all the initial comparisons a sixth factor, race, was automatically controlled by restricting the analysis to the white stratum in the national samples. Correspondingly, race is automatically controlled in all the later refined comparisons. Whatever group is examined—women, Catholics, etc.—is always homogeneously white. The detailed tables necessary to convey the findings for all items of knowledge naturally are very lengthy and therefore are presented in Appendix D. Only tables 17–24, summarizing the general results from the series of comparisons involving each of the control variables, are presented in Appendix A. In focusing on the big question of whether the *educational* effects persist, the reader should not neglect other important, if subsidiary, questions which are also illuminated by the findings in each set of tables. We shall stress these only in reviewing the first set of findings on the variable, sex, and readers can inspect the appropriate data for themselves in the relevant tables.

CONTROLS ON SEX

Tables D.1 to D.7 in Appendix D present the findings for all discrete items of knowledge where tests were made of effects of education separately for men and for women. The tables report whether the differences over *all* educational levels were significant (reaching the .05 level by a chi-square test) and what the association, over the full range of the variables, was (as measured by gamma). The items are arranged according to the two major spheres of knowledge, subareas of content, and by time periods. As noted in chapter 1, there was no need to make such controlled comparisons on the many items where men and women had been found to be equally knowledgeable or in the occasional surveys where the samples showed no significant differences in the total distribution of education by sex. Under these circumstances, the gross differences by educational level could not have arisen in the first place because sex was not controlled. Sex is not a determinant of that particular kind of knowledge or of the educational attainments among that particular sample of individuals. An entry indicates these instances. Table 17 summarizes the sets of findings for men and women respectively.

The emphatic answer these tables give to our *big* question is that the differences between educational groups persist among individuals matched in sex. In 123 such tests, there is hardly an instance where the findings are not significant both among women and among men (there are two such instances for women, and three for men). The association between education and knowledge when sex is controlled, as measured by gamma, is of about the same magnitude, on the average, as was found in the uncontrolled comparisons. Thus the earlier findings cannot be assailed by arguing that the gross differences between educational groups simply reflected the greater knowledgeability of men who, having been advantaged in the pursuit of education, are therefore disproportionately represented among the educated. Moreover, the central assumption in such an argument often is not warranted. On about a hundred items, the two sexes are equally knowledgeable (or, occasionally, equally educated), and there is no need to counter the argument by a controlled test.

Although education has a significant effect on both men and women, its effect may be *differentially* greater for one sex. Put another way, there may be some type of interaction between education and sex, rather than education's working uniformly or additively upon the individual no matter what the sex. The question surely is interesting and important to examine, and the hypothesis of differential effects is plausible on a number of grounds. If higher educational institutions have been more selective in recruiting one sex—perhaps, discriminatory—or if it has been less characteristic of one sex to pursue advanced education and only very unusual representatives have presented themselves to the institutions, one could well expect the effects to be differential. Certainly the kinds of institutions that have provided education exclusively for women have been different. And it may be argued that women and men, within the same schools, have not been instructed in the same way. The hypothesis, however plausible on these and other grounds, is not supported in the large by our findings from all kinds and levels of institutions. Table 17 presents seven pairs of gammas, showing the *average* effects on men and women in different periods and spheres of knowledge, and these turn out to be almost identical in magnitude. It may still be argued that the *means* obscure a world of differences. The respective *distributions* of gammas for men and women, showing the effects of education on each discrete item of knowledge, could be different and yet yield averages of the same magnitude. However, by inspecting the pair of gammas for men and women on each of the 123 items available in the detailed tables, one can almost always observe that they are similar in magnitude. The results of such an inspection are summarized in table 17, which shows that in the great majority of instances the magnitudes of the discrete coefficients differ by less than .10. For the items where the differences are large, there is no consistent pattern. Half the time, the association between education and a particular item of knowledge is markedly greater for men; in half the instances, greater for women; and these occurrences are not peculiar to one major content area or period.

The question of differential effects could, of course, be pursued to a point more subtle than that of time period or major sphere of knowledge. Perhaps the differential effects are limited to very particular kinds of knowledge. The reader can examine such subtle questions for himself in the detailed tables in Appendix D. We raise the issue only to alert the reader to the kinds of questions that can be examined in these and other detailed tables on the other variables.

The prime purpose of these tests was to protect the initial findings from being *spurious*. Since the sex of the individual *antedates* education, there was the risk that it governed both the educational attainment and the knowledge and receptivity to knowledge that the individual brought into the school. Then the uncritical could have been misled into drawing the false conclusion that education determined knowledge when in fact sex was responsible for the effects. The empirical findings just reviewed eliminate this danger and have a second implication of interest and importance.

The sex of the individual, apart from influencing chances for an education and the knowledge and orientation toward learning initially brought to that experience, also influences later life, the long chain of experience *subsequent* to the completion of education. It in no sense stereotypes the sexes or assumes that all American women or men have identical careers to assert that sex has important consequences for the roles and experiences of individuals throughout their lifetimes. The different paths taken by men and women conceivably could dampen the earlier effects of education for one sex and enhance them for the other. In our samples of mature individuals, ranging in age from twenty-five to seventy-two with a median age of about forty-five, there surely has been endless opportunity to experience the impress of the role, especially among those who are products of times when the roles were sharply prescribed. Yet in the generations of women who reached maturity and old age in the 1950s and more recently, we find no evidence that their specialized experiences have dampened or enhanced the effects of their earlier education to any differential degree. The same point could be made about the men. Whatever special burden or advantage they have had in adult life does not attenuate or exaggerate the effects of earlier education any more or less than is true for women.

The same series of questions are raised and answered by the sets of findings when other variables are controlled. Having alerted the reader, we shall not dwell on such subsidiary matters and shall focus only on the big question of whether the educational effects persist under various controls.

CONTROLS ON RELIGION

Tables D.8 to D.12 present the detailed findings when religion is controlled, and table 18 summarizes those findings. As noted in chapter 1, Jews are so small a minority in the general population that a separate analysis of educational effects among them would be too insubstantial and risky, and the tables examine only the effects of education separately for Catholics and for Protestants. Since our prime concern is to safeguard the conclusions against the danger that the initial findings were spurious, what should be controlled is the individual's religion *during childhood*. That is the variable that may have governed both educational attainment and the knowledge and propensities to learn that the individual brought into his schooling. To be sure, his early religious identity would also be likely to affect his experiences in later life, and the values and apperceptive mass established in childhood may long endure. We should not ignore these facets of the religious variable, but we cannot omit for our purposes consideration of the childhood status. Ideally the measurement should refer back to that time. As earlier noted, operationally defined, the variable measured in the surveys is the religious identity of the adult at the time of the inquiry. The slippage between ideal concept and measured variable, however, is of trivial consequence, since the proportion of white adults who have changed from their childhood affiliations as Protestants or Catholics is only about 3 percent.[1]

Apart from the way survey agencies measure the variable, religion, it should also be noted that they frequently omit its measurement altogether. Thus, the controls can be applied only to the analysis of 129 discrete items of knowledge; the 100-odd other items have been drawn from surveys where religion was not enumerated. At worst, it should be stressed that 129 items is hardly an inconsiderable number on which to base a generalization. Those items are distributed fairly widely over the various periods and content areas, and the reader can inspect the distribution for himself in the detailed tables. However, a reasonable assumption can be made about the items that, perforce, are omitted from the refined analysis. Since the agencies do not measure religion routinely, one may suggest that it is incorporated into surveys when the researchers have reason to believe that the topics under study are correlated with religion. Since their judgment is empirically based, one may assume that knowledge of the items on which we have been unable to impose the control would be even less likely to be influenced by religion.

The emphatic answer these tables give to the question of prime concern is that the differences persist when the broad constellations of factors covered by the labels "Protestant" and "Catholic" are controlled. In eighty-eight such tests, there is no instance where the differences in knowledge among Protestants of contrasted education are not significant, and in seventy-eight of the eighty-eight such tests among Catholics, the differences are significant. (On the remaining forty-one items examined, religion could not have been responsible for the earlier gross findings and no control is instituted.) The association between education and knowledge when religion is controlled, as indicated by the average values of the gammas, is substantial and of about the same magnitude among Catholics and Protestants as in the earlier gross comparisons. In general, there appears to be little interaction effect; education functions uniformly on both groups to increase knowledge.

In passing, we may note that these tests do more than guard the earlier findings against spuriousness. They also reduce one obscurity that was present in those gross comparisons. Our inquiry has focused only on the effects of given levels or *amounts* of education and not on the influence of particular *types* of schools contained within a level, although in our samples the students from all major types of schools and colleges across the nation should be represented in their proper weights. Within the samples of individuals, a considerable number who are products of *private* elementary and secondary schools are, in the earlier gross comparisons, inextricably mixed with those who attended public schools. This is mainly so for Catholics, among whom the proportion from parochial schools may be between 10 and 15 percent, although true figures for all cohorts are probably impossible to determine.[2] Whatever obscurities were introduced in the earlier comparisons by such a mix are resolved in the refined tests. Among Protestants, the individuals compared are with rarest exceptions all products of public schools. The comparisons among Catholics, of course, do include a considerable proportion of parochial school graduates. In general, those comparative findings suggest that individuals who obtain more education, even that founded on the base of parochial school, show benefits in knowledge equal to those whose education was completely secular.

Although education has a significant effect on Catholics and Protestants—on the average, an effect equal in magnitude for both groups—the tables also suggest that there may be some subtle differential effects limited to occasional items. The reader can locate the respective subtle patterns for himself within the detailed tables, but they may not warrant further study. For unknown reasons—including error—particular items may have behaved in strange ways, and what in the broad religious constellation might determine any real differential effects on special kinds of knowledge would be a matter of guesswork. One factor in the constellation normally accompanying religious membership in the United States, however, has been removed from these comparisons and cannot be implicated in any of the differential effects observed. The racial composition of Protestant and Catholic groups in America is not the same; blacks are rarely Catholics and are likely to be members of a few particular Protestant denominations. However, since blacks were excluded initially from all the samples, the religious groups and the educational strata within them that have been compared are homogeneously white.

EFFECTS OF EDUCATION AMONG THE NATIVE-BORN

Tables D.13 and D.14 present findings on the effects of education among individuals who are all native-born. As noted in the introduction, it was possible to examine the possible contribution of the variable only for the thirty-eight discrete items of knowledge contained within surveys where ethnicity was enumerated. This is far fewer than the number of tests one would like to make but surely provides considerable evidence about the variable. Again, one may assume that agencies make the unusual decision to measure ethnicity in surveys where they have reason to believe it influences the phenomena under study and that they omit it in inquiries where it is less likely to do so. And it should be noted that examination of twenty-three items of knowledge of *public affairs* provided empirical evidence that, in more than 40 percent of these instances, ethnicity had no significant effect. However, some may wish to reserve their decision and adjudge the agencies as guilty of careless neglect of a potentially important variable. In any case, we must make the best of the not insubstantial evidence available to us.

As noted in chapter 1, it was desirable to make tests among the native-born to eliminate the possibility that the effects traced to education represented to some small degree the potency of the educational systems of countries other than the United States, thus resulting in ambiguity. Although our inquiry is not concerned with the effects of particular types of schools, the implicit assumption in all the analyses presented in chapter 2 (and those to be presented in chapter 4) is that we are examining the American national system of education. However, among the older cohorts, a small proportion are immigrants who received their education in their home countries. By confining analyses to the native-born, we ensure that American education is being put to the test. These refined analyses also provide data on whether immigrant status, as noted in chapter 1, could have distorted some of the gross comparisons among age cohorts and educational levels. In addition, these tests provide safeguards against spurious conclusions, since, on various grounds such as discrimination and variations in language and financial resources, immigrants may have been less able to obtain an education and to become knowledgeable.

Table 19 summarizes the findings from comparisons of knowledge among native-born groups contrasted in education. No analysis of the differential effectiveness of education among immigrants is presented. The group is too diverse to be treated as if it had unity; and finer differentations by nationality subgroups cannot be made, since the subgroups are too many and diverse and the respective samples very small.

All fourteen tests on academic knowledge showed significant differences by education. The association on the average is high and of about the same magnitude as in the initial gross comparisons. In the realm of public affairs, analysis of the twenty-three items of knowledge revealed that ethnicity made no difference in ten of them. In another nine tests, when native birth was controlled, the differences by educational level remained significant. The evidence strongly suggests that conclusions about the effects of education in general or in particular age cohorts have not been distorted by the immigrants contained within the various groups.

CONTROLS ON SOCIAL CLASS ORIGINS

Measures of the socioeconomic position of the family at the time the individual was growing up were available on a fraction of the surveys. Nevertheless, it could be controlled in the analysis of the effect of education on knowledge for forty of the discrete items asked in some ten surveys between 1949 and 1971. Six of the items are the battery used to test knowledge of vocabulary. They were treated separately in the earlier analysis of academic knowledge because of the special nature of the indicators, but they are included here because of the need to broaden the limited evidence on the effects of education in this sphere, when social origins are controlled. Even so, only fourteen such tests could be made for 1949–71. However, by asking a question on father's occupation (at the time the respondent was growing up) in the 1974 survey on which we piggybacked the four items of academic knowledge, we were able to make four more tests controlling social origins. We thus increased the total evidence in this sphere to eighteen tests spread over 1949–74, making a grand total of forty-four tests.

It should be noted that three of the twenty-six items of public affairs knowledge are insensitive indicators of the effect of education or of any other source of knowledge, since they are so easy that they are almost universally known. Nevertheless, these three—knowledge of President Kennedy's religion, of President Johnson's home state, and of the name of the governor of the respondent's home state—are included in the findings presented, although they work strongly to depreciate the conclusions on the effects of education. The three items yield very low measures of association and nonsignificant differences by educational level, as would be expected.

Given the potency of social origins—the considerable evidence that a childhood milieu rich in cultural and financial resources can enhance the individual's opportunities for education and knowledge and stimulate his propensities to learn—it was most important to control such variables and protect our conclusions. The number of surveys and corresponding items for which adequately refined analysis could be made is unfortunately limited, but by applying three different analytic approaches to the data, we have at least introduced strong and multiple safeguards against false conclusions.

First, we have followed the conventional approach already used by comparing the knowledge of individuals contrasted in education but equated in the class position of their families when they were growing up. The indicator employed was the occupation of the father. Tables D.15 and D.16 present results separately for individuals whose fathers held professional or executive positions and for those whose fathers held blue-collar positions. These two levels provide a sharp contrast in the *richness* of childhood milieu. Although a rural milieu also presents a sharp contrast with an urban environment, the children of farmers are not examined in these tables, because the *class* positions of those in rural occupations are heterogeneous. (The indicator in these and almost all other surveys is too crude for precise location in the class structure.) Similarly, those whose fathers were white-collar workers are not included, again because they are a rather heterogeneous group.

In these detailed tables, we have departed from the earlier convention of reporting as "significant" all relationships between education and knowledge for groups of homogeneous class origins where the chi-square test yielded a probability of .05 or less. Since the results are mixed and more difficult to evaluate, we wanted some better sense of the weight of the cumulative or additive results from the multiple tests. The chi-squares are reported with greater exactitude. Three asterisks denote a p value of .001, two asterisks a p value of .01, and one asterisk a p value of .05. Table 20 summarizes the findings from this approach to controlling class origins. Among those from blue-collar backgrounds, education almost always makes a significant difference. The additive or combined result from many discrete, but highly significant, tests would clearly be positive. Recall also that three of the six nonsignificant findings out of the total of twenty-six tests made in the public affairs realm are based on the insensitive items that all people know no matter what their education or origin.

When one examines the effects of education among those whose origins were professional, the results are somewhat confusing. Only a little over half of the tests are significant. Three of the nonsignificant tests, of course, are again based on the insensitive items. And it should be stressed, as the evidence presented in table 21 shows, that the cells in these analyses are often exceedingly small. Those of lowly origins (a large class) who obtain high education may be a minority of their class but, since they come from a large class, they are considerable in number. It is exceedingly rare, however, for the children of high-status parents to be bereft of almost all education. Stemming from a small class to start with, this tiny minority is a negligible number that often produces a nonsignificant finding. One would be inclined to regard the results as reflections of the weakness of the tests rather than of the weakness of education. Consistent with this interpretation, the average values of the gammas, expressing the general association between education and knowledge for the two groups of contrasted origins, are about the same in magnitude and not dissimilar from the coefficients obtained for these items in the gross tests. Examining the summary table for differential effects of education by class, we find that the effect is enhanced on particular items about as often for one class as the other.

A second approach to these data may reduce the uncertainty. Again, the device of a contest or race with a built-in handicap has been employed. Instead of comparing the knowledge of groups with more and less education who are equated in social origins, we have examined a group of college graduates who have been "handicapped" by a relatively impoverished childhood milieu. These contestants, drawn from blue-collar families, have been raced forty-four times against others who have started with the advantages of class to see who shows superiority in knowledge of each of the items. Whenever possible, they have been compared with a group drawn from professional families who had not gone beyond *elementary* school. Since some may regard the educational disparity as too great, a third group has been entered: those from advantaged backgrounds who had graduated from high school. In passing, the reader will realize that, when these latter two groups are compared with each other, one has a test of the effect of an increment of education among individuals equated in social origins. Table 21 presents the results. As the reader will see from the appropriate entries, the cell containing those from professional backgrounds who did not go beyond elementary school is so small in some surveys as to preclude their entrance into some races. These tiny groups, however, were included in the first analytic approach to the problem, with the attendant difficulties noted.

There were twenty-five races where the performance of the three groups was examined. If we exclude the three contests involving tests of knowledge which was almost universal, the outcomes on the other tests indicate that the college educated, "handicapped" by low social origins, performed better than those from higher social backgrounds who had not gone beyond elementary school twenty out of twenty-two times. In these same three-way races, the handicapped college group performed better than those of higher social backgrounds who had even gone so far as to graduate from *high school* eighteen times out of twenty-two. In the instances where it was possible only to race the "handicapped" college group against the high school graduates of advantaged social background, the college group won seventeen out of nineteen times. In the races where the performance of two groups equated in high social origins, one with high school education and the other with only elementary education, can be compared, the better educated win in almost all the contests.

A third approach taken to the question of whether the earlier associations between knowledge and education could have been consequences of growing up in an enriched environment employed techniques of multiple and partial correlation. Throughout our earlier analyses, we could have summarized or expressed the relation between education and knowledge by correlation coefficients. Such a procedure would have been conservative, however, and very possibly misleading, since our items, although almost always monotonically related to education, are frequently not related to it in linear fashion.[3] However, in estimating the net effect of education after social origins are controlled, it seemed desirable to try more powerful statistical methods than we have used elsewhere in the analysis, obtaining in the process simultaneous control over multiple possible sources of spuriousness.

Five surveys in our original pool plus the 1974 survey contained at least some information on respondents' families of origin. These surveys and the knowledge items from them are listed at the left of table 22. In the first column of the table, we present a summary measure of the association between education and each item. In each case, a dichotomized dependent variable (correct/incorrect) was regressed against respondent's education, the five categories of which were entered seriatim as four dummy variables. (In the 1959 and 1967 NORC surveys, here and in the next chapter, "no schooling" and "1 to 8 years" were kept separate, so we entered *five* dummy variables.) The "R" in the first column is the square root of the variance explained by education in this fashion (or the "multiple r" of the items with the dummy variables).

The six surveys had rather different combinations of background variables. The first three (NORC 1959 and 1967, and SRC 1958) had measures only of father's occupation (categorized as professional or executive; white collar; blue collar; and agricultural) and of ethnicity (categorized as native- or foreign-born). The fourth survey (SRC 1964) had, in addition, an assessment by the respondent of whether his family background was "middle class" or "working class." The fifth survey (NORC 1966) had a measure of father's occupation (similar to the others) and measures of both father's and mother's educations (five categories each, similar to codes for respondent's education). The 1974 survey had only father's occupation. For each survey, each background variable was entered as a series of dummy variables to explain each knowledge item, with the results shown at the right of the table.

By and large, the joint effects of whatever background items are used are somewhat smaller than the effects of respondent's education alone. Notice that, by this standard, the more elaborate measures of family background, as might have been expected, do a somewhat better job than the simpler ones.

The crucial comparison, however, is that between the first and second columns of table 22. After the background measures had been entered into the regression equation, the respondent's own education was entered (as a series of dummy variables, as before), and the data in the second column address the question of whether education makes any difference in knowledge, after the effects of family background on knowledge have been statistically "removed." The number in the column is the square root of the proportion of *residual* variance (after background items have been entered) which is explained by education.

In most cases, there is some reduction of the difference education makes (and in a few cases, there is substantial reduction), but overall the magnitude of the reduction is not at all impressive. We can conclude, on the basis of these data, that education per se contributes to knowledge—both directly to "academic" sorts of knowledge and indirectly to other sorts of knowledge.

CONTROLS ON RESIDENTIAL ORIGINS

There is evidence that the residential milieu during childhood affected the educational levels attained by the populations sampled in our surveys. In the total population that was already adult in 1950 or that became adult as late as 1960, those reared on farms show the lowest educational attainment. Those from a rural nonfarm milieu, although not so disadvantaged, also trailed behind those brought up in urban areas.[4] It also seems plausible that, in the past before television and turnpikes invaded the countryside, the rural environment would have been poorer in information and could have hindered the growth of knowledge among those from such settings. The apparent effects of education on knowledge thus may represent the influence that residential origin has on each of the two variables, and controls on that possible source of spuriousness would be desirable.

It is a commentary on social research that only *one* of our many surveys included a direct question about the size of the community in which the respondent grew up. Table 23 presents the findings for

the five items of knowledge available to test the effects of education
where the residential milieu can be controlled with considerable precision. Unfortunately, all five items are from the domain of "public
affairs" and refer to one special category, knowledge of persons in
government. Granted these limitations, the effects of education persist, with occasional exceptions—notably on the one item, knowledge
about the mayor—when individuals are equated in residential origins.

The meager evidence from these five direct tests, fortunately, can
be strengthened by indirect evidence from the forty-four earlier tests
which controlled father's occupation during the respondent's childhood. That control serves to specify the respondent's *residential*
origins as well as his class origins, since professional, executive, and
blue-collar careers are generally practiced in *urban* settings. There
are, admittedly, country doctors and country lawyers, and some com-
muters who keep their families down on the farm, but these must be
a small fraction of the larger professional and executive group. The
city dwellers who send their children off to live with their country
cousins must also be exceptional. Farm managers and farm laborers,
following the routine coding practice in surveys, are never included
in code categories, "executive" and "blue collar." They are included,
along with sharecroppers and farm owners, in the heterogeneous
category "farmers." As noted earlier, that category is thus made too
crude to define class origins, which prevented our using those with
farmer fathers in the tests of educational effects when class origins
were controlled. However, it serves very well to screen out of the
professional or executive and blue-collar categories all the children
of farmers, only a few of whom would have been sent to grow up
with their city cousins.

The soundness of this formulation can be supported by empirical
evidence. The one survey that included the direct question on residential milieu during childhood also included a question on father's
occupation during the child's development. Among the white adults
aged twenty-five to seventy-two in 1967 (the date of the survey), of
those who had professional fathers 10 percent report that they grew
up on a farm. Among those with blue-collar fathers, the proportion
is 9 percent. Thus the educational levels compared earlier in table 20
are not only equated in class origins; with few exceptions, they are
"urban" in origin.[5] (For illustrative evidence that the educational
differences persist among those from rural origins, see note 5.) To be
sure, this is not a precise way to control the residential milieu, since
there is much variability, among these two "urban" occupational
groups, in the size of the community where they spent their childhood.

Many grew up in small cities and small towns, although the modal category is the big city.

CONTROLS ON CURRENT SOCIAL POSITION

Tables D.17 to D.23 examine the effects of education on knowledge, controlling the *current* social position of the adult at the time of the survey. As noted in chapter 1, these tables serve a different function and should be interpreted differently from the tables controlling other social characteristics. An obvious link in the long chain of effect from early education to later knowledge is the life style that the educated can achieve, because their entry into privileged occupations or into marriages with the more privileged eases the acquisition of, and buying of the facilities that lead to, knowledge.[6] When we control the current social position of either the respondent or the breadwinner in the family, we are not protecting the earlier findings from the risk of being spurious. Current position could not have antedated education; position follows education temporally and dynamically. The controls, however, test whether the hypothesized process is the only avenue by which mature educated adults obtain and maintain their greater knowledge, or whether such knowledge can endure despite the disadvantaged status to which those adults may fall. The tests also tell whether the uneducated who rise in status can compensate for the deficiencies of their earlier education. To be sure, these tests are not utterly unitary or pure in their implications. To some extent, privileged position is inherited from one's family, and the social disadvantages a child started with are often perpetuated in his later life. Thus the variable, current status, indirectly reflects, to some extent, social origin and partially controls that earlier status and its accompaniment, intellectual aptitude, in an indirect and approximate fashion.

Table 24 summarizes the findings from these analyses, which were made for all 222 discrete items of knowledge. What is examined in these sets of tables is the effect of education separately for two contrasted groups of individuals, those contained within professional families and those contained within blue-collar families. This states the matter neutrally, but it may also be formulated in a more dramatic fashion, admittedly speculative. The highly educated in lowly circumstances may perhaps be described as having wasted their opportunities and fallen below their proper stations. Perhaps they have been unlucky, but certainly they have not made the most of their credentials. The uneducated who have arrived at a high station in life may have been lucky—or, in contrast, they may be described as un-

usually talented in having got far with little training. The educated
of professional and the uneducated of blue-collar status may both
be described as in positions commensurate with their training. Thus,
in a way, in the comparisons at the professional level, "ordinary"
educated individuals are being contrasted with "extraordinary" uneducated individuals, and in the comparisons among blue-collar individuals, "average" uneducated individuals are being contrasted with
educated individuals who are in some way less than "average." The
two races are, possibly, not quite fair matches, the educated contestants in both instances being, in some subtle sense, handicapped.

In the great majority of tests, the effects of education persist even
when the opportunities provided by current class position are equated.
Among those living in a blue-collar milieu, this is almost invariably
so. Among those living in a professional or entrepreneurial milieu, it
is true in about 80% of the tests made, but the slight increase in the
number of findings that appear to wash out at this level may simply
represent the small numbers in some of the cells. The association
between education and knowledge, on the average, is of about the
same magnitude at the two class levels. However, when the detailed
distributions are examined, there is considerable evidence that education, although significantly effective no matter what the opportunities and life style available, functions differentially depending on the
circumstances. The effects of education are frequently enhanced
among those whose circumstances are advantaged and attenuated
among those in less-advantaged positions. This pattern occurs on a
substantial number of discrete items of knowledge, as the summary
table shows, and the reader can inspect the detailed findings presented in Appendix D. What is suggested is that it is harder for the
educated to obtain and maintain their knowledge under stringent conditions of life. Evidently, their greater knowledgeability is whittled
away but not to the extent that it withers or vanishes.

REFINING TESTS ON THE EFFECTS OF AGING BY COHORT ANALYSIS

Chapter 2 presented a great deal of evidence that the positive effects
of education endured in individuals who had reached as advanced an
age as sixty. Indeed, with only occasional exceptions, enduring effects were generally observed in individuals as old as sixty-one to
seventy-two. However, various difficulties in drawing inferences about
aging and the enduring effects of education from comparisons of
groups who had reached different ages on the date of a *particular* survey, or during one narrow time period when some particular set of
surveys had been conducted, were reviewed at length in chapter 1.
The contrasted individuals do represent those who have aged more

and less and who are removed from their schooling by few or many years, but they also represent cohorts born at different historical points who may therefore reflect the experiences of their respective generations and the particular kinds of education during those times.

Our comparisons, fortunately, involved age-groups drawn from many surveys clustered at four points over a twenty-year period. The uniform finding that the effects of education persisted among the old, no matter what birth cohort or generation was sampled, strongly suggests, to adopt a poetic view on education, that "age cannot wither nor custom stale her infinite" power. One would be hard pressed to argue in the face of the evidence that the effects endured simply because of the good fortune or unusual training and talent of some singular generation. The few exceptions to the general findings can be discounted on statistical or methodological grounds and surely do not deserve to be treated as weighty evidence against the conclusion.

Despite all the evidence, the question of whether the effects of education endure with aging is important enough that further tests were made by another method. As mentioned in chapter 1, changes in the very same birth cohort as it is aging can be brought under scrutiny by locating equivalent samples of the cohort at successive stages of life from surveys widely spaced in time. For example, the cohort aged twenty-five to thirty-six in our surveys of the early 1950s was easily relocated in the surveys of the early 1960s. By then members had aged a dozen years and were the individuals who fell into the age-group thirty-seven to forty-eight. The method of cohort analysis is not so simple and uncomplicated as just described, but the methodological difficulties and safeguards have been reviewed in chapter 1, and it does provide a direct, longitudinal approach to our problem.

The time span covered by the surveys and the fineness of the age codes were ideally suited to an extended cohort analysis in which a considerable amount of aging could be brought under observation. But in order to study whether the effects of education on *knowledge* persisted, declined, perhaps even enlarged, as individuals aged, we needed identical or equivalent items in widely separated surveys to provide comparable measures of knowledge or receptivity to knowledge. In the fifty surveys, of the 250 items, only 2 were found that had been repeated after a *long* interval, although many had been repeated in adjacent surveys to measure short-term trends. Table 25 (tiers A and B) presents the results for the 2 items, knowledge of the filibuster and of the electoral college, the former having been repeated in surveys separated by almost a fifteen-year interval and the latter after about an eleven-year interval.

Although both items measure knowledge in the same narrow area, civics, it should be noted that at no time were the two carried on the same surveys. Thus they yield two independent sets of tests of the changes that occur as a number of cohorts age a good deal and reach various advanced stages of life. And the limited area covered in these tests will be extended to some other tests soon to be reviewed. It should also be noted that the question about the filibuster had been asked in several adjacent surveys around the first time point, 1949. Two of these were pooled making the base point measurement more reliable and less susceptible to transient conditions. In this light, one may give more weight to the findings on "filibuster."

The two items are "academic" in the sense that they are taught in school. To be sure, they refer to contemporary institutions, and the knowledge may be reinforced, even learned for the first time, in later life. Thus it would not be unexpected if all groups gained a little knowledge with age, since there would have been ample opportunity for all individuals to learn about such common institutions, whatever their former education. Such a constant gain would not obscure the relative position of the various educational groups. If one group, however, were more receptive to learning in later life as a result of its education, or more or less prone to remember its earlier academic lessons, that would show up in differential changes with aging.

Tier A shows changes in knowledge about filibuster for contrasted educational groups contained within three birth cohorts as they age some fifteen years between the dates of the surveys. The youngest cohort has moved on to the mature stage of being forty to fifty-one; the older cohort has moved along as far as the early sixties; the oldest cohort has advanced to the point where its oldest members are seventy-five by the time of the later survey. Looking down the *columns* shows the change in the prevalence of knowledge in the particular educational stratum with aging. The elementary school group shows trivial or modest gains tailing off with very old age. It is surely dramatic to find that knowledge has increased strikingly among the college graduates in the oldest cohort as they move into "very old" age, although the small numbers suggest caution. The consequences of aging for the high school stratum within these cohorts appear to be quite different. A decline begins to occur around age fifty, and the loss in knowledge is substantial as this stratum in the oldest cohort studied reaches old age. We shall reserve judgment on these distinctive patterns until we examine other items. Whatever decline occurs does not change the relative positions of the contrasted educational groups as they age. Inspecting the three pairs of *rows* in the table, one observes that the disparity in knowledge between educational levels is just as great or even greater, despite fifteen years of aging, which has taken some of these cohorts far along in the aging process.

Tier B presents an equivalent analysis of changes in knowledge about the electoral college. There is an apparent *decline* in knowledge among the college educated in the oldest cohort studied as they move into very old age, but again it should be stressed that the base or cell size for estimating the knowledge of this group when the members were in their fifties is only twelve cases. Conservatism would urge that the finding be treated most tentatively. Among the high school educated, no decline in knowledge with aging is observed. If anything, they seem to show unusually large gains. The discrepant findings from the analyses of the two items leaves the issue cloudy or leads to the conclusion that there is neither a consistent gain nor a consistent loss in knowledge with aging. In any case, again we observe, by examining the pairs of rows in the table, that the large differences between educational groups persist despite aging.[7]

The four items of academic knowledge piggybacked in 1974 are themselves diverse in content and difficulty, but all refer to another broad area, history and geography, and had been asked in three of our early surveys from 1955 to 1957. Thus they permit us to extend the interval over which cohorts can be aged—to almost twenty years and almost up to age eighty—and to examine changes in knowledge over a wider area. The four sets of cohort analyses are presented in tiers C–F of table 25.

Examining the changes in knowledge of each discrete item within each educational level of each cohort as it ages and reaches some life stage is a complex and bewildering task. We shall try to highlight the general patterns that characterize the three items presented in tiers C–E and the two items already reviewed in all the cohorts as they reach "middle age" and in all the cohorts as they move into "old age." The former label is used somewhat arbitrarily for the first pair of rows in each tier, which take various cohorts up to about age fifty. The latter label is used perhaps arbitrarily for both the second and third pairs of rows in each tier, but it surely applies to the last rows, which take all cohorts as far as age seventy and some almost to their eightieth year. We have violated our earlier standard practice and have included these very old individuals in this one analysis so as to devise the most dramatic test possible of the enduring effects of education. Changes in knowledge about the sixth item, Mt. Vernon, presented in tier F of the table, will be reviewed separately because of one distinctive feature of the pattern.

No matter what changes have occurred with aging in any of the educational levels, one thing remains unchanged in all of the tests and all of the cohorts. The large differences in knowledge between educational groups persist. Within each educational level, over the five items examined, declines and gains in knowledge are about equally common up to middle age. Many of the changes are small, and a decline on one item, even when substantial, is offset by a substantial gain on another item. The net change in "general knowledgeability," averaging the changes on all items, is close to zero. The same pattern of change occurs as the cohorts move into old age. Gains and declines are about equally common and offset each other, the net change in "general knowledgeability" being close to zero.

In contrast with the first five items of academic knowledge where knowledge remained fairly constant over the ten- to twenty-year interval, by 1974 knowledge of the location of Mount Vernon, for reasons unknown, was much more prevalent in the total population than it had been in 1957. As noted earlier, various events can have a temporary or permanent effect in heightening the knowledge about some item. However, any differential sensitivity of a group to such stimulation because of either age or education should still be revealed, and the prior differences in knowledge, if substantial enough, should persist despite whatever quantum of later knowledge is added to or subtracted from the earlier scores. In the cohort advanced from age thirty-seven to forty-eight to ages fifty-four to sixty-five, as shown in the middle pair of rows, the great gains in knowledge at the lower levels of education have washed out the earlier differences. But in the other cohorts, the differences persist with aging. For the college educated within the oldest cohort studied, their gain is the greatest as they move up into their seventies, and their earlier superiority is even enhanced as a result.

We can make use of the batteries of items on domestic public figures to broaden the evidence still more. The fourteen items asked in the early 1950s had an average index of difficulty of 30, and the twenty-four items asked after about an interval of a dozen years in the surveys of the early 1960s had an average difficulty index of 34. Although not identical, they are equivalent in content and difficulty. The same situation applies to the twelve items asked in the late 1950s and the fifteen items from the late 1960s, whose average difficulty index was 42 in both instances. Thus two more independent sets of tests can be made. The length of the batteries and the fact that the items were drawn from multiple surveys should make the estimates more reliable and less subject to transient sources of error. These items, of course, were not taught in school, and knowledge of them is indicative of *receptivity* to learning in adult life. The equivalence of the batteries had permitted the analysis reported in table 10, where the influence of generation had been found to be negligible. The findings from the same batteries, appropriately rearranged to show changes in knowledge as cohorts are aged, are presented in table 26.

Given the small sample sizes, we surely should regard changes of five percentage points as negligible and nonsignificant, easily accounted for by sampling error.[8] The general findings from the two sets of analyses presented in tiers A and B of the table suggest that knowledge and receptivity to knowledge in this domain do not grow with aging—but neither do they wane. The differences among educational strata endure into old age. There is the suggestion that the lesser educated may gain a little as they mature and move into middle age, but they never come close to catching up. The last two rows of tier A of the table suggest that the college educated stratum may become slightly less receptive with old age, but here again the numbers in the cells are so small as to make the finding tentative. These nine sets of cohort analyses, combined with the many findings reported in chapter 2, support the general conclusion that educational effects long endure.

4 Continuing Learning: Mass Media Exposure and Information Seeking

Lessons may stop once an individual exits through the classroom door, and the formal institutionalized period of schooling ends, in most instances, with the final year of classwork completed or the highest degree earned. But human learning goes on, far beyond the days and years of school. It is more than a cliché to say that one of the functions of early formal education is to prepare the individual for a lifetime of learning.

Numerous authorities agree that to educate means more than to inform and instruct an individual about his society's current culture, although this is an important part of the educational process. Education also tries to equip him with the motivation, intellectual outlook, and skills that will give him the power to continue to learn, to seek, and to be receptive to new information and culture that exist beyond the classroom, and to participate fully in the larger world of communication that surrounds him and forms a vital part of his intellectual environment.[1]

Outside the schoolhouse, the major sources of information about what is going on in the world (ranging from current political events to more enduring scientific and technical discoveries) are, for most citizens in modern societies, the several channels of mass communication. Some information, to be sure, reaches individuals from specialized sources (e.g., scientists talk to one another and read technical journals), and all individuals receive some kinds of information from personal sources (e.g., neighborhood gossip), but the bulk of the news and interpretation about the larger world surrounding the individual and his family and neighbors is mediated through our system of mass communication. Therefore the use of such media or the failure to use them is one indicator of the individual's continued interest and involvement in society. Communications exposure may be seen as one prerequisite to informed social participation.

Adult communications behavior and information seeking may be regarded as important products of education in their own right. They also may serve as mechanisms by which adults, with varying amounts of formal schooling, acquire additional knowledge, especially on non-

80

academic matters such as current events, but also on academic subjects. In this chapter, we direct our attention to establishing the link between level of education and subsequent adult communications behavior, by cohorts.[2]

We examine survey data on the differences in communications behavior among respondents who have had varying amounts of formal education. We begin with what is, in one sense, a broad indicator of continuing learning and information seeking—general exposure to mass media. Then we consider somewhat more purposive, but informal, means of potential adult learning, namely, the use of the mass media for following specific topics. Two realms of public affairs are considered, national and foreign affairs, parallel to the distinction observed in earlier chapters. Limited data are also available on the use of the media to keep informed about a more personal and private topic, health. Finally, there are data on purposive and formal acts of lifetime learning—enrollment in adult education classes or efforts at self-instruction. Information seeking in relation to the sphere of "academic knowledge," treated in the earlier chapters, of course is not included, since the topics involved are not in the purview of adult mass media (except in connection with adult education classes, where they are subsumed).

In presenting the data, we depart from the pattern of explication and analysis followed in the previous chapters dealing with levels of information. Findings are presented, in accordance with our model, for each of four age cohorts, but the surveys are not grouped into the established periods. The main reason for this departure is that there were too few replications of specific items to permit such systematic comparisons across time. Nevertheless, a wide spread of time (twenty years) is covered by the various surveys to be used, and this temporal span will be reported and taken into account in our analysis. It provides grounds for confidence that our generalizations about the relation between formal education and subsequent adult communications behavior and information seeking are not based on data limited to one period.

MASS MEDIA EXPOSURE

Our findings, quite consistent with those of other researchers, are that higher proportions of individuals with more formal schooling, compared to those with less, regularly use the print media (newspapers, magazines, and books). They also are more likely to attend motion pictures. On the other hand, education shows no consistent relation to daily television viewing and is not positively related to daily radio listening.

Newspaper Reading: An Example of the Analytical Procedures

Seven national surveys ranging from 1951 to 1967 with a combined total of thousands of respondents show a significant relation between level of education and newspaper readership. We shall examine these data in some detail in order to illustrate the mode of analysis that we shall use subsequently (see table 27.).

Let us consider, first, the percentage of individuals in each of our four age cohorts who read a daily newspaper, for each of the surveys conducted between 1951 and 1967. As an example, in 1967, 44 percent of the respondents aged twenty-five to thirty-six who had only an elementary school education reported that they read a daily newspaper. In the same age-group, 74 percent of those who had graduated from high school (but had gone no further) read a paper daily, as did 86 percent of those who were college graduates. Comparable figures among the age-group thirty-seven to forty-eight were: 53 percent readers among the elementary school educated, 87 percent among the high school graduates, and 89 percent among the college graduates. For the age-group forty-nine to sixty, the figures were 60 percent, 91 percent, and 95 percent for the elementary school, high school, and college groups, respectively. And the corresponding figures for the elderly (sixty-one to seventy-two) were 70 percent, 88 percent, and 89 percent. Thus the 1967 survey showed that newspaper readership increased with each step in higher education, within each age-group, although the gains appear small in some instances.

The relation between level of education and newspaper readership in 1967, if we use the full range of education and all cases—that is, if we do not restrict the comparisons to those who had *graduated* from high school or college—also was statistically significant, by chi-square measure, within each age-group. The probability that such differences would occur by chance is less than one in one thousand (.001). The strength of this overall association, as measured by gamma, ranges from .40 to .54 among the four age cohorts.

The relation between education and daily newspaper readership holds for all seven national surveys and within each of the four age cohorts, with one exception. Examination of the twenty-eight tests of significance (column P) reveals that the relation is significant (at the .05 level or better) for twenty-seven of the tests. Indeed, in half the tests the relation is significant at the .001 level, and if one were to use the additive property of x^2, the probability that twenty-eight independent tests of the relation of this magnitude would occur by chance is infinitesimal. The strength of the association ranges from gammas of .03 to .79, most being above .40.

In all four age cohorts and throughout all seven national surveys, the proportion of high school graduates who read a daily newspaper is greater than the proportion of those whose schooling stopped with elementary school who do so. Further gains in newspaper readership appear between high school and college graduates, in nineteen of the twenty-eight comparisons, although the size of these gains is often smaller than those between elementary school and high school.

This examination of the findings separately for each of the seven independent national surveys, spanning sixteen years of recent history and representing the work of different agencies, strengthens our confidence in the general relationship discovered. It is not an artifact of a particular survey or of a moment in time.

A crude but convenient summary measure of daily newspaper readership among individuals of varying age and schooling is presented in table 28. This measure is the average of the percentages of newspaper readership for each educational level in each age cohort across the seven independent national surveys. These summary figures make it clear that persons with high school education are more likely than those without it to be daily newspaper readers—whether young, middle-aged, or elderly. The relation between education and adult reading habits does not fade with time; some of these elderly respondents have been out of school for the past half-century.

While the actual differences in percentage of newspaper readers found among individuals of varying levels of education are important in their own right, we were also, as before, interested in determining the relative impact of each increment in schooling. For this purpose, we have computed indexes of effectiveness for high school graduates vs. elementary school only, college graduation vs. high school graduation only, and college graduation vs. elementary school only. These indexes have been explained earlier, so we need only summarize them here to refresh the reader's memory. Each index is the ratio of actual gain to total possible gain between the two levels of education being compared. As examples, 44 percent of the young elementary school educated individuals in 1967 read a newspaper daily; 56 percent did not. If the additional schooling provided by high school graduation had the impact of making everyone a newspaper reader, then the gain would be 56 percent. The index would be expressed as 56/56 or 1.0; but to avoid decimals we follow the convention of multiplying by 100; thus the index in this case would be 100. Actually, 74 percent of the young high school graduates were newspaper readers in 1967. The gain is 30 (74-44) and the index of effectiveness is 30/56 (x100), or 53. This means that high school graduation was effective in achieving newspaper readership among

53 percent of those who, presumably, would not have been news-paper readers if their schooling had stopped at the elementary school level. The impact of college graduation vs. high school only, for this age-group in 1967, was 46; and the impact of college graduation vs. having gone to elementary school only was 75. With this refresher, we are now ready to inspect the findings. The indexes of effectiveness are presented in three columns in table 27. The averages of these indexes are computed in the same way as described in chapter 2.

High school education has considerable impact on increasing the ranks of newspaper readers. In all surveys, for all cohorts, there is a sizable index of effectiveness for high school, ranging from 43 to 100. The relative improvement in newspaper readership brought about by college graduation vs. high school only is smaller but considerable. Nineteen of the twenty-eight indexes of effectiveness of college (vs. high school only) range from 8 to 100; six have reached this upper limit. In eight of the twenty-eight comparisons, there was a decrease in percentage of readers between high school and college graduates, and in one instance there was no change. Overall, when the impact of college graduation is compared with elementary schooling only, gains in newspaper readership are found in every one of the twenty-eight comparisons across all surveys and for all age-groups, the indexes of effectiveness ranging from 13 to 100, most on the high side.

Indexes of the average effectiveness across the seven surveys are presented in table 29. Inspection of these averages enables us to determine whether there is a pattern of differential impact of education by age cohorts. For example, if the impact of education on news-paper reading weakens as the individual grows older, then the average of the indexes of effectiveness should decrease as he moves from the younger to the older cohorts. This clearly is not the case. The impact of high school education on newspaper reading ranges from 63 to 71, with no apparent trend among age-groups. The overall index of the effect of college graduation vs. having only an elementary school education was 76 among the very youngest and 65 among the oldest cohort. These data, taken in conjunction with the increase in percentages of readership as the individual moves up the educational levels, show that this very substantial impact of education on subsequent newspaper readership persists throughout a lifetime. It does not wither with age.

To summarize, there is impressive evidence that education is positively related to daily newspaper reading. This relation occurs in seven independent national surveys from 1951 to 1967. It is consistent over the four age cohorts under study, indicating that the impact of education persists over an adult's lifetime. The major gains in newspaper readership appear with graduation from high school, but completion of college also increases the proportion of individuals who read the newspapers every day.

Our presentation of these findings has been lengthy and, perhaps, labored, because we wanted to exemplify our mode of analysis. We move now to briefer presentations of the findings about the impact of education on our other measures of communication behavior and information seeking.

Magazine Reading

The effects of education on subsequent adult reading of magazines is even more dramatic than its impact on newspaper readership (see table 30).

Data are presented from five independent national surveys from 1955 to 1967. The proportion of magazine readers increases with educational level in fifty-nine of the sixty comparisons possible. The relation is, for all practical purposes, monotonic. The probability of such differences' occurring by chance is less than .01 in each of the twenty comparisons over the full range of education by age cohort. And the strength of the relationship (gamma) ranges from .30 to .58.

The largest gain in absolute percentages of magazine readership occurs between elementary school and high school. But the additional years of college education also increase the proportion of readers. The combined impacts of high school and college graduations yield indexes of effectiveness ranging from 64 to 100.

The impact of education on subsequent adult magazine readership, as with newspaper reading, does not deteriorate with age. For example, the indexes of average effectiveness of college graduation vs. elementary school education is 81 among those aged twenty-five to thirty-six and it is 91 for those aged sixty to seventy-two. And the averages of the percentage of college graduates who are regular magazine readers is 95% for the elderly compared with 88% for the young adults.

Book Reading

The probability that an individual will read books is also clearly a function of amount of education (see table 31).

Data from five independent national surveys between 1952 and 1963 indicate that the relation between book reading and education (over the full range of education), among the four age cohorts under study, was statistically significant in sixteen of the twenty possible comparisons. The strength of these associations (gamma) ranged from .32 to .68.

Sizable gains in the proportion of persons who read books occur when high school graduates are compared to individuals with elementary school background only, but equally sizable and sometimes larger gains occur between college and high school graduates. The effectiveness indexes for college/high school are greater than those for high school/elementary in all but one or two instances.

An average of 7 to 10 percent of the elementary school educated in any age cohort were reading a book at the time of any of three independent surveys. In contrast, from 46 to 60 percent of the college graduates (on average) were currently reading a book. An average of 22 to 32 percent of the elementary school educated had read a book during the year preceding each of two surveys, while an average of 72 to 94 percent of the college graduates had done so*

Moviegoing

Though hardly a direct measure of information seeking, moviegoing provides exposure to one mode of our popular culture and an opportunity to become knowledgeable about it. Three of the surveys contained informative data about this behavior (see table 32).

Educational background is related to motion picture attendance. The relationship was statistically significant in nine of the twelve possible comparisons across the full educational range. Gammas range from .15 to .72.

The greatest gains in proportions attending the movies occurred between high school graduates and the elementary school educated, at all ages. The impact of college was greater among the young and middle-aged adults and weakened among the advanced middle-aged and the elderly.

In general, motion picture attendance dropped with age, regardless of educational background. Even so, about half of the elderly high school graduates attended movies, in contrast to about a quarter of those elderly individuals who had not gone to high school.

Daily Television Viewing

Our data on television viewing come from three national surveys conducted in 1956, 1962, and 1967 (see table 33). Obviously, the prevalence of television viewing increased in all educational strata and all age cohorts during this eleven-year span, so that by 1967 most respondents were television viewers.

Differences in proportion of daily television viewers by the full range of educational levels were statistically significant in seven of the twelve comparisons. Gammas ranged from .01 to .24.

---

*Because specific question wording varied among the five national surveys, two summary average measures are presented in the table, one for 1952–57, the other for 1962–63.

On average, the relation between education and television viewing is not monotonic. It increased slightly between grade school education and high school graduation, then decreased for the college graduates. An exception is among the the elderly, where viewing was essentially unrelated to educational level.

Daily Radio Listening

Although we have data from only two national surveys bearing on radio listening, it is quite clear that daily listening is not positively related to educational background (see table 34). The differences in proportions of listeners among individuals with various amounts of schooling, for each of the four cohorts, is not statistically significant in seven of the eight comparisons.

KEEPING INFORMED ABOUT ELECTION CAMPAIGNS AND ABOUT PUBLIC AFFAIRS

Following Presidential Election Campaign News in the Mass Media

In the preceding sections, we have examined gross data on general exposure to mass media by individuals with varying educational backgrounds. These data demonstrate that persons with more formal schooling are more likely to "tune in" to mass communications as adults; as a consequence of general media usage, they may be exposed to information of social and political consequence.

We turn now to data on communications exposure focused directly on one realm of civic importance—following mass media coverage of presidential election campaigns. We draw upon data from four surveys conducted by the University of Michigan's Survey Research Center in 1952, 1960, 1964, and 1968.

The percentage of individuals who specifically follow presidential campaigns in their newspapers is considerably lower than the percentages of individuals who are daily newspaper readers. Nevertheless, this particular use of the daily papers to follow campaigns clearly increases with level of education (see table 35). The differences between individuals with varying amount of schooling are statistically significant in eleven of the sixteen comparisons. The associations range in strength, by gamma, from .12 to .46. The relation is monotonic, increasing somewhat as we move from adults with no high school education to high school graduates to college graduates. The increase in proportions of those reading election news is generally greater between the high school and college educated populations than between those with elementary school vs. high school backgrounds. In addition, the indexes of effectiveness show that the additional schooling provided by college graduation has a somewhat greater impact than high school graduation has over elementary education alone. The impact of additional formal schooling prevails among all age cohorts, again demonstrating that it persists far beyond the era immediately following graduation.

Relatively few people read about election campaigns in magazines. This activity is more common among individuals with more formal schooling than among those with less (see table 36). All of the sixteen comparisons were statistically significant, with associations (gamma) ranging in strength from .31 to .58. Readers of such magazine material are most rare among individuals with less than high school education (the average of percentages ranging from 1 to 6 percent and not much more prevalent among high school graduates (averages ranging from 8 to 14 percent). It is only among college graduates that a sizable minority follow information about the presidential election campaigns in magazines. The indexes of effectiveness show that college graduation has a greater impact on this behavior than high school graduation alone.

Educational background did not influence viewing election campaigns on television (see table 37). Only three of the sixteen comparisons were statistically significant. On average, approximately one-third to one-half of the respondents, from each cohort and from each educational level, used television for this purpose.

Radio listening to election campaigns also was not a function of educational background (see table 38). Few of the sixteen comparisons were statistically significant. On average, from about one-tenth to one-quarter of the respondents from each cohort and educational level listened to the campaigns on the radio.

We conclude our examination of adult exposure to news about presidential election campaigns with a relevant psychological variable, interest in politics. One function of education, we have held, is to stimulate the individual's interest in social and civic matters. Interest, in turn, may lead the individual to continue to seek information about such topics as an adult. Studies have suggested, especially for presidential election campaigns, that interest in politics and communications exposure about campaign events are intertwined in a mutually causative fashion that is impossible to unravel. Interest is related to higher media exposure on the topic; higher communications activity, in turn, appears to lead to greater interest. We will not attempt to sort out the causal circuit here. But we can examine the extent to which formal schooling is associated with expressed interest in politics during the later postschool adult years. Data on this relationship are presented from seven independent national surveys spread from 1952 to 1971 (see table 39).

Education is clearly related to adult interest in politics. (Unfortunately, the questions did not distinguish between interest in local politics and interest in national politics—a distinction which will prove to be important in chapter 5.) In twenty-five of the twenty-eight comparisons, the differences are statistically significant; the strength of the associations (gammas) ranges from .22 to .53.

College graduation appears to have a substantially greater impact on the development or continuation of this interest than high school alone, although both contribute. The result is that while, at best, somewhat fewer than three out of every ten individuals with no high school education are very interested in political events, about two-thirds to three-quarters of the college graduates express strong interest.

In summary, the previously described relation between level of education and subsequent adult general exposure to newspapers and magazines is further supported when we consider the specific use of these media for keeping informed about an important civic event, presidential election campaigns. Television viewing and radio listening, neither especially related to educational background, were also not any more or less likely to be used as sources of information about election campaigns by persons with different amounts of formal schooling. Adult interest in political events is clearly related to education.

Following Public Affairs

The second specific media usage we examine is following public affairs coverage in the mass media. Data about following public affairs in general were obtained from a national survey in 1960, and data on paying attention to a specific topic—the Vietnam War—come from two independent national surveys in 1968 and 1970 (see table 40).

With only one exception, the more formal schooling the members of any age cohort had, the more likely they were to follow news about public affairs regularly—to follow newspaper accounts of these events every day and magazine accounts at least every week. These results were statistically significant in all but one of the twelve comparisons. Both high school and college education contribute to sizable increases in the proportion of individuals who follow public affairs in the press; the index of effectiveness of college/high school usually is greater than high school/elementary. Findings on the effects of education on following public affairs on radio and television are less definite.

National survey data on interpersonal communications about public affairs are rare. Therefore we are fortunate in having one question about this area in the 1960 survey. We find that the probability of the individual's talking about public affairs every day increased with his level of formal schooling, although only a minority of the public discussed such matters daily.

One particularly salient issue in recent American foreign policy has been the Vietnam War. Data from two national surveys indicate that this concern cuts across educational levels. In six of the eight comparisons between persons having different educational backgrounds within each age cohort, there is no statistically significant difference in the proportion of individuals who paid attention to the war.

In summary, adult attention to public affairs, whether the individual is exposed to them through the print media or through personal discussions, is directly related to the amount of formal schooling he obtained earlier in life. Occasional exceptions appear to be media-specific (e.g., broadcast news) or tied to an especially salient political and social problem (e.g., the Vietnam War).

KEEPING INFORMED ABOUT HEALTH NEWS

Our prior examples have concentrated on information seeking or communications exposure in the political and civic realms. For contrast, we turn now to two surveys containing data on following mass media accounts about a more personal matter, health. Does prior education make a difference in whether individuals continue to keep informed, by mass media, about developments in the field of medical and dental care?

A national survey in 1955 reports the percentage of adults who frequently read the health columns in the newspaper and in magazines, and who listened to programs about health on radio or on television (see table 41).

From youth through early middle age, the individual's level of education is related to his subsequent reading about health in newspaper columns. The greatest increase in readership is attributable to the individual's having completed high school. Education is more consistently related to reading the health columns in magazines; both high school and college have impacts within each age cohort from young to elderly. By contrast, education appears unrelated to the probability of the individual's listening to health programs on radio and television.

Data from a national survey in 1959 shed light on adult exposure to communications about dental health (see table 42). The more formal schooling individuals had had, the more likely they were to recall seeing articles about dental hygiene in papers or magazines and frequently reading such articles in the press. Seeking advice directly from a dentist is more common than reading articles on dental health, but its relation to formal schooling is questionable. This could be expected, since the opportunity to seek such firsthand advice depends on so many factors other than schooling.

These limited data on communications behavior concerning the personally relevant area of health indicate, on balance, that prior schooling makes a difference. Persons with more formal education appear more likely than those with less to make the effort as adults to keep informed about health matters.

Continuing Education as an Adult

The most formal evidence of continuing lifetime learning that we have comes from three surveys, made in 1950, 1962, and 1963, providing data on participation in adult education. The 1962 survey also provides data on whether the individual had ever tried to teach himself some subject through self-instruction. The relation between these adult educational activities and prior formal schooling is shown in table 43.

Participation in adult education is clearly related to earlier formal schooling, whether the adult education takes the form of enrollment in courses or of self-instruction. Furthermore, this relation is found among all four age cohorts under examination, no matter which survey or period is under scrutiny. Both high school graduation and college graduation (but the latter more so) contribute to the likelihood that an individual will continue his search for learning after graduation, and these impacts are found at all age levels, from the very young adults to the elderly.

Differences between individuals with varying levels of formal schooling are rather large. For example, only 7 percent of the youngest adult age cohort in 1950 who had not gone to high school had ever subsequently taken an adult education course, in contrast with 52 percent of the college graduates; comparable figures in 1962 were 24 percent vs. 77 percent. If the time span is extended to include most of the individual's lifetime and considers the history of those who were elderly at the times of the surveys in 1950 and 1962, it still is the case that those with college education were more likely to have taken some additional course work as adults than were those with elementary school backgrounds. Also, for both young and elderly, individuals who had graduated from high school were more likely to have taken some adult education courses than those who had not gone to high school.

High school graduates were more likely than the elementary school educated to have tried some form of self-instruction, as were college graduates except among the elderly.

Conclusion

A variety of measures, ranging from general exposure to mass communications through specific enrollment in courses in adult education, have shown that individuals' chances for continued learning are greater for those who have had the benefits of a greater amount of formal schooling before adulthood. If we accept the argument that one of the long-range goals of formal education is preparation for a lifetime of learning, then our data present strong evidence for the conclusion that our schools are achieving this goal to an observable degree.

In some cases, it is apparent that the experience of a high school education is sufficient to influence the individual far into his adulthood. In others, the additional years of college schooling leave their mark. In most cases, the combined impact of high school and college is quite substantial.

Taken as a whole, the data presented in this analysis of a large number of national surveys, covering two decades of recent history and reflecting the impact of education on individuals of varying ages who have been out of school for few to many years, lead us to the conclusion that some of the enduring effects of such schooling are seen in adult communications behavior and information seeking. Adults who start out with more formal schooling are more likely to exploit the communications opportunities in their society that will keep them informed about significant social, political, personal, and academic matters of concern to them. .

A Postscript on Controls

We have described the various ways in which we have tried to take into account the possible contributions of sex, social background, religion, and various other characteristics of the individual that may have been associated with his level of schooling and possibly with the dependent phenomena which we are attributing to schooling. Parallel analyses were conducted for the communication variables. Overwhelmingly, the relation reported between level of education and subsequent adult communications behavior (or the lack of relation, in some instances) appeared to hold up under controls for these other characteristics. With so many items to be considered, there were bound to be rare instances, of course, in which the impact of education was reduced or differentially important for individuals classified by sex, religion, and ethnicity. Since our conclusions are based on the general pattern of relation disclosed, we shall not present the lengthy detailed tables for specific controls.

One important factor deserves special consideration, however. This is the social origin of the respondent and its possible impact on the relation between education and adult communications behavior.

Two of our surveys had social background information on respondents in a form which allowed us to control for the effects of these factors, as we have in the previous chapter. Table 44 shows the results of this procedure.[3] NORC study 4018 (1967) allowed us to control for father's occupation and for ethnicity. It is evident from the table that education makes substantially more difference in media exposure of almost every sort examined than do these two background factors jointly, and—the critical point—that the difference education makes in media exposure is affected only negligibly by controls for these factors. NORC study 447 (1962) allowed us to control for both parents' education and father's occupation.[4] These factors jointly make about as much difference in media exposure as— actually, a little more than—respondent's education alone. Here, the controls reduce the difference education makes in media exposure somewhat, but, as in chapter 3, we can conclude that the association between education and our dependent variables is for the most part not spurious.

To summarize, the impact of the respondent's schooling on his subsequent adult communications behavior was reduced only very slightly by the influence of his social background. These various tests increase our confidence that the differences in adult behavior of persons having more or less schooling are not due to initial differences in the social origins of our respondents.

5 The Relative Effectiveness of Secondary and Higher Education

We have seen that the relation between education and specific learnings, although almost always monotonically positive, is very often not linear. For many of our items, although the proportion giving a correct response increases as education increases, it does not do so at a steady rate. We remarked this fact earlier, but in this chapter it will be the center of our attention. In contrast with the earlier chapters, we shall ignore the problems of aging and of different generations and look at variations in the shape of the relation between education and different learnings for the whole population.[1]

If one thinks for a moment of the subjects taught in American schools, perhaps one will not be surprised that competence in them does not increase by a constant amount each year. The alphabet, for instance, is taught to almost all students in the first grade. Almost everyone who is going to learn it has done so by the second grade and, although the proportion who know it may continue to increase, it will do so at a slower rate. Similarly, the multiplication tables are taught, to almost everyone, somewhat later. The curve relating years of schooling to knowledge of the multiplication table will show an abrupt increase in the middle years of primary school and then level off. This leveling off is not simply an artifact, a "ceiling effect" (although it may resemble one); it reflects the positioning of the subject matter in the curriculum. A relatively low proportion even of college graduates, for instance, will have mastered calculus. The curve relating education to this skill will not, in other words, rise very far, but what rise there is will be concentrated some time after the last years of high school.

In some cases, the positioning of subjects reflects the fact that some are prerequisites for others. An individual must be able to read before he can do almost anything else; he cannot study calculus until he knows algebra. In other cases, however, hoary tradition seems to be at work. In this country, in this century, the study of foreign languages has usually begun in high school (far too late, some have said), while philosophy and most of the social sciences have been reserved for college (still too early, some may say). In situations

where the positioning of a subject is a matter of individual taste or of
local school board finances, we would expect to find learnings more
steadily increasing with years of schooling. Some subjects (like foreign languages) will be begun by some people in primary school, by
some in high school, and by still others in college. (The same effect
would be expected for subjects where people are exposed to the same
topics, if in greater depth, year after year. It has not been unusual,
for instance, for college students to have studied American history for
three or more years between the first and the twelfth grades and to
be "taking it" again as freshmen or sophomores.)

Common sense, then, would dictate a nonlinear, although positive,
relation between years of schooling and "academic knowledge,"
broadly defined. Many of our items measure various sorts of "academic knowledge," and we can ask at what stages in the curriculum
these learnings have been acquired. (There are methodological problems, of course, some of which will be discussed below.) Although
the earlier chapters have touched on the relative "effectiveness" of
high school and college, clearly the question at the heart of our concern here is: do (or, in what respects do) high school graduates
know as much as college graduates?

In the case of "current events" knowledge, it is less clear that we
should expect marked departures from linearity—just as it was less
clear that we should have expected the overall association with education that we have already observed. If, however, this knowledge
reflects habits of inquiry and attentiveness acquired in the course of
schooling, we can inquire whether *these habits* are acquired gradually
and steadily (i.e., linearly) over the course of the individual's education, or whether they are acquired rather abruptly. Moreover, we can
use our pool of items to distinguish among sorts of topics (personal-
ities vs. issues, foreign vs. domestic affairs), as in the earlier chapters, and between relatively superficial knowledge (e.g., recognition
of a name) and more thorough understanding (e.g., correct definition
of a concept), and we can ask when the corresponding interest and
skills were developed.

AN INDEX OF "PLACEMENT"

The nature of the problem to be examined in this chapter is illustrated by the data in tables 45–47. The items in each set are similar
to each other in their "difficulty" (indexed by the proportion of people
with little schooling who respond correctly) and the overall "effect"
of education (indexed by the difference between those with little
schooling and college graduates). Within each set, however, there
are substantial differences in the proportion of *high school graduates*

who respond correctly. Although persons with a grade school education were unlikely to know where either the Leaning Tower or the Suez Canal is, and college graduates were likely to know both, high school graduates were quite likely to know the former and relatively unlikely to know the latter. If we pretend that these data came from the same group of people as they moved through the educational system (recognizing that the image may be misleading), we can say that, although most will eventually know both, they learned the location of the Leaning Tower *before* they learned that of the Suez Canal—or, more precisely, that most who were going to learn where the Leaning Tower is (and had not learned it in grade school) had done so by the time they graduated from high school, while most who learned where the Suez Canal is, between grade school and college, did so in college.

A similar sort of reckoning can be applied to the data in table 46. Note that very few *ever* learn four symptoms of cancer or the name of the planet nearest the sun. Most of the small number who learn the former, however, do so in high school, while the latter is learned— if at all—in college. Similarly, table 47 can be interpreted as showing that most people who are going to be able to identify the authors of *Tom Sawyer* and *A Midsummer Night's Dream* can do so by the time they leave high school (although some additional learning takes place in college), while familiarity with Tolstoy and Freud are more clearly distinctive marks of a college education.

Obviously, what is needed is an index *locating* each of our items within the educational sequence, preferably one which is independent of the issues (considered in previous chapters) of how prevalent knowledge about the item is, and of how much difference—overall— education makes in knowledge.[2] One likely index could be the ratio of the percentage difference between the elementary school educated and high school graduates to the percentage difference between the former and *college* graduates. This measures, in effect, how much of the difference between those with a grade school education and the college educated is in fact simply a difference between those with a grade school education and high school graduates (which, of course, nearly all college graduates are). We are examining, in other words, the effectiveness of high school compared to that of high school *plus college*.[3] If we adopt the convenient fiction that our percentages represent measures on the same individuals at different points in their educational careers, then the ratio is the proportion of those *who are going to learn an item* between grade school and college graduation who have done so by the time they become high school graduates. For example, in table 46, there is an increase of 13 percent (3 to 16 percent) in the ability to name four cancer symptoms between elementary school and college graduation: 89 percent of this increase has occurred by the stage of high school graduation. By the same stage, in contrast, only 16 percent of the elementary school to college increase in the ability to name the planet nearest the sun has taken place.

This is the index of "placement" (P) which we shall use in this chapter. We shall, however, subtract the percentage from 100: thus, the larger the index, the "later" the stage at which an item (whether it measures an academic learning or, indirectly, a skill) is "learned."[4] The measure is admittedly crude, but it will serve to order the items in our pool according to their average location in the American school curriculum. Table 48 shows the items from tables 45–47 ranked according to their scores on this index. A small index value means that the learning is one which distinguishes chiefly between high school graduates and those with only a grade school education; a large value means that the item distinguishes the college educated from high school graduates. A value of 50 would mean that high school graduates are exactly halfway between the grade school educated and college graduated—or, put differently, that half of those who are going to learn it have done so by the time they graduate from high school. Table 48 is shown primarily to illustrate the way in which this index orders items of quite different difficulties that also vary in the strength of their relation to education. It is for the reader to say whether the order generated is "surprising" or not, and we shall reserve discussion of the *content* of learning at different stages for later.

SEQUENCING OF ACADEMIC LEARNINGS

Clearly, one factor affecting the stage at which an item is learned is its difficulty. For instance, learnings which are difficult because they presuppose *other* learnings must come relatively late in the educational sequence. Similarly, as we observed above, specialization comes relatively late in most American school systems, so learnings reserved for specialists, which appear (from the data) "difficult," should also be acquired relatively late.

The placement index allows us to verify these speculations (and their verification, in turn, supports our interpretation of what the placement index is measuring). One way in which we can generate a set of items ordered by difficulty is by taking *one* item and putting greater and greater restrictions on what is to be considered a "right" answer to it. We can ask, for instance, whether the ability to name five or more cabinet positions is acquired earlier or later than the ability to name at least one cabinet position. (Obviously, for a given *individual*, it will be acquired later—if only a few minutes later. But, far fewer people can name five positions than can name one: the question is whether they learned to name five at the same time that— or earlier than—others were learning to name one). Table 49 presents four cases in which this has been done. Observe that three of the four show the typical (and expected) pattern: the more difficult (i.e., more inclusive) response was acquired later.

If the ability to name each country (or cabinet position or Gospel or cancer symptom) were independent of each of the others, of course, purely probabilistic logic would dictate that the ability to name several would be more positively accelerated in relation to education than would the ability to name one. In cases where a "compound item" is *less* positively accelerated with relation to education than one of its components, we are led to examine the assumptions in the probabilistic model. This is the case with the question in table 49 asking for symptoms of cancer: it appears that detailed knowledge is "acquired earlier" (if it is going to be acquired at all) than the relatively superficial knowledge implied by the ability to name one or more symptoms. (Put another way, although high school graduates are somewhat less likely than college graduates to be able to name a symptom of cancer, they are almost as likely to be able to name four. In fact, among those who can name *any* symptoms of cancer, high school graduates are slightly more likely than college graduates to be able to name four or more). What this means is that learning one cancer symptom is not independent of learning others, and that these learnings are more strongly related for high school graduates than for college graduates. If a high school graduate is going to learn about cancer at all, he is a little more likely than a college graduate to "specialize" in it.

With this exception, however, these data suggest that persons with more education are not only more likely to have learned about a given subject—they are even more "more likely" to have learned about it in some depth and to have retained this knowledge into later life. Notice that one could easily have argued, in the absence of these data, that one result of higher education is a nodding acquaintance (or the ability to pick up or simulate such an acquaintance) with many subjects which one does not really know well. Our data suggest, to the contrary, that, for most subjects, superficial "acquaintance" is acquired at a relatively early stage; more detailed knowledge is acquired later (if at all).

Table 50 supports this conclusion. Occasionally the survey organizations coded answers more precisely than simply "right" or "wrong," indicating, for instance, that an answer was "probably correct" or "vague" or "partly correct" or "correct but less explicit [than a thoroughly 'correct' answer]." Usually when responses were coded in this fashion, the data show that the more superficial, less precise information is acquired earlier.

Once again, however, there is an exception, and it is interesting because it suggests an explanation for the earlier exception. Among the items testing knowledge of geography was a question asking for the location of Manchuria. As in the question dealing with the symptoms of cancer, the ability to give at least an approximate answer appears to be picked up, on the average, at a *later* stage than the ability to give a precise answer—again, if high school graduates are able to give an answer at all, they are slightly *more* likely than college graduates to give a precise one. Perhaps, however, for many high school graduates, at the peak of the Korean War in 1951 (when the question was asked), the location of Manchuria was not exactly an "academic" question—just as, for many people, knowledge of the symptoms of cancer is not. On these matters, as on most others, superficial knowledge increases with education; the "problem" is that there is relatively little increase in *detailed* knowledge between high school graduation and college graduation. We may suppose that many people will respond to conditions like having a friend or relative fighting in Korea, or stricken by cancer, with increased attention, resulting in detailed knowledge. We may also suppose that war and cancer affect people whether they are college graduates or not. In other words, if the information is in some respects "academic" (i.e., it *can* be learned in school) but relates to situations in which many people are personally involved, we may expect that superficial knowledge will appear to have been acquired later than detailed knowledge. When we turn to an examination of "current events" knowledge, we shall look for additional examples.

So far, we have distinguished between "superficial" and "detailed" knowledge—between "easy" and "difficult" questions—by manipulating the possible responses to individual questions. In earlier chapters, of course, we have operationalized the notion of "difficulty" by saying that a question answered correctly by a large proportion of the relatively unschooled is an "easy" one. By the logic of the argument above, we should expect to find that such "easy" items have been learned at a relatively early stage.[5]

Table 51 shows that this is obviously true for the items in our pool that tap academic knowledge of the humanities. The survey organizations do not report what constitutes a "correct" identification of the several artists and philosophers about whom their respondents have been asked, but one suspects not much was required. (Note the similarity in response frequencies between at least "partly correct" identification of Plato and "correct" identification of Aristotle—there was no "partly correct" category for the latter.) Evidently it is easier to "identify" Shakespeare than to recall the author of *A Midsummer Night's Dream*—and the former is learned earlier.

Substantively, the result of high school seems mostly to be familiarity with the names of some illustrious composers and with the works of such prominent authors as Shakespeare and Mark Twain. Most of the other items we have—dealing with philosophy, psychology, the fine arts, and literary figures—seem to be reserved for college.

When we turn to the items which tap knowledge of history (table 52), we find the same pattern: easier (or less specialized) items are learned earlier. In fact, compared to the humanities items, these items are quite easy and nearly all are learned before graduation from high school by most of those who are going to learn them. It is difficult to generalize about content from our limited sample of items: can we say that names of exemplary figures are taught before military history?

Knowledge about the Battle of the Bulge (specifically, in what war it occurred) is included in table 52, even though it could hardly be "academic" knowledge for these respondents; since they were answering in 1957, all had to have been at least teen-agers when the battle took place. Notice, however, that it is related to education in much the same way as knowledge of the war in which the Battle of Gettysburg was fought—with the significant exception that it was "learned earlier." Like the symptoms of cancer and the location of Manchuria, we may surmise that the Battle of the Bulge was personally important for many of our respondents.

The same pattern of earlier learning of easier or less specialized material is revealed in table 53, which shows items related to civics and government. In this table, we also have some evidence above the reliability and stability of the index of "placement." Respondents were asked four times in 1949 (once on a split ballot) and once in 1963 to define "filibuster." For the four 1949 ballots, the value of P ranged only from .34 to .38; by 1963 it had risen to .49, an increase which over a fourteen-year period is probably as due to actual trend as to response instability (and a value which still locates the learning—if only barely—as taking place in high school, for a majority). Notice, in any event, that by 1963 the learning had become less specialized (as measured by "% College"). The index values for the definition of "electoral college" show more variation—they are above .60 for 1950 and 1951, but substantially lower for 1954 and 1961. The corresponding variation in the percentage giving "correct" definitions suggests that the criteria for acceptable answers may have changed from survey to survey. This would affect P, but there is no clear connection between "easiness" and "placement" in these four observations, and the possibility of unreliability remains open.

Tables 54–55, presenting data on knowledge of geography and of science and mathematics respectively, contain no surprises. The easier (or less specialized) geographical material—United States geography, major world capitals, the countries and tourist attractions of Western Europe—are learned before high school graduation, if at all. More exotic spots—most places east of the Rhine or south of Mexico, apparently—are situated cognitively only by the college educated (unless, as suggested above, the U.S. army is likely to be engaged there). Scientific knowledge related to personal health or other aspects of daily life appears to be learned early, if at all, while learnings more thoroughly "academic" (in the sense of the word which means "irrelevant") are acquired later (again, if at all).

To summarize: although we have seen in previous chapters that knowledge of *all* sorts increases from grade school to high school and from high school to college, it is clear that there is considerable variation among our items in the degree to which they distinguish chiefly between high school graduates (including those who go on to college) and persons with only a grade school education, as opposed to distinguishing chiefly between college graduates and those without a college education (including those with only a grade school education). By and large, it appears that "easier" learnings are acquired at an earlier stage. Many of these "easier" items require relatively undetailed or imprecise acquaintance with a subject—knowledge that Formosa is somewhere in Asia, or that Shakespeare wrote (unspecified) plays, for instance—or hinge on the association of two words or phrases—"Eiffel Tower" and "Paris," or "Einstein" and "relativity." Others may simply appear "easy" by our measures of difficulty because—like the name of the ocean between the United States and Britain, or Christopher Columbus's major accomplishment, or how many times 3 goes into 75—they are taught to most people in *grade school.*

In many of the cases we have examined, an easy item appears to be "learned early" because of ceiling effects. The item is one which is known to nearly all high school graduates, and there is nothing a college education can do to increase that knowledge. Nearly all high school graduates can name at least one cabinet position; what college can (and does) do is surround that knowledge with related information. It fills in the names of past incumbents, locates the department within the broader structure of the executive, identifies the department's "job," teaches the names and functions of other cabinet departments (thus, the ability to name five or more cabinet offices is located by our index somewhere after high school graduation). Not many people learn in college where the Eiffel Tower is; most high school graduates know that. A somewhat higher proportion, however, learn after high school graduation where *France* is, and nearly everyone who ever learns where Bulgaria is does so in college. Most high school graduates have at least a vague idea of what "monopoly" means, but not until college graduation can most define it with any precision.

In some other cases, however, we have located relatively "difficult" learnings ("difficult" in that relatively few persons ever learn them) early in the educational process. Often this is clearly because these subjects are emphasized in American secondary education—the major works of Shakespeare and Mark Twain, American geography and military history, weights and measures. If these subjects are learned at all (and the data show that they frequently are not—or are forgotten), they are likely to be learned before high school graduation. In other cases, relatively difficult or specialized items appear to have been "learned early" because—we have suggested—they are important in the daily lives of at least as many high school graduates as college graduates.

All of these learnings are at least *possibly* academic—i.e., learned by respondents in school and retained by them into adulthood. At least two separate processes underlie our data, however. The first, implicit in the previous discussion, is that people who have gone further in school have simply been exposed to a larger body of knowledge (of which, presumably, our items and the "learnings" they measure are indicators). The other process rests on the fact that, as we have seen in chapter 4, education trains people in habits of media exposure and of self-education that continue the process of learning long after formal education has ended. Not only have educated people learned more, that is, but they have also learned to behave in ways that ensure (1) that they are less likely to forget what they have learned, and (2) that they continue to acquire new information.

They are less likely to forget what they have learned because even the more specialized material is in a sense more relevant to their everyday lives. They continually reencounter it in the course of their reading, television viewing, conversation, and other daily activities— the nature of which has been shaped by their education. Thus, while in 1951 Manchuria may have figured as often in the concerns of high school graduates as of college graduates, the former were probably less likely than the latter to be reminded that they once knew the capital of American Samoa, the name of the British commander at Quebec, or the name of the planet nearest the sun.

Better-educated people, moreover, are more likely to continue to learn after they leave school. They have the prerequisite knowledge and habits of attention necessary to acquire knowledge that was neglected in their formal education or that did not exist at the time they were in school. It is impossible to say how much of the difference in academic knowledge between educational levels is due to differences in what was learned initially, how much to differences in what has been retained, and how much to differences in what has been learned subsequently (although much of the terminology in the above discussion assumes that the first is the principal factor). We can, however, as in chapters 2 and 3, examine current public affairs knowledge as a case where we can say with certainty that the observed differences are due to the last factor—learning which has occurred after (often long after) the end of formal schooling. We can ask whether the generalizations we have made about learnings which are presumably in large part academic apply as well to those which could *not* have been learned in school at all.

THE "PLACEMENT" OF PUBLIC AFFAIRS KNOWLEDGE

In this section, it will be appropriate to drop the interpretation of the placement index as measuring whether an item is "learned early," since such an interpretation is clearly not applicable. We can fall back on the interpretation of the index as measuring whether high school graduates more nearly resemble college graduates or persons with only a grade school education. If high school graduates are as likely as college graduates to know about some public affairs item, it is because their information-gathering skills and habits are as efficient, in that respect. If they resemble those with only an elementary school education, it is because the requisite skills and habits are, in that respect, lacking. In other words, the placement index, when applied to public affairs knowledge, is presumably measuring the stage at which information-gathering skills sufficient for different tasks are acquired.

Table 56 shows that "compound" items made up of current events items behave very much like those made up of academic items. As the criterion gets harder and harder, high school graduates resemble college graduates less and less. (Incidentally, the items asking respondents to name their senators give some additional evidence on the stability of the index, as applied to similar items asked at different times by different survey organizations. The table also shows that ceiling effects can be as much of a problem when *no one* knows an item as when everyone does. Note that the value of P begins to decrease, for the question asking for Supreme Court justices, after we have reached the point where essentially no high school graduates are responding correctly.)

These data basically support our earlier conclusions, but the evidence in table 57 is less clear-cut and suggests an important qualification. Although here, as in table 50, the usual pattern is for high school graduates to resemble college graduates more with respect to "approximate" knowledge than to detailed knowledge, the differences are in general smaller, and a substantial minority of the items show a reversal of the pattern. We have suggested that this reversal was likely for knowledge which is of equal importance in the lives of high school and college graduates. Perhaps we can assume that this is more likely to be so for "public affairs" knowledge (at least of the sort which makes its way into public opinion polls) than for most strictly "academic" knowledge.

The three largest reversals occur on the items asking for an identification of Richard Nixon (in 1963), a definition of the 38th Parallel (in 1951), and a definition of automation (in 1957). The first is seemingly due to the relatively small proportion of college graduates who gave an entirely "correct" answer and the relatively high proportion of high school graduates who did so—both puzzling when compared to the figures for other politicians (e.g., Rockefeller)—and also at least possibly due to sampling error. (The reader should recall that, in 1963, Richard Nixon had recently lost a California gubernatorial election and was languishing in political obscurity. Although this does not explain the reversal, it does account for what may seem, to some, to be relatively small proportions who identified him correctly.) The item asking about the 38th Parallel is a much better example in support of our general explanation of these reversals and could have been predicted from the similar results for the item asking for the location of Manchuria. The automation item is perhaps even more to the point. In the late 1950s, high school graduates who had *any* idea of what automation meant were relatively likely to know *exactly* what it meant—not surprising, when we reflect about whose jobs were supposedly threatened by automation.

A related set of data are shown in table 58. Here we see that high school graduates resemble college graduates more when they are asked simply whether they have "heard of" a public figure or agency than when they must give more precise identification. (The data bearing on the identification of J. Edgar Hoover come from different surveys over a period of several years. However, the consistency of the results with those found elsewhere strongly suggests that the difference in index values is due to the greater difficulty of the more detailed questions rather than to actual change over time.)

Finally, we can ask whether high school graduates resemble college graduates more with regard to items which are relatively "easy" or unspecialized, as measured by the proportion of the unschooled or of college graduates who respond correctly. In particular, we can look at questions which have been repeated over time and ask what happens to public knowledge as an issue emerges from an obscurity where knowledge of it is of interest only to "specialists," becomes salient for a larger public of "well-informed citizens," perhaps comes to dominate the media to the point where it is difficult *not* to know something about it, and finally recedes from public attention. Unfortunately, we do not have data for any single bit of knowledge through all of these phases, but we may be able to locate repeated items each of which illustrates one or more of the transitions suggested.[6]

For instance, although it is unclear how close answers to the items in table 59 had to be to be "correct" (and that may have varied from one survey to the other), clearly in 1951 virtually no one knew the population of China, regardless of his education. A few months later, differences by education may have begun to emerge (although the differences are still small). High school graduates and the grade school educated were still almost certain not to have the information, but a respectable 10% of college graduates did. Presumably, that information was "at large" during the Korean War, and the college educated had their information-gathering nets cast more widely.[7] Notice that the information was still not widely known: whatever their education most people did not know it and it was not important or topical in the same way that the location of the 38th Parallel or of Manchuria was at the same time. Had it become so, we expect that high school graduates would have begun to acquire it sooner than the grade school educated, thus differentiating themselves from the latter and eventually coming to resemble the college educated with respect to this knowledge.

This is evidently the process at work in table 60. In these cases, the rate of increase for the college educated has slowed; nearly all who are going to know the information know it. (In the first three instances, nearly all of the college educated are "going to know it," but this obviously need not be the case.) The questions are still becoming "easier," however; the proportions of the grade school educated and of high school graduates responding correctly continue to increase. (In nearly every instance, a dramatic, newsworthy event involving the knowledge intervened between the first and the second asking of the question.) Because the high school graduates have more sensitive antennae than the grade school educated, their rate of correct responses increases faster. This is the point in the process at which our original formulation becomes relevant. As the question becomes "easier," high school graduates increasingly differ from the grade school educated (and—after a point—come to resemble the college educated), thus reducing the index of placement.

If the process continues, it seems likely that the proportion of high school graduates responding correctly will reach its maximum and level off, while the proportion of the grade school educated responding correctly will continue to increase. This will have the effect of increasing the relative resemblance of high school graduates and the grade school educated and of increasing the index of placement. This may be what is taking place in table 61.

For many items of knowledge, no doubt, the process is arrested before this last stage is reached. The topic involved passes from the news and from conversation. Some, like that of the population of China, probably never reach the second stage. Sooner or later (perhaps much later), we may suppose that nearly all public affairs knowledge—even the meaning of the word "wiretapping"—will become "academic" and then pass from the public mind altogether. When this happens, we would expect that the process sketched here will be reversed: the knowledge will be "forgotten" first and fastest by the least well educated, since they are least likely to be reminded of it by the media and in conversation, and they have probably related it to fewer other matters.

Table 62 gives data on four areas about which the level of public knowledge was declining during the period of the surveys. For the first set of two items, dealing with Arab-Israeli conflict, if there had been any "forgetting" at all it had occurred only among the grade school educated—the process, in other words, had only just begun. The other four items show a rather more advanced stage of the process. In each case, there had been relatively little change for the college educated. Both the other groups, however, show fairly substantial declines. The *rate* of decline is greater, in almost every case, for the grade school educated, as predicted. The absolute percentage decline is greater for the high school graduates, thus increasing the value of P.

Tables 63–66 present data on the rest of our public affairs items. (To reduce the size of some otherwise very bulky tables, the items treated in tables 56–62 are not reproduced here. The data for these items are, however, included in the averages presented at the bottoms of tables 63–66.) As in chapter 2, the items are grouped by topic. In all four tables, as for the "academic" items and for most of the public affairs items already discussed, the index of placement is larger for the more "difficult" items—i.e., high school graduates resemble college graduates less. The model outlined above suggests an explanation which does not require assumptions about the "interests" of persons with different education. Information about the more "difficult" items is not widely available (by definition, for one thing: fewer people know it), and only those with energetic information-gathering habits —the college educated—will have picked it up. As the information becomes more widely available, others will begin to acquire it; high school graduates first, then the grade school educated.

If we introduce the idea of interests which result in special attention to information of various sorts, a number of the exceptions to the general rule become less puzzling. In particular, where "difficult" items show high school graduates to be as well informed as college graduates, the items often seem to be those where interest is unrelated, or even negatively related, to education. Thus, the college graduates' being generally well informed may sometimes be offset by the fact that as many, or more, of the less well educated have *special* interests in the topic. This was, by hypothesis, the case with "academic" knowledge of cancer and of Manchuria, and, perhaps more frequently, of public affairs knowledge, like the definitions of automation and of the 38th Parallel.

Where we find that college graduates are no more—or even less— likely to know about a topic than those with less education, it is usually plausible that interest in the topic is negatively related to education. When high school graduates resemble college graduates in their knowledge of some item, in other words, it seems to be because the proportion of college graduates who know the item is close to 100 percent and cannot be much higher, *or* because a relative lack of interest by college graduates imposes a low ceiling on the proportion who know the item. This could well be so for some of the "celebrity" items discussed in chapter 2. As another case in point, notice that five of the six items in table 62 with P values less than 40 and percent college less than 80 (marked with asterisks) deal with *local* political figures.

By and large, however, the data in tables 63–66 support the general conclusion that high school graduates are most likely to resemble college graduates when the knowledge in question is relatively "easy"—which is to say, in this context, widely available. If this is so, we have suggested the information-gathering habits of high school graduates will begin to be as likely as those of college graduates to lead them to the knowledge. If the knowledge is arcane, specialized, or "difficult," it requires the more systematic efforts of the college educated if it is to be acquired as part of the general knowledge of nonspecialists.

The reader will judge for himself but should note that (obvious, but perhaps not emphasized, in previous chapters) a *high school* education makes a very large difference and is quite "effective"—both in absolute terms and even relative to the additional effects of college —for a great variety of subjects of knowledge and behaviors.[8] Since our pool of items cannot be taken as representative of the "universe" of knowledge, we shall not dwell on the point, but it is striking how often high school graduates more nearly resemble college graduates than they do those with grade school educations. Our discussion in this chapter of the circumstances under which high school and college educations are differentially important should not obscure the fact that America's high schools have made substantial contributions to the creation of a better-informed citizenry.

6 Conclusion: Toward Further Studies of Enduring Effects through Secondary and Semisecondary Analysis

Many and varied measurements on thousands of adults, drawn from a long series of national samples and thus representing the students taught in all the nation's schools and colleges over a long period, lead us to conclude that education produces large, pervasive, and enduring effects on knowledge and receptivity to knowledge. To the reader grown accustomed to the common, severe, and manifold criticism of education, the conclusion may come as a refreshing surprise. Yet he may have come so much to believe the criticisms that he may find our conclusion *un*believable—apparently contradicted again and again by all that has been said so authoritatively. He has been told, to cite but one extreme example, that the schools "have forever been at the edge of failure."[1] Perhaps he is not urged to feel complete pessimism about education, but surely he is pushed right to the bitter edge and may not take comfort from our findings. Indeed, he may reject them as too aberrant to be true.

Our findings that the schools succeed in increasing *knowledge-ability*, it should be stressed, are not incompatible with the schools' failing in many other respects. Jencks's assertion, for example, that "some schools are dull, depressing, even terrifying places,"[2] could well apply to *many* schools. Yet it could still be true that the students have learned a great deal, albeit at too heavy a psychic cost. The criticisms that too many students drop out and that some groups have been discriminated against and denied equal access to advanced education could be true and not incompatible with finding that more education creates more knowledge. Indeed, our findings give real point and meaning to such arguments. They establish how valuable a thing is being disdained by some and denied to others.

Some critics assert that too little money is being invested in education; others say too much money is or that too much of it is being allocated in trivial, wasteful, and inefficient ways; still others, that money is being allocated unfairly and in a fashion that discriminates against certain groups in the population. These criticisms are not in conflict with our findings. They are simply pointed in a different direction from our inquiry, although our conclusion is not without relevance to such controversies. Clearly, the investment cannot be an utter waste. The learners generally are reaping substantial benefits in knowledge.

The criticisms that the schools are segregated by race or by class with undesirable consequences for the progress of the pupils similarly are pointed at important, but different, questions from those we address. The differential effects of social contexts and the detriments produced by student bodies of particular narrow social composition do not negate that schools in general may produce increments in learning.

The schools and colleges are also criticized for neglecting to build character or liberal values; for inculcating the wrong character traits and values; for suppressing the best impulses the students start with; for homogenizing the perspectives of students and destroying individuality; for molding the young to accept their lot in life, their slot in society, and the larger imperatives of a technological or military society. Much of such criticism is polemic and cannot be taken at face value. It is often based on meager evidence or none at all, or on empirical inquiries fraught with ambiguity. After examining 1,500 studies on the impact of college, Newcomb and Feldman remark about many of them that the "misfortune is not so much that their findings are wrong as that they cannot be interpreted."[3] Surely, many of these putative bad effects should be regarded as exaggerated in magnitude and overgeneralized in extent—and providing no adequate basis for impugning our findings. That some of these bad effects are, in fact, produced in some students from some institutions we have no doubt, but it could also be true that the students had grown in knowledge. The relation between different psychic realms, the cognitive and the realm of attitude or value or conduct, is complex and often loose. Some of the strangest—and apparently paradoxical—psychic constellations can be observed in individuals.

The putative bad effects in noncognitive realms also can be questioned, not merely on methodological grounds but also on the basis of our findings. Some, if not all, bad attitudes and values and forms of conduct certainly stem from ignorance or misinformation and could not survive in the presence of fuller knowledge. The gains in knowledge effected by education are no cure for all kinds of undesirable tendencies and acts, but surely they must have reduced the total prevalence. Indirectly, our general findings work to cast a reasonable doubt on some extreme claims by the critics, and particular findings provide direct evidence against certain of the accusations. Surely the image of the school as stultifying the student, as destroying the natural passion for learning and the love of intellectual discovery, is not compatible with our finding that with more education there is more information seeking and more receptivity to new knowledge, implanted so well that they survive old age and other circumstances of life. Thus our present findings have at least some bearing on such criticisms, and the general mode of inquiry will lead in the future to substantial, generalizable findings on the important question of the noncognitive effects of education. It had been our intention to conduct a parallel secondary analysis of the effects of education on specified values and forms of conduct. Indeed, many of the surveys already in our pool contain questions appropriate for such a study and were chosen with the twin objectives in mind. The very same design would be employed, simply substituting the noncognitive measures for the knowledge measures. The present analysis, however, became so elaborate and laborious that the second study was tabled until some future time.

We have not attempted to catalogue completely all the criticisms of education. The brief review should suffice to make the reader realize that analysis of the effects of education is multidimensional and that many of the variables scrutinized may have only loose connections to each other or no connections at all. Many kinds of criticisms, assuming they are valid, are irrelevant to appraising our findings; and our findings, though they bear on some of the controversies that rage, are irrelevant to the questions other critics have posed. But if our study can shed no light on some of the heated questions now raging about education, should it be regarded as trivial? To the contrary.

As we remarked in the opening lines of this work, to increase knowledge is a fundamental purpose of the entire educational enterprise. Some of the most heated current controversies have to do with just what the schools accomplish in the cognitive realm, and evidence generalizable to the nation for even *one* time point has been very rare. Evidence on the same scale for a series of points representing several cycles of operation of the educational system seems nonexistent, and evidence on the same scale about how long the effects endure into adult life is without doubt nonexistent. No wonder that two weighty studies dealing with the *cognitive* effects of education have been the subject of endless discussion, lengthy published symposia, and even thorough reanalysis eventuating in a book about one of the books. No wonder the studies have fallen like blockbusters upon the schools and that the massive negative findings, like heavy bombs, have shattered hopes. But if Coleman and his colleagues' report on *Equality of Educational Opportunity* and Jencks and his colleagues' work on *Inequality*, both dealing with cognitive effects, yield such negative findings, it surely must cast doubt on our positive findings.[4] No brief review can do justice to these monumental studies, but it can certainly show how sharply they differ from our inquiry and resolve the apparent contradiction.

The two studies are blockbusters not merely because they have a shattering impact but also because they are heavyweight, intricate works. The Coleman report is 1,285 pages long; the Jencks book, although far shorter, is a close rival in complexity of content and statistical apparatus involved. Understandably, they have been popularized, vulgarized. What many people take to be the problems treated and the findings obtained are far removed from the original facts. It should also be noted that the findings have been subjected to much criticism and should not be regarded as inviolate. But taken at face value, the studies do not address the same questions as our inquiry, nor do they refer to the populations we have studied. The cognitive realm is most spacious, and many distinct and important questions can be explored over and over again in different populations and temporal contexts.

The Coleman report refers strictly to the population of *children* enrolled in specified grades in the nation's elementary and high schools in 1965. A gigantic sample was drawn. *Academic* knowledge was tested, and by complex analyses the contribution of various factors of two major types to such knowledge *at that given point* was determined. The report cannot tell us what those who went to college know—or what adults with any level of education know about academic matters and especially about what they know of nonacademic matters. It is not impossible or illogical that little seeds of knowledge can flower and perhaps, with enough time, even bloom in profusion. One recalls Bateson's old and neglected, lovely concept, "deutero-learning," *the learning to learn*, which is contrasted with the specific first learning or "proto-learning," although it is implicit in and derived from it.[5] Measurements of the child's cognitive achievement at an incipient stage of development may reveal only proto-learning. Give deutero-learning enough time (in Bateson's model, the curve becomes progressively steeper) and the individual will show more and more and wider and wider knowledge, for he has learned how to learn, and he has had time to put that skill to work. If not incipient in all children, the deutero-learning has somehow been acquired by some proportion of them. Bateson may have been expressing an overly optimistic note, more appropriate to some favored subgroup and to better times, when he wrote in 1942 (reprinted 1947) about the potentialities of deutero-learning: "We might be kept on our toes by a nameless, shapeless, unlocated hope of enormous achievement. For such a hope to be effective, the achievement need scarcely be defined. All we need to be sure of is that, at any moment, achievement may be just around the corner, and true or false, this can never be tested."[6] The findings in chapter 4 above on continuing learning and information seeking among the educated have some of the flavor of Bateson's prophetic passage.

The major questions Coleman asks are whether *variations in the resources* of schools make a difference in the cognitive accomplishments of the pupils, and whether the individual differences in knowledge found among the pupils are better explained by other factors, such as personal and family backgrounds. The related questions examined are whether the schools, and what features of them, have differential effects on nonwhite and white pupils. These questions are quite different from our inquiry into the effects of *amounts of* education in increasing knowledge. Mosteller and Moynihan, the learned editors of the book about the Coleman book, make the distinction very clear:

> Schools receive children who already differ widely in their levels of educational achievement. The schools thereafter do not close the gaps between students aggregated into ethnic/racial groups. Things end much as they begin. To the simple of mind or heart, such findings might be interpreted to mean that "schools don't make any difference." This is absurd. Schools make a very great difference in children. . . . But given that schools have reached their present levels of quality, the observed variation in schools was reported by EEOR to have little effect upon school achievement.[7]

The Coleman finding that the variation among schools in 1964 made little difference may seem shocking, but surely it is not in contradiction of our finding that big amounts of education make a difference.[8] When one compares the effects of sixteen years of schooling with eight years of it, one is studying an enormous range of variation. It is on a far greater scale than obtainable from examining the effect on two sixth-grade pupils of having a small or large library or one teacher rather than another, or on two ninth-grade pupils of having one chemistry laboratory or another. However big the range of the latter variables may turn out to be in any particular universe of schools, it would still seem minuscule compared to the variation in our variable. Moreover, by 1964, the range between schools may very well have diminished. As Mosteller and Moynihan remark, "it is likely we shall find that American school systems are more like one another than otherwise."[9]

One of our major findings is quite consistent with the Coleman findings. When we compare adults who were the products of the high schools of 1920 with those from the high schools of 1940, we, like Coleman, are studying the range of variation between schools at a given educational level, no doubt bringing under scrutiny a much larger range of variation in the variable. Thus our results are even more surprising, but we also found that such a variable made little or no difference, *in the long run,* among tne adults who were removed from their respective schools by many years.[10]

Coleman examines a second set of questions on the differential effects of schooling, the type of school environment and the progressive amount of education up and through high school, on white and nonwhite children. Although we did examine *differential* effects of education, for example, among men and women and religious groups, our analysis was always confined to whites. Thus we do not address the same specific question. In principle, our inquiries could have converged at this point, and we could have added depth to Coleman's dramatic findings that American education contributes too little to the knowledge of racial minorities. His data show that the gap between such pupils and the white pupils is not reduced with progressive amounts of education, but widened. (The knowledge displayed by the minorities does improve with increasing education, but more slowly than that of whites.)

We could have explored what the gap would have been when the respective populations had become adult or very old and what the enduring effects of education are for racial minorities by a secondary analysis of national surveys of the same design as we employed, but, for the methodological reasons outlined in chapter 1, it seemed too risky an undertaking at this time. Given the importance of the problem and the absence of evidence, it may just possibly be worth taking the risk in the future. The findings on whites are already in hand, providing one side of the comparison. The general skills needed to operate such secondary analyses are already in hand. One is not overwhelmed all at once by all the technical problems that must be solved, and one can face the special problems of the quality of measurement and sampling for the minority with greater confidence and experience. And in the future the pool of data will enlarge, reducing the risks involved.

Jencks and his associates are concerned with the *enduring* effects of education, and their many reanalyses of existing data do lead them to generally gloomy conclusions. It should be stressed, however, that the measures on *adults* at their disposal refer not to knowledge but *exclusively to money and position.* These are variables of great importance, and their measurement provides the basis for Jencks's argument that education will not eliminate inequality. But status is not the same thing as knowledge, even if the latter can sometimes be exchanged for the former at a modest rate of exchange. Jencks's data provide no direct evidence about the question we have examined.

He is, of course, very interested in the variables of cognitive accomplishments and abilities, their determinants in the school and outside of the school, and, in turn, their consequences for worldly success. But here again he has to use the data available, and he relies essentially on the survey Coleman had already conducted—on *children*. He is simply going around in the same circle of data, extracting from them more and more findings by finer and finer analyses but obviously never escaping from the limitations inherent in the materials. Indeed, he often asks the same questions as Coleman did, the survey being suited to those purposes, although he examines the policy implications from his own perspective. The issue once again is the effect of differences *between schools*: "There is no evidence that school *reform* can substantially reduce the extent of cognitive inequality. . . . Neither school *resources* nor *segregation* has an appreciable effect. . . . We cannot blame economic inequality on *differences* between schools, since differences between schools seem to have very little effect."[11]

Other studies have been reexamined. Project Talent provided materials for another analysis of the cognitive effect on pupils of *differences* between high schools. The Plowden survey yielded a parallel analysis for English children. Jencks is still moving in the same circles, testing the same question. It is appropriate that the editors of a special symposium on *Inequality* emphasize the very point that Mosteller and Moynihan made in introducing their book about the Coleman report. Coakley and Foster-Gross remark: "This is not to say, of course, that the schools teach nothing. All children learn more by going to school. . . . It is only when one moves from the absolute effects of schooling to the comparison of schools with each other that differences in achievement become slight."[12]

Occasionally, Jencks poses the question of the effects of amounts of education but stresses the severe limitations of the data at his disposal. Recall his remark "that virtually no research has been done on these issues." Although he must be tentative, here his conclusion is far from gloomy: "We also infer that equalizing the amount of schooling people get might do quite a lot to equalize cognitive skills."[13]

This brief review will suggest the utility and uniqueness of national data on the enduring effects education has on the knowledge of adults. It will also suggest, until such time as other large-scale secondary analyses or primary data collections appropriate in scope and scale are accomplished, that the merits of our investigation can be examined only by analytic means or by comparison with the few secondary analyses of national surveys of the adult population that already provide some information on the problem. Such findings by

Withey and his associates document positive effects of *college* education on knowledge, media behavior, values, and civic conduct.[14]
Schramm and his associates document the cognitive effects of education, examining the variable over its full range. To be sure, their
evidence is based in some degree on the same studies we examined;
but it should be noted that three studies, two of which had become
fugitive by the time of our inquiry, are the major sources of their
evidence and that these were analyzed by multiple regression procedures, which we employed only rarely. Yet they arrive at similar
conclusions and are worth quoting:

> Education must be contributing to the skills, the ability to under-
> stand, the interest in serious information, and the habit of
> seeking it. Education, as we have suggested before, must be
> outlining a cognitive map which the individual spends the rest
> of his life filling out and, to some extent, revising. Education
> must be arousing a curiosity that lasts after the school years.[15]

Further Studies Through Secondary and Semisecondary Analysis

The critic who inspects our study from a utopian perspective may
accept the findings but discount the conclusions about the positive
effects of education. He may argue that the educated do appear
knowledgeable, but only in light of the ignorance of the uneducated
with whom they are compared. He may indict the lower schools for
having taught the common man so little and the higher schools for
not having taught their students more. Each can bring his own standards, and those who wish can look down on our findings from an
Olympian position. We do not urge complacency about the schools,
but we do suggest applying a modest standard somewhere between
what would be ideal and what seems to be realistic accomplishment
for ordinary human beings confronting the business and burdens of
life. The findings on adults from cross-sections of our society in
different times who reflect all the kinds of schooling that Americans
devised in an extended period should give some sense of the limitations of human beings and of schools. From this perspective, the
effects represent no mean accomplishment.

Admittedly, many of our questions, even by lenient standards,
could not be described as difficult. But this simply means that we
must reserve our judgment. If more stringent tests had been given in
the course of these surveys, of course, more people would have failed
them. But the *differences* between educational strata could well have
been bigger, and the effects attributable to education even greater.

Indeed, our analyses would incline us to that prediction. But we can take the guesswork out of the problem.

The national surveys that have accumulated since 1971 and those that will accumulate in the future will produce a natural growth of questions about knowledge that could lead to further secondary analyses of the effects of education. Some of the items may simply replicate the present ones—all to the good, as we shall suggest—but surely some of the new questions will enlarge the domain within which effects can be examined. No matter what special area within the domain of knowledge these items represent, the new data will soon bring us to the point where the effects of another cycle of education operating on a more recent cohort or generation can be examined. We can also anticipate that some of the new surveys will enumerate religion, ethnicity, social origins, and residential origins and thus strengthen the evidence about the effects of education under controlled conditions at the points where the present analysis was weaker than we would have liked.

But we should not rely exclusively on a process of *natural* growth. Judging by the past performance of survey agencies, we can anticipate that measures of some of the variables desirable as controls in refined tests of the effects of education will probably be few and far between. Social and residential origins are examples. And the indicators of such variables, when they are enumerated at all, are less refined than one would like. Some, for example, may regard *two* aspects of the residential milieu in childhood as relevant to control: the size and rurality of the community and the *region* in which the child lived. The first aspect was measured in only one of our pool of more than fifty surveys; the second, in *none* of them. We found enough surveys to make forty tests controlling social origins, using the father's occupation as the indicator. We found very few surveys where father's and/or mother's education could be used for a more refined classification of the socioeconomic setting in which the child developed—a refinement which our data suggest makes a difference.[16]

Judging by the trend of inquiry, we perceive that explorations into the *academic* knowledge of adults are diminishing, curtailing the analysis of effects in this sphere for the 1960s and likely to curtail it even more in the 1970s. Cohort analysis provided a direct avenue for tracing changes in the effects of education with aging, and, within the sphere of academic knowledge, identical questions repeated after a long interval were the ideal raw materials for such analysis. We found only *two* such questions in our total pool. Among the many questions in this sphere, and among the even greater number in the sphere of public affairs, there were few that tapped the depths of knowledge or reached its top heights, needed to test the full extent of the effects of education.

In these instances, reliance on the *natural* growth of surveys will not yield enough data to strengthen secondary analyses of the effects of education, and these are the very points that most need to be buttressed. To be sure, the present secondary analysis may have sensitized survey agencies to the utility their normal inquiries have for those interested in the effects of education. It may have made salient the gaps in their present measures of personal and social background, the discontinuities in their trend questions, the lack of powerful items that may be criteria of the higher learning. The agencies may respond to our needs. But we should not expect them to bear the full expense necessary to enrich the potential materials for our future secondary analyses. A strategy of *semi*secondary analysis is called for. The appropriate measures of background characteristics and the batteries of knowledge items can be piggybacked on future national surveys the agencies conduct, and these strategic services can be bought and paid for out of special funds. The tiny supplement piggybacked on a Gallup survey in 1974 shows how much is gained with one small expenditure. Merely by repeating four of the questions on academic knowledge asked in the 1950s and the one item on father's occupation, we obtained nationwide evidence on enduring effects produced by the schools of another, more recent period in a cohort of adults born more recently and on changes in the earlier cohorts after long aging; and additional tests of effects purified of the influence of social class origins could be made.

The totality of future data, part created in the course of natural growth and part specially produced to suit the need, will provide the basis for more powerful semisecondary analyses of the enduring effects of education. In view of how much will still come to us free of charge, and how little the supplementary costs are when compared with current investment in studies of the *immediate* effects of education, it will be quite a bargain.

Comparative Studies of the Effects of Education: Canada

It had been our intention to conduct a comparative secondary analysis of the enduring effects of the education in another country, drawing on the many surveys of national samples that have been conducted over a long period in many countries. Any differential effects observed would lead to a better understanding of the context of conditions that hamper or facilitate the long-run effectiveness of schools and would lead to a sounder judgment's being made about the American educational system. Against the standard of the enduring effects achieved in other places, we may look very good or very bad.

Uniformity across nations would truly give the sense of the limitations inherent in the universe of people and the universe of schools. By marking off the boundaries of the possible in more than one time and place, we could then set our aspirations in a more realistic way. This is the promise of a comparative design, but the promise cannot be realized at the present time.

Many comparative secondary analyses were only in the distant vista, but one comparative case seemed an immediate prospect. This prospect receded quickly as we examined the fairly long list of countries where survey research had been well established. France, Norway, Denmark, Holland, Germany, Italy, and Japan were scratched from our list, although the survey data seemed promising on first inspection. It is a commentary on our times that either the cohorts of adults involved or the educational systems in all these places had been scarred for an extended period by forces of war or totalitarianism. To those interested in the workings of education under such disruptive conditions, these may have seemed strategic sites for inquiry. But to us, they seemed to provide unfair tests of the enduring effects of education. England had also suffered the hazards of war, and the generations educated and maturing during certain periods were not ideal vehicles for our inquiry, but scarcity led us to entertain this prospect seriously. It is a commentary on theoretical and methodological perspectives that most English surveys, for mysterious reasons, do *not* enumerate educational attainment, the variable at the heart of our inquiry. We then turned to Australia, whose domestic society has been far away enough from war to offer a good site. For unknown reasons, educational attainment is almost never enumerated in Australian surveys.

We finally settled on Canada, which meets the required criteria and differs enough to provide instructive comparisons.[17] In a way it provides two comparative cases for the price of one, since it is divided into two subcultures and two subsystems of education. Higher education has characterized only a small minority in Canada—a situation similar to that in many European countries and in sharp contrast with that in the United States. In many respects, there are similarities to the United States, but these, as in comparative research generally, reduce the problems in trying to decide what, in the complex of factors in a society, accounts for the differences observed.

Another commentary on the perspectives of researchers is provided by the practices in Canadian surveys. Education, fortunately, is enumerated routinely, although not with the degree of refinement ideal for our inquiry. Asking the age of the respondent, however, was only a recent innovation, thus restricting the analysis to one narrow period in the mid-1950s, and age is coded into only a few broad categories which do not match the U.S. ones. Canada is far from an ideal choice, but sufficient data were available from eleven surveys of the Canadian Gallup Poll to provide substantial evidence of the enduring effects on knowledge produced by the schools and colleges of another country.

Tables 67–69 follow the same format as the tables of chapter 2, and report eleven tests of knowledge of public affairs for each of three age cohorts. The findings are uniform over all the tests. There is not a single instance where education does not have a significant effect or where the relationship is not monotonically positive and of considerable magnitude. The effects endure among those over age fifty, and judged by the average gamma and the means of the other scores and indexes, they have not waned with age. Tables 70–72 present a parallel analysis for five items of popular culture. Here again we find consistent evidence that education increases knowledge, and that the effects are strong and endure in the older age-groups. These, of course, are simply the gross findings. To establish the net effects of education, the influence of other variables would have to be controlled, paralleling the procedures earlier employed on the U.S. data.

Such controls were instituted, but only the summary findings, rather than the detailed tables, will be presented. When sex and *contemporary* socioeconomic position are controlled, the findings remain significant; the effects are of the same substantial magnitude and follow the pattern observed in the U.S. data. When the effects are examined among those who are native-born, they are found to be significant and not reduced in magnitude. In the Canadian case, the differences between those of French and those of English ethnicity and language would be of substantive interest, representing, as earlier noted, two comparative cases rather than one, although at the subcultural level. But the control is also necessary for methodological reasons. The French-speaking group have lower educational attainment and could well show less knowledge, if only because many of the items involved have a somewhat "English" tone and phrasing and would come easier to those with that background and language. This control also works to equate roughly the contrasted educational levels in geographical location and the corresponding opportunities provided, because of the ecology of French Canada. Every discrete test remains significant among contrasted educational groups, equated in language and ethnicity (as was also true when sex and status and nativity were equated), and the associations are of about the same magnitude as in the gross comparisons. Controls on religion, which partially duplicate the control on ethnicity but also control other factors, reveal the same patterns.

It would be reckless to draw invidious conclusions from the two *overall* sets of findings—the Canadian and the U.S. The way the continuum of age was cut did not bring the two sets of individuals to the same stages of aging; the Canadians were not tracked so far out toward the extreme of old age. The much wider span of time covered in the U.S. surveys includes generations exposed to events quite different from the Canadian experiences under study. The contents of the items of knowledge are not the same in the two sets of surveys, although the levels of difficulty are roughly equivalent. The Canadians and their schools were put to far fewer tests and thus far not tested at all on matters of academic knowledge. But surely we can draw the tentative conclusion that the effects of Canadian education are also positive, substantial, and enduring, and not unlike those found for the U.S.

Uniformities in the effects observed across nations, as remarked earlier, lead to a sense of the inherent limitations of people and schools. The Canadian findings, although not strictly comparable, suggest some restraint on the tendency to be overly critical about education in the United States. Canadian education has marked effects, but it, too, has not made all its former pupils into paragons of knowledge. Ideally, the two systems of education should have been put to the same series of tests before judgment was rendered. Given the surveys available in both countries, only one such test could be made. In 1955, a difficult ten-word spelling test was incorporated into a Gallup national survey in each country. In table 73 the effects of education on spelling ability are compared for United States white adults and for Canadian adults of English ethnicity and language. We excluded the French-Canadians since, obviously, they would enter this race with an unfair handicap.

In each of the three birth cohorts representing a particular generation at a certain stage of aging, one finding is so consistent and dramatic in magnitude that it may monopolize the reader's attention. At every level of education, Canadians are better spellers. Some may jump to the conclusion that Canadian education, from the lowest to the highest levels, has greater enduring effects in this sphere than its United States counterpart.

Inspected from another perspective, the findings lead to more cautious conclusions. The fact that spelling ability is far more widespread in Canadian society and even characterizes those with rudimentary education suggests an alternative hypothesis. Canadians, for reasons unknown but located outside of the school, simply start out with a special aptitude in spelling. Since that putative base line is higher, the added effect of education naturally brings them up to a higher end point—which is a deceptive datum to interpret. Examining the *gain* in spelling ability with higher education over each country's own base line is a more meaningful measure of effect. That datum is presented in the last columns of the two halves of the table. Using it as the standard, we can state that Canadian education does not consistently produce larger enduring effects in the three cohorts or generations studied.

Expressing the gains in terms of *absolute* magnitude, however, may also be misleading, because the different base points alter the ceiling and limit the maximum gain that can be recorded. The index of "effectiveness" used in chapters 2 and 4 was designed to resolve just this technical problem. Such indexes were therefore computed. Although not presented in the table, they also support the conclusion that Canadian education does not consistently produce larger gains.[18]

The issue of *relative* effectiveness remains unresolved, but we should not lose sight of the *major* finding from this particular comparative analysis. We have added, to the many United States findings, one more finding that bears on an aspect of academic knowledge not previously measured; and the Canadian findings, previously devoid of any evidence in this sphere, have now been enriched by data from a lengthy multiple-item test. In both countries, there are marked effects of education that endure beyond age fifty. The pattern is monotonic in all the cohorts. Let us hope that survey research in Canada and elsewhere will grow and expand greatly the comparative secondary analysis of the enduring effects of education.

The Contribution of Secondary Analyses of Knowledge to the Social Sciences

We have said as much as need be said and demonstrated as well as we could the value of secondary analyses of knowledge in appraising the enduring effects of education. We cannot close without some brief remarks about the value such findings and further analyses have for other social scientists as well as for educators. Throughout our examination of aging, we have stressed only the fact that the *educational* effects endured. That told us something about the power of education, but it also tells us something about the powers of the aged. The picture of the aged, not highlighted before and possibly lost to sight, is certainly not one of an enfeebled group, detached from current affairs, uninterested in stimulation, remote from popular culture. Our findings are contrary to the theorizing of some social scientists and surely of interest to many social psychologists and sociologists who are concerned with the aged.

The analyses also can serve to examine the merits of theory about the concept, "generation," which has been a topic of lively concern for sociologists and social psychologists. It has been applied mainly to studies of ideology and behavior, but surely its claims in the sphere of knowledge should be examined. In a way, the theory is implicated in discussions of social change. There are some who have argued that, for the recent generations living in a world enriched by mass media, where travel is easy, where knowledge blankets the total society, formal education is not so important as it once was. People have alternative avenues to knowledge. So the argument goes. We find no evidence that education has lost its importance among the more recent cohorts we studied. To be sure, none of our cohorts yet represent the age of television, the McLuhan generation, but they will soon drop into place in the secondary analyses of the future. Provisionally, however, our evidence suggests the continuing power of education. The persistent disparities between the educated and the uneducated, the knowers and the know-nots, remind one of the classic distinction between the haves and the have-nots. Perhaps it is an equally important form of division in society and it certainly should attract the interest of students of social stratification.

Our comparisons of knowledge among groups contrasted in education but equated in other social characteristics served us to examine the net effects of education. But if examined once again and with simple rearrangement, these same comparisons would illuminate a central problem in the sociology of knowledge. Do males and females, old and young, poor and rich, Catholics and Protestants—of *equal* education—have different concerns about and degrees of knowledge? Do the patterns of knowledge they assimilate correspond to the realms which implicate their special collective interests? The answers are there in the tables ready to be sifted, just waiting for the sociologist of knowledge who grasps the opportunity to illuminate central questions in a discipline that has been long on theory and short on data.

On these notes of hope for the growth of secondary analysis and the enlargement of other social sciences as well as education, we close.

Appendix A
Basic Tables

TABLE 1. Comparisons of Educational Attainment of the Population

	Census	NORC
1959, 1960, Population		
18 Years and Over[a]		N = 970
8 years or fewer	34.8	34.8
9–12 years	48.5	45.8
More than 12 years	16.7	19.4
1967, Population		
20 and Over[b]		N = 2,549
8 years or fewer	28.7	27.8
9–12 years	50.7	50.9
More than 12 years	20.5	22.0

[a]Gabriel Almond and Sidney Verba, **The Civic Culture** (Princeton: Princeton University Press, 1963), p. 522. Reprinted by permission of the authors and Princeton University Press.

[b]S. Verba and N. Nie, **Participation in America** (New York: Harper & Row, 1972), p. 349. The census estimates of education presented are drawn from 1969, introducing a slight element of incomparability. A portion of this table is reprinted with the permission of the authors and their publisher, Harper & Row.

TABLE 2. Acquaintanceship and knowledge of the Hoover Commission Documented in Two Gallup Surveys[a]

	January 1950 Survey Percentage of Group Who			May 1952 Survey Percentage of Group Who		
	Claim Acquaintanceship	Can Define Its Nature		Claim Acquaintanceship	Can Define Its Nature	
	(1)	(2)	Ratio 2:1	(1)	(2)	Ratio 2:1
Age 25–36						
Elementary school	7%	5%	.71	13%	6%	.46
High school	49	36	.73	33	22	.66
College	84	71	.84	80	70	.87
Age 37–48						
Elementary school	23	17	.73	11	5	.45
High school	57	47	.82	47	31	.65
College	89	82	.92	75	61	.81
Age 49–60						
Elementary school	28	21	.75	22	11	.50
High school	62	51	.82	47	32	.68
College	71	58	.81	81	67	.82
Age 61–72						
Elementary school	33	24	.72	22	12	.54
High school	79	71	.89	66	45	.68
College	85	77	.90	92	77	.83

[a]To sharpen the essential comparisons, the number of cases in the various cells is not included in the table. These can be found in Appendix B, tables 1.1 through 1.4, where these same data are presented for their substantive value.

TABLE 3. Error in the Measurement of Acquaintanceship as Revealed in a 1951 Gallup Survey by a "Fictitious" Item[a]

	Percent Who Have Heard of Howard C. Backer		N
Age 25–36 (all educational levels)	5%		345
Elementary school		7	73
High school graduates		4	116
College graduates		7	27
Age 37–48 (all educational levels)	6%		299
Elementary school		5	88
High school graduates		9	58
College graduates		4	28
Age 49–60 (all educational levels)	10%		224
Elementary school		9	110
High school graduates		8	26
College graduates		6	16
Age 61–72 (all educational levels)	10%		126
Elementary school		12	69
High school graduates		8	13
College graduates		0	6

[a]Gallup Survey 474, April 1951.

TABLE 4. Estimates of Knowledge Obtained from the Two Half-Samples of Gallup Split-Ballot Surveys

	Percentage of National Sample on	
	Form T	Form K
Survey 443[a]		
Heard of recent criticism of Atomic Energy Commission	58.9%	60.3%
Know what wiretapping is	46.0	48.3
Followed the discussion of the Taft-Hartley Law	52.8	56.5
Heard about civil war in China	78.0	80.6
Heard of Rita Hayworth–Aly Khan marriage	88.4	88.3
Heard about NATO	63.1	67.6
Survey 438[b]		
Heard about NATO	52.6	47.7
Know meaning filibuster	56.1	55.9

[a]June 1949. Form T sample size is 1,117; Form K, 1,061.

[b]March 1949. Form T sample size is 1,220; Form K, 1,235. There are slight variations in the number of cases for the various estimates because of occasional omissions on particular questions.

TABLE. 5 Number of Chi-Square Tests of the Relationship between Education and Knowledge not Significant at the .05 Level by age Cohorts over all Periods

	Age 25–36	Age 37–48	Age 49–60	Age 61–72
Knowledge of public affairs (140 tests for each cohort)	7	8	15	36
Academic knowledge (82 tests for each cohort)	4	6	8	12

TABLE 6. Average Magnitude of Associations between Knowledge and Education

SURVEYS IN THE EARLY 1950s

On domestic public figures—14 tests	Mean Gamma[a]
Age 25–36	43
37–48	43
49–60	53
61–72	46
On domestic events—20 tests	
Age 25–36	48
37–48	47
49–60	46
61–72	47
On foreign public figures—7 tests	
Age 25–36	49
37–48	48
49–60	49
61–72	50
On foreign events—14 tests	
Age 25–36	49
37–48	48
49–60	48
61–72	46
On history—4 tests	
Age 25–36	56
37–48	58
49–60	60
61–72	62
On humanities—13 tests	
Age 25–36	58
37–48	61
49–60	61
61–72	62
On geography—5 tests	
Age 25–36	44
37–48	48
49–60	50
61–72	51
On civics—9 tests	
Age 25–36	50
37–48	54
49–60	54
61–72	48
Miscellaneous academic items—2 tests	
Age 25–36	39
37–48	37
49–60	24
61–72	76

SURVEYS IN THE LATE 1950s

On domestic public figures—12 tests	
Age 25–36	43
37–48	40
49–60	38
61–72	37

TABLE 6—Continued

	Mean Gamma
On domestic events—6 tests	
Age 25–36	36
37–48	41
49–60	34
61–72	37
On foreign Public figures—3 tests	
Age 25–36	52
37–48	48
49–60	51
61–72	35
On foreign events—no tests	
On history—8 tests	
Age 25–36	54
37–48	52
49–60	48
61–72	54
On humanities—6 tests	
Age 25–36	65
37–48	65
49–60	62
61–72	58
On geography—16 tests	
Age 25–36	56
37–48	42
49–60	42
61–72	47
On civics—no tests	
On science and miscellaneous—13 tests	
Age 25–36	43
37–48	44
49–60	41
61–72	49

SURVEYS IN THE EARLY 1960s

On domestic public figures—24 tests	
Age 25–36	50
37–48	47
49–60	46
61–72	36
On domestic events—5 tests	
Age 25–36	43
37–48	46
49–60	37
61–72	35
On foreign public figures—no tests	
On foreign events—4 tests	
Age 25–36	47
37–48	55
49–60	53
61–72	39
On civics—3 tests	
Age 25–36	67
37–48	71
49–60	60
61–72	41

TABLE 6—Continued

SURVEYS IN THE LATE 1960s

On domestic public figures—15 tests	Mean Gamma
Age 25–36	38
37–48	38
49–60	35
61–72	33
On domestic events—7 tests	
Age 25–36	38
37–48	42
49–60	44
61–72	40
On foreign public figures—3 tests	
Age 25–36	45
37–48	51
49–60	50
61–72	36
On foreign events—6 tests	
Age 25–36	35
37–48	47
49–60	50
61–72	34
On civics—3 tests	
Age 25–36	38
37–48	42
49–60	37
61–72	38

[a]For convenience, the decimal points on the gammas are omitted in this and subsequent tables.

TABLE 7. Aggregated Size of Samples for Various Estimates of the Effect of Education on Knowledge

	Elementary School Educated	College Graduates	Total Sample For Estimating Effects of All Levels of Education
Early 1950s			
(17 surveys ca. 1951)			
Age 25–36	1,269	967	7,371
37–48	2,002	930	6,923
49–60	2,226	545	5,388
61–72	1,780	215	3,136
All ages	7,277	2,657	22,818
Late 1950s			
(9 surveys ca. 1956)			
Age 25–36	425	338	3,247
37–48	837	296	3,451
49–60	1,030	180	2,466
61–72	984	84	1,755
All ages	3,276	898	10,919
Early 1960s			
(10 surveys ca. 1963)			
Age 25–36	564	639	4,582
37–48	1,365	620	5,625
49–60	1,864	395	4,639
61–72	1,790	217	3,486
All ages	5,583	1,871	18,332
Late 1960s			
(15 surveys ca. 1968)			
Age 25–36	550	1,085	6,656
37–48	1,165	933	7,305
49–60	1,804	569	6,187
61–72	2,072	370	4,454
All ages	5,591	2,957	24,602
All time periods			
Age 25–36	2,808	3,029	21,856
37–48	5,369	2,779	23,304
49–60	6,924	1,689	18,680
61–72	6,626	886	12,831
Grand Total: All ages over all time periods	21,727	8,383	76,671

TABLE 8. Average Levels of Knowledge Related to Education for Various Times and Ages

	Mean Percentage Informed among			Diff.
	Elementary School (1)	High School Graduates (2)	College Graduates (3)	3 vs. 1
SURVEYS IN THE EARLY 1950s				
On domestic public figures—				
14 tests				
Age 25–36	26%	46%	65%	39
37–48	29	52	62	33
49–60	32	53	71	39
61–72	33	51	64	31
On domestic events—20 tests				
Age 25–36	28	54	78	50
37–48	36	60	78	42
49–60	40	64	77	37
61–72	41	67	78	37
On foreign public figures—				
7 tests				
Age 25–36	24	50	83	59
37–48	29	57	81	52
49–60	33	62	83	50
61–72	29	68	73	44
On foreign events—14 tests				
Age 25–36	33	53	71	38
37–48	36	56	68	30
49–60	39	57	71	32
61–72	37	59	66	29
On history—4 tests				
Age 25–36	33	59	89	56
37–48	36	70	90	54
49–60	42	70	96	54
61–72	38	68	92	54
On humanities—13 tests				
Age 25–36	13	41	73	60
37–48	13	46	78	65
49–60	15	43	70	55
61–72	15	47	75	60
On geography—5 tests				
Age 25–36	31	53	69	38
37–48	33	53	77	44
49–60	39	60	68	29
61–72	30	50	71	41
On civics—9 tests				
Age 25–36	36	60	85	49
37–48	38	67	82	44
49–60	44	67	87	43
61–72	41	64	80	39
Miscellaneous academic				
items—2 tests				
Age 25–36	75	90	96	21
37–48	85	94	99	14
49–60	86	90	96	10
61–72	85	95	100	15

TABLE 8—Continued

	Mean Percentage Informed among			Diff.
	Elementary School (1)	High School Graduates (2)	College Graduates (3)	3 vs. 1
SURVEYS IN THE LATE 1950s				
On domestic public figures—				
12 tests				
Age 25–36	29%	56%	73%	44
37–48	39	61	72	33
49–60	44	64	73	29
61–72	48	61	83	35
On domestic events—6 tests				
Age 25–36	45	65	89	44
37–48	46	69	85	39
49–60	59	72	85	26
61–72	58	75	89	31
On foreign public figures—				
3 tests				
Age 25–36	20	51	79	59
37–48	28	54	75	47
49–60	31	63	80	49
61–72	34	58	60	26
On foreign events—no tests				
On history—8 tests				
Age 25–36	27	60	84	57
37–48	34	66	78	44
49–60	38	62	79	41
61–72	36	68	88	52
On humanities—6 tests				
Age 25–36	00	34	62	56
37–48	05	40	69	64
49–60	11	35	75	64
61–72	09	31	62	53
On geography—16 tests				
Age 25–36	33	64	81	48
37–48	40	67	80	40
49–60	44	69	82	38
61–72	37	72	93	56
On civics—no tests				
On science and				
miscellaneous—13 tests				
Age 25–36	42	65	75	33
37–48	48	68	77	29
49–60	48	65	74	26
61–72	42	65	76	34
SURVEYS IN THE EARLY 1960s				
On domestic public figures—				
24 tests				
Age 25–36	28%	47%	66%	38
37–48	33	52	69	36
49–60	36	50	66	30
61–72	37	54	60	23

TABLE 8—Continued

| | Mean Percentage Informed among | | | |
	Elementary School (1)	High School Graduates (2)	College Graduates (3)	Diff. 3 vs. 1
On domestic events—5 tests				
Age 25–36	45	69	88	43
37–48	47	73	92	45
49–60	60	76	88	28
61–72	61	72	83	22
On foreign public figures— no tests				
On foreign events—4 tests				
Age 25–36	63	81	97	34
37–48	65	87	97	32
49–60	68	88	97	29
61–72	72	89	96	24
On civics—3 tests				
Age 25–36	05	45	81	76
37–48	14	61	89	75
49–60	27	64	94	67
61–72	29	41	86	57
SURVEYS IN THE LATE 1960s				
On domestic public figures— 15 tests				
Age 25–36	31%	52%	69%	38
37–48	39	60	70	31
49–60	43	60	70	27
61–72	46	62	69	23
On domestic events—7 tests				
Age 25–36	34	40	69	35
37–48	29	45	65	36
49–60	29	56	77	48
61–72	32	56	65	33
On foreign public figures— 3 tests				
Age 25–36	30	72	91	61
37–48	41	77	84	43
49–60	45	74	86	41
61–72	48	58	78	30
On foreign events—6 tests				
Age 25–36	57	73	91	34
37–48	57	77	95	38
49–60	57	80	96	39
61–72	63	81	86	23
On civics—3 tests				
Age 25–36	36	42	71	35
37–48	31	41	75	44
49–60	28	53	64	36
61–72	32	55	62	30

TABLE 9. Declines in Knowledge with Increments of Education as Related to Age over 222 Tests[a]

	Decline Occurs between		
	High School Grad. and Elementary School	College Grad. and High School Grad.	College Grad. and Elementary School
Age 25–36:			
Number of declines	7	7	2
Mean percentage decline	6%	4%	11%
Age 37–48:			
Number of declines	3	15	3
Mean percentage decline	2%	5%	7%
Age 49–60:			
Number of declines	7	15	4
Mean percentage decline	3%	7%	5%
Age 61–72:			
Number of declines	12	32	10
Mean percentage decline	3%	13%	5%

[a]For the index "knowledge of cancer," the educational groups were compared using several cutting points at different locations on the scale, and the several comparisons have been presented in the earlier tables. In making the tally of declines, we entered only one of the comparisons for this test item.

TABLE 10. The Effects of Education on Different Generations Enrolled in Institutions at Different Times

	Difference between College Graduates and Elementary School Group in Mean Percentage Informed on Items in the Battery
A.	
Early 1950s—knowledge of "domestic public persons"	
Average difficulty of 14-item test—30	
Age 25–36	39%
37–48	33
49–60	39
61–72	31
Early 1960s—knowledge of "domestic public persons"	
Average difficulty of 24-item test—34	
Age 25–36	38
37–48	36
49–60	30
61–72	23
B.	
Late 1950s—knowledge of "domestic public persons"	
Average difficulty of 12-item test—42	
Age 25–36	44
37–48	33
49–60	29
61–72	35
Late 1960s—knowledge of "domestic public persons"	
Average difficulty of 15-item test—42	
Age 25–36	38
37–48	31
49–60	27
61–72	23
C.	
Early 1950s—knowledge of "domestic events"	
Average difficulty of 20-item test—36	
Age 25–36	50
37–48	42
49–60	37
61–72	37
Late 1960s—knowledge of "domestic events"	
Average difficulty of 7-item test—31	
Age 25–36	35
37–48	36
49–60	48
61–72	33

TABLE 10—Continued

	Difference between College Graduates and Elementary School Group in Mean Percentage Informed on Items in the Battery
D.	
Early 1950s—knowledge of "humanities"	
Average difficulty of 13-item test—14	
Age 25–36	60
37–48	65
49–60	55
61–72	60
Late 1950s—knowledge of "humanities"	
Average difficulty of 6-item test—08	
Age 25–36	56
37–48	64
49–60	64
61–72	53
E.	
Early 1950s—knowledge of "geography"	
Average difficulty of 5-item test—34	
Age 25–36	38
37–48	44
49–60	29
61–72	41
Late 1950s—knowledge of "geography"	
Average difficulty of 16-item test—40	
Age 25–36	48
37–48	40
49–60	38
61–72	56
F.	
1955–57	
Four miscellaneous items[a] of academic knowledge	
Age 25–36	51
37–48	42
49–60	39
61–72	50
1974 Piggyback	
Identical four items	
Age 25–36	41
37–48	47
49–60	42
61–72	45

[a]Inventor of telephone, location of Mount Vernon, profession of Florence Nightingale, war in which Battle of Bunker Hill fought.

TABLE 11. Indexes of Average Effectiveness for Various Periods and Age Cohorts

SURVEYS IN THE EARLY 1950s	Mean Effectiveness of		
	High Sch. Grad. Elem. School	College Grad. High School	College Grad. Elem. School
On domestic public figures— 14 tests			
Age 25–36	27	35	53
37–48	32	21	46
49–60	31	38	57
61–72	27	27	46
On domestic events—20 tests			
Age 25–36	36	52	69
37–48	38	45	66
49–60	40	36	62
61–72	44	33	63
On foreign public figures—7 tests			
Age 25–36	34	66	78
37–48	39	56	73
49–60	43	55	75
61–72	55	16	62
On foreign events—14 tests			
Age 25–36	30	38	57
37–48	31	27	50
49–60	30	33	52
61–72	35	17	62
On history—4 tests			
Age 25–36	39	73	84
37–48	53	67	84
49–60	48	80	93
61–72	48	75	87
On humanities—13 tests			
Age 25–36	32	54	69
37–48	38	59	75
49–60	33	47	65
61–72	38	53	71
On geography—5 tests			
Age 25–36	32	34	55
37–48	30	51	66
49–60	34	20	48
61–72	29	42	59
On civics—9 tests			
Age 25–36	38	63	77
37–48	47	45	71
49–60	41	61	77
61–72	39	44	63
Miscellaneous academic items— 2 tests			
Age 25–36	60	60	84
37–48	60	83	93
49–60	29	60	71
61–72	67	100	100

TABLE 11—Continued

SURVEYS IN THE LATE 1950s	Mean Effectiveness of		
	High Sch. Grad. Elem. School	College Grad. High School	College Grad. Elem. School
On domestic public figures— **12 tests**			
Age 25–36	38	39	62
37–48	36	28	54
49–60	36	25	52
61–72	25	56	67
On domestic events—6 tests			
Age 25–36	36	69	80
37–48	43	52	72
49–60	32	46	63
61–72	40	56	74
On foreign public figures—3 tests			
Age 25–36	39	57	74
37–48	36	46	65
49–60	46	46	71
61–72	36	05	39
On foreign events—no tests			
On history—8 tests			
Age 25–36	45	60	78
37–48	48	35	67
49–60	39	45	66
61–72	50	63	81
On humanities—6 tests			
Age 25–36	30	42	60
37–48	37	48	67
49–60	27	62	72
61–72	24	45	58
On geography—16 tests			
Age 25–36	46	47	72
37–48	45	39	67
49–60	45	42	68
61–72	56	75	89
On civics—no tests			
On Science and miscellaneous— **13 tests**			
Age 25–36	40	29	57
37–48	38	28	56
49–60	33	26	50
61–72	40	31	59

SURVEYS IN THE EARLY 1960s

On domestic public figures— **24 tests**			
Age 25–36	26	36	39
37–48	28	35	54
49–60	22	32	48
61–72	27	13	37

TABLE 11—Continued

| | Mean Effectiveness of | | |
	High Sch. Grad. Elem. School	College Grad. High School	College Grad. Elem. School
On domestic events—5 tests			
Age 25–36	44	61	78
37–48	49	70	85
49–60	40	50	70
61–72	28	39	56
On foreign public figures—no tests			
On foreign events—4 tests			
Age 25–36	49	84	92
37–48	63	77	91
49–60	63	75	91
61–72	61	64	86
On civics—3 tests			
Age 25–36	42	65	80
37–48	55	72	87
49–60	51	83	92
61–72	17	76	80

SURVEYS IN THE LATE 1960s

On domestic public figures— 15 tests			
Age 25–36	30	35	55
37–48	34	25	51
49–60	30	25	47
61–72	30	18	43
On domestic events—7 tests			
Age 25–36	09	48	53
37–48	23	36	51
49–60	41	48	68
61–72	35	20	49
On foreign public figures—3 tests			
Age 25–36	60	67	87
37–48	61	30	73
49–60	53	46	75
61–72	19	48	58
On foreign events—6 tests			
Age 25–36	37	67	79
37–48	47	78	88
49–60	53	80	91
61–72	49	26	62
On civics—3 tests			
Age 25–36	09	50	55
37–48	14	58	64
49–60	35	23	50
61–72	34	16	44

TABLE 12. Knowledge of Vocabulary (1966)

	Percentage Informed among			Index of Effectiveness			Relationship over Full Range on Variables	
	Elem. School	High Sch. Grad.	College Grad.	High Elem.	Col. High	Col. Elem.	Chi-Sq. (P)	Assoc. (γ)
Individuals Age 25–36								
Can define								
"accustom"	74 (31)	92 (119)	86 (44)	69	—	46	**	32
"edible"	76 (33)	95 (130)	100 (54)	79	100	100	***	60
"cloistered"	31 (32)	39 (131)	67 (54)	12	46	52	***	40
"pact"	28 (32)	77 (131)	93 (54)	68	70	90	***	54
"allusion"	03 (32)	13 (131)	46 (54)	10	38	44	***	67
"emanate"	09 (33)	15 (130)	48 (52)	07	39	43	***	58
MEAN =	37	55	73	29	40	57		
Individuals Age 37–45								
Can define								
"accustom"	68 (31)	87 (102)	82 (39)	59	—	44	NS	15
"edible"	74 (35)	98 (109)	100 (44)	92	100	-00	***	75
"cloistered"	27 (34)	57 (108)	77 (43)	41	47	68	***	41
"pact"	43 (35)	91 (108)	96 (44)	84	56	93	***	65
"allusion"	06 (35)	16 (109)	39 (44)	11	27	35	**	46
"emanate"	00 (32)	33 (105)	67 (43)	33	51	67	***	71
MEAN =	36	64	77	44	36	64		

TABLE 13, Part 1. Knowledge of Tools and Duties of Occupations among Individuals 25–36 (1965)

	Percentage Informed among			Index of Effectiveness			Relationship over Full Range on Variables	
	Elem. School	High Sch. Grad.	College Grad.	High Elem.	Col. High	Col. Elem.	Chi-Sq. (P)	Assoc. (γ)
Tools Used by Metal Caster								
Correct on "cold chisel"	24 (25)	34 (116)	33 (36)	13	–	12	NS	07
Correct on "tongs"	80 (25)	72 (116)	89 (36)	–	61	45	NS	06
Correct on "blowtorch"	20 (25)	24 (118)	31 (36)	05	09	14	NS	09
Mean =	41	43	51	03	14	17		
Tools Used by Boilermaker								
Correct on "jackhammer"	56 (25)	57 (118)	69 (36)	02	28	30	NS	01
Correct on "crowbar"	32 (25)	24 (118)	42 (36)	–	24	15	NS	06
Correct on "welding torch"	92 (25)	89 (120)	86 (36)	–	–	–	NS	–05
Mean =	60	57	66	–	21	15		
Duties of Newspaper Proofreader								
Correct on "rumor checking"	36 (25)	85 (118)	94 (36)	77	60	91	***	61
Correct on "rewriting"	40 (25)	64 (118)	75 (36)	40	31	58	***	36
Correct on "checking typesetting"	54 (24)	87 (119)	78 (36)	72	–	52	**	21
Mean =	43	79	82	63	14	68		
Duties of Personnel Director								
Correct on "administering tests"	20 (25)	64 (118)	72 (36)	55	22	65	***	48
Correct on "telling workers their jobs"	32 (25)	64 (119)	81 (36)	47	47	72	***	37
Mean =	26	64	77	51	36	69		

TABLE 13, Part 2. Knowledge of Tools and Duties of Occupations among Individuals 37–48 (1965)

	Percentage Informed among			Index of Effectiveness			Relationship over Full Range on Variables	
	Elem. School	High Sch. Grad.	College Grad.	High Elem.	Col. High	Col. Elem.	Chi-Sq. (P)	Assoc. (γ)
Tools Used by Metal Caster								
Correct on "cold chisel"	30 (46)	42 (102)	38 (29)	17	—	11	NS	12
Correct on "tongs"	61 (46)	87 (104)	87 (30)	67	0	67	**	28
Correct on "blowtorch"	33 (46)	32 (103)	35 (29)	—	04	03	NS	14
Mean =	41	54	53	22	—	20		
Tools Used by Boilermaker								
Correct on "jackhammer"	52 (46)	56 (101)	63 (30)	08	16	23	NS	08
Correct on "crowbar"	39 (46)	29 (102)	30 (30)	—	01	—	NS	−04
Correct on "welding torch"	89 (46)	86 (103)	90 (30)	—	29	09	NS	11
Mean =	60	57	61	—	09	03		
Duties of Newspaper Proofreader								
Correct on "rumor checking"	35 (46)	84 (102)	93 (29)	75	56	89	***	61
Correct on "rewriting"	37 (46)	71 (102)	86 (29)	54	52	77	***	50
Correct on "checking typesetting"	63 (46)	82 (102)	88 (30)	51	33	68	*	32
Mean =	45	79	89	62	48	80		
Duties of Personnel Director								
Correct on "administering tests"	39 (46)	63 (103)	80 (30)	39	46	67	***	43
Correct on "telling workers their jobs"	24 (46)	58 (104)	83 (29)	45	60	78	***	43
Mean =	32	61	82	43	54	74		

TABLE 13, Part 3. Knowledge of Tools and Duties of Occupations among Individuals 49–60 (1965)

	Percentage Informed among			Index of Effectiveness			Relationship over Full Range on Variables	
	Elem. School	High Sch. Grad.	College Grad.	High Elem.	Col. High	Col. Elem.	Chi-Sq. (P)	Assoc. (γ)
Tools Used by Metal Caster								
Correct on "cold chisel"	42 (66)	55 (66)	27 (11)	22	–	–	NS	–03
Correct on "tongs"	76 (67)	82 (68)	100 (11)	25	100	100	*	37
Correct on "blowtorch"	35 (66)	50 (66)	36 (11)	23	–	02	*	–07
Mean =	51	62	54	22	–	06		
Tools Used by Boilermaker								
Correct on "jackhammer"	47 (66)	61 (66)	55 (11)	26	–	15	NS	07
Correct on "crowbar"	38 (66)	36 (66)	81 (11)	–	70	69	*	16
Correct on "welding torch"	90 (67)	87 (68)	91 (11)	–	31	10	NS	–12
Mean =	58	61	76	07	38	43		
Duties of Newspaper Proofreader								
Correct on "rumor checking"	34 (65)	80 (65)	100 (11)	70	100	100	***	66
Correct on "rewriting"	49 (65)	69 (65)	90 (10)	39	68	80	***	50
Correct on "checking typesetting"	60 (65)	72 (67)	82 (11)	30	36	55	*	32
Mean =	48	74	91	50	65	83		
Duties of Personnel Director								
Correct on "administering tests"	45 (67)	55 (66)	82 (11)	18	60	67	*	27
Correct on "telling workers their jobs"	33 (64)	56 (66)	64 (11)	34	18	46	**	33
Mean =	39	56	73	28	39	56		

TABLE 13, Part 4. Knowledge of Tools and Duties of Occupations among Individuals 61–72 (1965)

	Percentage Informed among			Index of Effectiveness			Relationship over Full Range on Variables	
	Elem. School	High Sch. Grad.	College Grad.	High Elem.	Col. High	Col. Elem.	Chi-Sq. (P)	Assoc. (γ)
Tools Used by Metal Caster								
Correct on "cold chisel"	37 (79)	56 (25)	46 (11)	30	—	14	*	03
Correct on "tongs"	81 (79)	84 (25)	46 (11)	16	—	—	*	−07
Correct on "blowtorch"	28 (79)	20 (25)	36 (11)	—	20	11	NS	−08
Mean =	49	53	43	8	—	—		
Tools Used by Boilermaker								
Correct on "jackhammer"	24 (79)	54 (24)	36 (11)	39	—	16	NS	29
Correct on "crowbar"	47 (79)	25 (24)	46 (11)	—	28	—	NS	−03
Correct on "welding torch"	85 (79)	80 (25)	73 (11)	—	—	0	NS	−03
Mean =	52	53	52	02	—	—		
Duties of Newspaper Proofreader								
Correct on "rumor checking"	32 (79)	88 (24)	82 (11)	82	—	74	***	64
Correct on "rewriting"	37 (79)	88 (24)	91 (11)	81	25	86	***	54
Correct on "checking typesetting"	68 (79)	88 (25)	64 (11)	63	—	—	*	15
Mean =	46	88	79	78	—	61		
Duties of Personnel Director								
Correct on "administering tests"	39 (79)	68 (25)	64 (11)	48	—	41	**	39
Correct on "telling workers their jobs"	19 (79)	62 (26)	73 (11)	53	29	67	***	62
Mean =	29	65	69	51	11	56		

TABLE 14, Part 1. Knowledge of Popular Culture among Individuals 25–36

	Percentage Informed among			Index of Effectiveness			Relationship over Full Range on Variables	
	Elem. School	High Sch. Grad.	College Grad.	High Elem.	Col. High	Col. Elem.	Chi-Sq. (P)	Assoc. (γ)
Heard Rita Hayworth marriage '49	76 (131)	97 (240)	100 (79)	88	100	100	***	68
Know Bob Hope new movie '50	00 (40)	03 (154)	03 (40)	03	0	03	NS	
Know Loretta Young new movie '50	00 (40)	00 (154)	00 (40)	0	0	0	NS	
Know Joan Bennett '52	53 (59)	78 (102)	85 (33)	53	32	68	***	39
Know Casey Stengel '52	10 (59)	31 (102)	36 (33)	23	07	29	*	30
Know author of **From Here to Eternity** '53	02 (59)	10 (158)	29 (51)	08	21	28	***	49
Know winner World Series '55	22 (68)	42 (164)	67 (45)	26	60	58	***	34
Know heavyweight boxing champ '55	43 (68)	68 (164)	78 (45)	44	31	75	***	35
Know what an Oscar is '55	62 (68)	94 (164)	100 (45)	84	100	100	***	76
Know Elizabeth Taylor '63	97 (91)	96 (252)	95 (97)	–	–	–	**	−11
Know John Glenn '63	85 (91)	96 (252)	95 (97)	73	16	67	***	36
Mean =	41	56	63	25		37		

TABLE 14, Part 2. Knowledge of Popular Culture among Individuals 37–48

	Percentage Informed among			Index of Effectiveness			Relationship over Full Range on Variables	
	Elem. School	High Sch. Grad.	College Grad.	High Elem.	Col. High	Col. Elem.	Chi-Sq. (P)	Assoc. (γ)
Heard Rita Hayworth marriage '49	75 (201)	99 (143)	98 (87)	96	—	92	***	72
Know Bob Hope new movie '50	01 (85)	01 (79)	00 (40)	0	—	—	NS	
Know Loretta Young new movie '50	01 (85)	00 (79)	00 (40)	—	0	—	NS	
Know Joan Bennett '52	45 (86)	71 (68)	84 (32)	47	45	71	***	44
Know Casey Stengel '52	09 (86)	44 (68)	38 (32)	38	—	32	**	37
Know author of **From here to Eternity** '53	01 (100)	10 (112)	30 (33)	09	22	29	***	57
Know winner World Series '55	36 (106)	47 (107)	53 (40)	17	11	27	NS	19
Know heavyweight boxing champ '55	52 (106)	70 (107)	63 (40)	38	—	33	NS	17
Know what an Oscar is '55	69 (106)	98 (107)	100 (40)	94	100	100	***	77
Know Elizabeth Taylor '63	86 (218)	96 (274)	99 (92)	71	75	93	***	67
Know John Glenn '63	86 (218)	94 (274)	98 (92)	57	67	86	**	45
Mean =	42	57	61	26	09	33		

TABLE 14, Part 3. Knowledge of Popular Culture among Individuals 49–60

	Percentage Informed among			Index of Effectiveness			Relationship over Full Range on Variables	
	Elem. School	High Sch. Grad.	College Grad.	High Elem.	Col. High	Col. Elem.	Chi-Sq. (P)	Assoc. (γ)
Heard Rita Hayworth marriage '49	74 (181)	98 (95)	98 (53)	92	0	92	***	61
Know Bob Hope new movie '50	00 (94)	04 (52)	00 (37)	04	—	0	NS	
Know Loretta Young new movie '50	00 (94)	02 (52)	00 (37)	02	—	0	NS	
Know Joan Bennett '52	36 (114)	78 (40)	42 (12)	66	—	09	***	43
Know Casey Stengel '52	13 (114)	23 (40)	17 (18)	12	—	05	NS	47
Know author of **From Here to Eternity** '53	02 (113)	07 (45)	18 (17)	05	12	16	NS	50
Know winner World Series '55	42 (116)	54 (48)	53 (19)	21	—	19	NS	16
Know heavyweight boxing champ '55	43 (116)	63 (48)	58 (19)	35	—	26	NS	21
Know what an Oscar is '55	66 (116)	98 (48)	100 (19)	94	100	100	***	83
Know Elizabeth Taylor '63	92 (212)	95 (155)	100 (58)	38	100	100	***	53
Know John Glenn '63	92 (212)	95 (155)	97 (58)	38	40	62	**	52
Mean =	42	56	53	24	—	18		

TABLE 14, Part 4. Knowledge of Popular Culture among Individuals 61–72

	Percentage Informed among			Index of Effectiveness			Relationship over Full Range on Variables	
	Elem. School	High Sch. Grad.	College Grad.	High Elem.	Col. High	Col. Elem.	Chi-Sq. (P)	Assoc. (γ)
Heard Rita Hayworth marriage '49	63 (118)	94 (35)	96 (27)	84	33	98	***	74
Know Bob Hope new movie '50	01 (75)	00 (14)	00 (12)	–	0	–	NS	
Know Loretta Young new movie '50	00 (75)	00 (14)	00 (12)	0	0	0	NS	
Know Joan Bennett '52	28 (71)	40 (25)	60 (5)	17	33	44	NS	35
Know Casey Stengel '52	06 (71)	12 (25)	20 (5)	06	12	15	*	47
Know author of **From Here to Eternity** '53	00 (78)	10 (20)	33 (6)	10	26	33	**	73
Know winner World Series '55	33 (109)	50 (28)	40 (10)	25	–	10	NS	27
Know heavyweight boxing champ '55	39 (109)	64 (23)	70 (10)	41	17	51	NS	33
Know what an Oscar is '55	51 (109)	79 (23)	100 (10)	57	100	100	***	71
Know Elizabeth Taylor '63	90 (241)	94 (77)	97 (31)	40	50	70	***	44
Know John Glenn '63	83 (241)	92 (77)	100 (31)	53	100	100	*	21
Mean =	36	49	56	20	13	31		

TABLE 15. Knowledge Relevant to Labor, When "Handicap" of Union
Membership Is Introduced

	Elementary School Respondent in Union Household (1)	College Graduate in Nonunion Household (2)	High School Graduate in Nonunion Household (3)
Heard of Following[a] **Labor Leaders:**			
John L. Lewis	73%	86%	80%
Walter Reuther	45	74	53
James Petrillo	40	74	57
David McDonald	19	23	12
Dave Beck	67	95	74
George Meany	41	60	31
Heard about congressional investigation of unions[a]	75	99	84
Heard about Taft-Hartley Law[b]	66	95	76
Know meaning of automation[c]	5	25	17

[a]Survey 581; April 1957. Both the elementary and college groups contain
approximately 100 cases, and the high school group about 250 cases.

[b]Survey 505; October 1952. The college group is 74 cases; the grammar
school group, 88 cases; the high school group, 177 cases.

[c]Survey 587; August 1957. Both the elementary and college groups contain
about 100 cases and the high school group about 200 cases.

TABLE 16. Knowledge of Sports, When the "Handicap" of Sex Is Introduced[a]

	Elementary-School Educated		College Graduate	
	Women	Men	Women	Men
Can identify Casey Stengel	5% (145)	14% (185)	12% (41)	54% (41)
Know heavyweight boxing champion	26 (193)	61 (206)	54 (48)	82 (66)
Know winner Baseball World Series	25 (193)	44 (206)	42 (48)	68 (66)

[a]Gallup Survey 549; June, 1955.

TABLE 17. Effects of Education When Sex Is Controlled

Public Affairs	Early 1950s		Late 1950s		Early 1960s		Late 1960s	
Number of items examined and control not needed	29		7		3		8	
Number where control needed and test made	26		14		30		23	
	Male	Female	Male	Female	Male	Female	Male	Female
Number of such tests where chi-square reaches .05 level	26	26	12	13	29	30	23	22
Mean gamma	.50	.51	.38	.34	.47	.47	.38	.40
Number of tests where gammas differ by less than .10	20		9		21		15	
Number of tests where gamma is at least .10 higher among males	2		4		5		3	
Number where gamma is at least .10 higher among females	4		1		4		5	

Academic Knowledge	Early 1950s		Late 1950s		Early and Late 1960s Combined	
Number of items examined and control not needed	19		32		0	
Number where control needed and test made	14		10		6	
	Male	Female	Male	Female	Male	Female
Number of such tests where chi-square reaches .05 level	14	14	10	10	6	6
Mean gamma	.59	.63	.53	.51	.50	.49
Number of tests where gammas differ by less than .10	8		9		6	
Number of tests where gamma is at least .10 higher among males	2		1		0	
Number where gamma is at least .10 higher among females	4		0		0	

TABLE 18. Effects of Education When Religion Is Controlled

Public Affairs	Early and Late 1950s Combined		Early 1960s		Late 1960s	
	Protestant	Catholic	Protestant	Catholic	Protestant	Catholic
Number of items examined and control not needed	8		8		10	
Number where control needed and test made	3		25		21	
Number of such tests where chi-square reaches .05 level	3	3	25	24	21	18
Mean gamma	.47	.50	.41	.34	.38	.36
Number of tests where gammas differ by less than .10	2		17		13	
Number of tests where gamma is at least .10 higher among Protestant	0		7		5	
Number of tests where gamma is at least .10 higher among Catholic	1		1		3	

Academic Knowledge	Early and Late 1950s Combined		Early and Late 1960s Combined	
	Protestant	Catholic	Protestant	Catholic
Number of items examined and control not needed	14		1	
Number where control needed and test made	34		5	
Number of such tests where chi-square reaches .05 level	34	29	5	4
Mean gamma	.54	.50	.47	.47
Number of tests where gammas differ by less than .10	22		2	
Number of tests where gamma is at least .10 higher among Protestant	9		2	
Number of tests where gamma is at least .10 higher among Catholic	3		1	

TABLE 19. Effects of Education Among the Native-born

	Public Affairs (All Periods Combined)	Academic Knowledge (All Periods Combined)
Number of items examined and control not needed	10	1
Number where control needed and test made	13	14
Number of such tests where chi-square reaches .05 level	9	14
Mean gamma	.33	.55

TABLE 20. Effects of Education When Class Origins Are Controlled (All Periods Combined)

Public Affairs

	Professional	Blue-Collar
Number of items examined and control not needed	0	
Number where control needed and test made	26	
Number of such tests where chi-square reaches .001 level	0	2
.01 level	5	16
.05 level	9	2
Nonsignificant	12	6
Mean gamma	.28	.30
Number of tests where gammas differ by less than .10	10	
Number of tests where gamma is at least .10 higher among professional	7	
Number where gamma is at least .10 higher among blue-collar	9	

Academic Knowledge

	Professional	Blue-Collar
Number of items examined and control not needed	0	
Number where control needed and test made	18	
Number of such tests where chi-square reaches .001 level	5	7
.01 level	5	7
.05 level	2	2
Nonsignificant	6	2
Mean gamma	.43	.42
Number of tests where gammas differ by less than .10	7	
Number of tests where gamma is at least .10 higher among professional	5	
Number where gamma is at least .10 higher among blue-collar	6	

TABLE 21. Levels of Knowledge among Highly Educated Individuals with Low Social Origins and among Lesser Educated Individuals with High Social Origins

	College Graduates with Blue-Collar Fathers		High Sch. Graduates with	Professional Fathers	Elem. Sch. Individuals	
Domestic Affairs—Persons						
Know Kennedy's religion	100%	(25)	100%	(32)	100%	(8)
Know Kennedy's home state	81	(26)	72	(32)	63	(8)
Know Nixon's religion	46	(26)	50	(32)	25	(0)
Know Nixon's home state	85	(26)	78	(32)	63	(8)
Know Johnson's home state	92	(25)	91	(46)	88	(16)
Know Goldwater's home state	92	(25)	89	(46)	56	(16)
Know own two senators	63	(62)	36	(25)	33	(6)
Know own congressman	74	(62)	48	(25)	0	(6)
Know own mayor	79	(62)	72	(25)	83	(6)
Know own governor	97	(62)	88	(25)	100	(6)
Know head local school board	65	(62)	52	(25)	50	(6)
Know two or more Supreme Court justices	88	(9)	29	(7)	*	
Index of knowledge 1958 candidates—"high score"	50	(20)	30	(23)	20	(15)
Domestic Affairs—Events						
Index of political information 1966—"high score"	56	(9)	57	(7)	*	
Index of political information 1970—"high score"	58	(19)	44	(9)	*	
Index of information on issues 1970—highest score	76	(21)	58	(26)	50	(18)
Index of knowledge, Mainland China—"high score"	100	(23)	87	(45)	50	(14)
Heard of Taft-Hartley Act	100	(24)	79	(52)	82	(17)
Know party with congressional majority before election:						
1958	76	(21)	54	(26)	61	(18)
1960	81	(26)	83	(30)	88	(8)
1964	100	(23)	73	(45)	57	(14)
1970	90	(19)	80	(10)	*	
Know party with election majority:						
1958	95	(21)	89	(26)	83	(18)
1960	73	(26)	70	(30)	63	(8)
1964	96	(23)	89	(45)	79	(14)
1970	90	(19)	70	(10)	*	
Academic Knowledge						
Know number of terms president can serve	84	(19)	70	(10)	*	
Know length of Senate term	79	(19)	70	(10)	*	
Know length of Congressional term	90	(19)	50	(10)	*	

TABLE 21—Continued

	College Graduates with Blue-Collar Fathers		High Sch. Graduates with Professional Fathers		Elem. Sch. Individuals	
Vocabulary test[a]						
Can define						
"accustom"	80	(25)	94	(34)	*	
"edible"	100	(28)	94	(34)	*	
"pact"	100	(28)	85	(34)	*	
"cloistered"	67	(27)	56	(34)		
"allusion"	43	(28)	15	(34)	*	
"emanate"	46	(26)	32	(34)	*	
Heard of fluoridation:						
1959	96	(22)	91	(76)	75	(36)
1966	96	(28)	85	(33)	*	
Index knowledge of cancer:						
Know 4 or more symptoms	13	(31)	12	(92)	02	(43)
Know 1 or more symptoms	84	(31)	77	(92)	51	(43)
Know diabetes not						
contagious	97	(31)	92	(92)	79	(43)
Know meaning of pyorrhea	86	(22)	90	(76)	72	(36)
Know inventor of telephone[b]	100	(29)	87	(47)	*	
Know Florence Nightingale's						
profession[b]	93	(29)	79	(47)	*	
Know Bunker Hill war[b]	83	(29)	40	(47)	*	
Know location Mt. Vernon[b]	86	(29)	60	(47)	*	

*Fewer than 5 respondents in this cell.
[a]Asked only of respondents 45 or under.
[b]1974 piggyback.

TABLE 22. Effects of Education on Knowledge with Social Origins Controlled by Correlational Methods

(Survey) Item	RItem and Education	RItem and Education with Origins Controlled	RItem and Origins
(SRC 1958)			
Know party with Congressional majority before election	.25	.20	.19
Know party with election majority	.24	.20	.15
Average	.24	.20	
(NORC 1967)			
Name mayor	.11	.11	.08
school board head	.21	.21	.11
governor	.17	.16	.05
senators	.32	.31	.09
Average	.20	.20	
(NORC 1959)			
Know meaning of pyorrhea	.19	.16	.14
Heard of fluoridation	.37	.33	.21
Average	.28	.25	
(SRC 1964)			
Know party with Congressional majority before election	.24	.18	.19
Know party with election majority	.20	.15	.17
Know LBJ's home state	.10	.09	.08
Know Goldwater's home state	.21	.15	.19
Average	.19	.14	
(NORC 1966)			
Can define "pact"	.32	.26	.27
"allusion"	.32	.24	.33
"cloistered"	.28	.20	.27
"accustom"	.17	.14	.17
"emanate"	.40	.33	.34
"edible"	.34	.33	.16
Average	.31	.25	
(Gallup piggyback 1974)			
Know inventor of telephone	.33	.30	.19
Know Florence Nightingale's professsion	.35	.31	.17
Know Bunker Hill war	.40	.36	.22
Can locate Mt. Vernon	.24	.23	.10
Average	.33	.30	
Average of survey averages	.26	.22	

**TABLE 23. Effects of Education When Residential Origins Are Controlled
(NORC Survey 4018—1967)**

	Main Residence during First Fifteen Years of Life							
	Farm		Small Town		Small City		Big City or Suburb	
	Chi-Square	γ	Chi-Square	γ	Chi-Square	γ	Chi-Square	γ
Know own senators	***	20	***	26	**	13	***	11
Know congressman	***	37	***	39	NS	14	***	32
Know governor	**	47	***	46	**	26	NS	32
Know mayor	**	19	NS	09	NS	12	NS	11
Know school board head	***	43	***	31	*	24	***	31

TABLE 24. Effects of Education When Opportunities Provided by Class Position Are Equated

Public Affairs

	Early 1950s		Late 1950s		Early 1960s		Late 1960s Early 1960s	
	Prof.	Blue-Collar	Prof.	Blue-Collar	Prof.	Blue-Collar	Prof.	Blue-Collar
Number of items examined and control not needed	3		0		1		5	
Number where control needed and test made		52		21		32		26
Number of such tests where chi-square reaches .05 level	42	48	14	16	28	29	21	24
Mean gamma	.41	.36	.33	.34	.40	.30	.36	.33
Number of tests where gammas differ by less than .10	27		9		13		13	
Number of tests where gamma is at least .10 higher among professionals	20		8		15		9	
Number where gamma is at least .10 higher among blue-collar	5		4		4		4	

Academic Knowledge

	Early 1950s		Late 1950s		Early and Late 1960s Combined	
	Prof.	Blue-Collar	Prof.	Blue-Collar	Prof.	Blue-Collar
Number of items examined and control not needed	1		2		0	
Number where control needed and test made		32		41		6
Number of such tests where chi-square reaches .05 level	27	32	35	39	5	6
Mean gamma	.44	.47	.45	.42	.46	.37
Number of tests where gammas differ by less than .10	17		21		3	
Number of tests where gamma is at least .10 higher among professionals	6		13		3	
Number where gamma is at least .10 higher among blue-collar	9		7		0	

TABLE 25. Changes in Knowledge as Cohorts of Given Educational Attainment Age

	Elem. School Group		High School Graduates		College Graduates	
A. Informed on Filibuster						
Age 25–36 In						
1949 surveys[a]	29%	(197)	65%	(431)	90%	(133)
Age 40–51 In						
1963 survey[b]	35	(226)	70	(232)	97	(64)
Change	+ 6		+ 5		+ 7	
Age 37–48 In						
1949 surveys	28	(313)	72	(263)	88	(135)
Age 52–63 in						
1963 survey	37	(205)	58	(98)	97	(33)
Change	+ 9		− 14		+ 9	
Age 49–60 in						
1949 surveys	40	(368)	70	(171)	83	(78)
Age 64–75 In						
1963 survey	42	(230)	51	(53)	100	(28)
Change	+ 2		− 19		+17	
B. Informed on Electoral College						
Age 25–36 In						
1950 survey[c]	05%	(76)	40%	(114)	96%	(23)
Age 36–47 In						
1961 survey[d]	09	(150)	56	(211)	94	(63)
Change	+ 4		+16		− 2	
Age 37–48 In						
1950 survey	13	(105)	44	(54)	78	(27)
Age 48–59 in						
1961 survey	22	(255)	66	(156)	89	(46)
Change	+ 9		+22		+11	
Age 49–60 in						
1950 survey	19	(108)	36	(28)	100	(12)
Age 60–71 In						
1961 survey	30	(273)	47	(88)	87	(38)
Change	+11		+11		−13	
C. Informed on Inventor of Telephone						
Age 25–36 In						
1955 survey[e]	57%	(68)	95%	(164)	96%	(45)
Age 44–55 In						
1974 survey	67	(36)	94	(89)	96	(48)
Change	+10		− 1		0	
Age 37–48 In						
1955 survey	62	(106)	92	(107)	100	(40)
Age 56–67 in						
1974 survey	57	(54)	90	(59)	95	(19)
Change	− 5		− 2		− 5	

TABLE 25—Continued

		Elem. School Group		High School Graduates		College Graduates	
Age 49–60 In							
1955 survey		60	(116)	92	(48)	95	(19)
Age 68–79 In							
1974 survey		51	(45)	84	(25)	100	(14)
	Change	− 9		− 8		+ 5	
D. Informed on Florence Nightingale's Profession							
Age 25–36 In							
1955 survey[c]		47%	(68)	87%	(164)	96%	(45)
Age 44–55 In							
1974 survey		61	(36)	84	(89)	98	(48)
	Change	+14		− 3		+ 2	
Age 37–48 In							
1955 survey		52	(106)	86	(107)	90	(40)
Age 56–67 In							
1974 survey		41	(54)	76	(59)	95	(19)
	Change	−11		−10		+ 5	
Age 49–60 In							
1955 survey		44	(116)	83	(48)	90	(19)
Age 68–79 In							
1974 survey		31	(45)	72	(25)	86	(14)
	Change	−13		−11		− 4	
E. Informed on Bunker Hill War							
Age 25–36 In							
1957 survey[f]		13%	(48)	49%	(167)	83%	(42)
Age 42–53 In							
1974 survey		3	(32)	32	(96)	78	(54)
	Change	−10		−17		− 5	
Age 37–48 In							
1957 survey		11	(85)	56	(136)	79	(28)
Age 54–65 in							
1974 survey		14	(49)	42	(57)	79	(19)
	Change	+ 3		−14		0	
Age 49–60 in							
1957 survey		24	(122)	52	(68)	81	(16)
Age 66–77 In							
1974 survey		20	(51)	54	(35)	72	(18)
	Change	− 4		+ 2		− 9	
F. Informed on Location of Mt. Vernon							
Age 25–36 in							
1957 survey[g]		17%	(47)	37%	(159)	65%	(31)
Age 42–53 In							
1974 survey		53	(32)	64	(96)	85	(54)
	Change	+36		+27		+20	

TABLE 25—Continued

		Elem. School Group		High School Graduates		College Graduates	
Age 37–48 in							
1957 survey		26	(102)	46	(129)	52	(27)
Age 54–65 in							
1974 survey		59	(49)	68	(57)	63	(19)
	Change	+33		+22		+11	
Age 49–60 in							
1957 survey		32	(127)	54	(54)	50	(18)
Age 66–77 in							
1974 survey		45	(51)	69	(35)	94	(18)
	Change	+13		+15		+44	

aThis estimate is based on the pooled data from two surveys, Gallup 436 in January 1949 and Gallup 438 in March 1949.
bGallup Survey 674, June 1963.
cGallup Survey 452 (TPS), February 1950.
dGallup Survey 649, August 1961.
eGallup Survey 549K, June 1955.
fGallup Survey 581K, July 1957.
gGallup Survey 580K, March 1957.

TABLE 26. Changes in Receptivity to Knowledge as Cohorts of Given Educational Attainment Age (Mean percentage)

		Elem. School Group	High School Graduates	College Graduates
A. Informed on Domestic Public Figures in Early 1950s and Early 1960s				
Age 25–36 in early 1950 surveys		26%	46%	65%
Age 37–48 in early 1960 surveys		33	52	69
	Change	+ 7	+ 6	+ 4
Age 37–48 in early 1950 surveys		29	52	62
Age 49–60 in early 1960 surveys		36	50	66
	Change	+ 7	− 2	+ 4
Age 49–60 in early 1950 surveys		32	53	71
Age 61–72 in early 1960 surveys		37	54	60
	Change	+ 5	+ 1	−11
B. Informed on Domestic Public Figures in Late 1950s and Late 1960s				
Age 25–36 in late 1950 surveys		29%	56%	73%
Age 37–48 in late 1960 surveys		39	60	70
	Change	+10	+ 4	− 3
Age 37–48 in late 1950 surveys		39	61	72
Age 49–60 in late 1960 surveys		43	60	70
	Change	+ 4	− 1	− 2
Age 49–60 in late 1950 surveys		44	64	73
Age 61–72 in late 1960 surveys		46	62	69
	Change	+ 2	− 2	− 4

TABLE 27. Daily Newspaper Reading

	Percentage of Readers			Index of Effectiveness			Relationship over Full Range on Variables	
	Elem. School	High Sch. Grad.	College Grad.	High Elem.	Col. High	Col. Elem.	Chi-Sq. (P)	Assoc. (γ)
Age 25–36								
1951	73 (79)	92 (167)	88 (84)	70	—	55	*	03
1956	64 (62)	86 (136)	89 (37)	61	21	69	*	04
1957A	60 (48)	85 (166)	85 (41)	62	0	62	**	36
1957B	65 (43)	91 (177)	93 (43)	74	22	80	***	42
1959	54 (43)	82 (162)	94 (49)	61	67	87	***	46
1962	53 (45)	85 (150)	94 (48)	68	60	87	***	48
1967	44 (39)	74 (228)	86 (79)	53	46	75	***	40
Mean =	59	85	90	63	33	76		
Age 37–48								
1951	72 (104)	88 (119)	93 (68)	57	42	75	**	09
1956	67 (100)	90 (124)	89 (45)	70	—	67	***	05
1957A	53 (85)	96 (136)	100 (28)	91	100	100	***	79
1957B	75 (95)	94 (129)	97 (35)	76	50	88	**	55
1959	62 (85)	83 (144)	88 (25)	55	29	68	***	36
1962	71 (90)	92 (135)	88 (41)	72	—	59	*	37
1967	53 (94)	87 (194)	89 (47)	72	15	76	***	51
Mean =	65	90	92	71	20	77		
Age 49–60								
1951	77 (155)	87 (95)	96 (48)	43	69	83	***	13
1956	78 (93)	89 (37)	100 (19)	50	100	100	**	18
1957A	74 (123)	94 (67)	100 (16)	77	100	100	***	66
1957B	82 (130)	96 (50)	93 (29)	78	—	61	*	44
1959	72 (143)	92 (82)	86 (22)	71	—	50	**	43
1962	69 (109)	86 (72)	100 (20)	55	100	100	*	50
1967	60 (140)	91 (134)	95 (38)	77	44	87	***	54
Mean =	73	91	96	67	56	85		

Age 61–72

1951	77 (128)	89 (28)	80 (15)	52	—	13	*	11
1956	78 (115)	90 (20)	100 (15)	54	100	100	**	21
1957A	76 (109)	92 (25)	93 (14)	67	12	71	**	52
1957B	77 (113)	98 (41)	100 (6)	91	100	100	***	64
1959	78 (146)	93 (27)	92 (12)	68	—	64	***	68
1962	82 (109)	100 (22)	92 (13)	100	—	55	NS	56
1967	70 (169)	88 (40)	89 (27)	60	08	63	***	52
Mean =	77	93	92	70	—	65		

SOURCES: 1951, Gallup 475K; 1956, Gallup 576K; 1957A, Gallup 581K; 1957B, Gallup 582; 1959, NORC 423A; 1962, NORC 447; 1967, NORC 4018.

TABLE 28. Mean Percentage of Individuals Who Read Newspapers Daily, among Four Age Cohorts, over Seven National Surveys, 1951–67

Age Cohort	Elem. School Education	High School Graduates	College Graduates
25–36	59	85	90
37–48	65	90	92
49–60	73	91	96
61–72	77	93	92

TABLE 29. Indexes of Average Effectiveness of Various Levels of Education on Daily Newspaper Reading, over Seven National Surveys, 1951–67, by Age Cohorts

Age Cohort	High School Graduation Compared with Elem. School	College Graduation Compared with High School	College Graduation Compared with Elem. School
25–36	63	33	76
37–48	71	20	77
49–60	67	56	85
61–72	70	—	65

TABLE 30. Magazine Reading

	Percentage of Readers[a]			Index of Effectiveness			Relationship over Full Range on Variables	
	Elem. School	High Sch. Grad.	College Grad.	High Elem.	Col. High	Col. Elem.	Chi-Sq. (P)	Assoc. (γ)
Age 25–36								
1955	34 (76)	75 (194)	86 (55)	62	44	79	***	50
1957	42 (43)	78 (177)	88 (43)	62	45	79	***	52
1959	19 (43)	70 (162)	88 (49)	63	60	85	***	55
1962	52 (46)	76 (150)	88 (48)	50	50	75	***	33
1967	31 (39)	71 (228)	90 (79)	58	65	85	***	47
Mean =	36	74	88	59	53	81		
Age 37–48								
1955	47 (122)	76 (133)	93 (41)	55	71	87	***	43
1957	43 (95)	83 (129)	94 (35)	70	65	89	***	58
1959	38 (84)	75 (143)	88 (25)	60	52	81	***	47
1962	51 (90)	79 (135)	98 (41)	57	90	96	***	39
1967	45 (94)	78 (194)	94 (47)	60	73	89	***	57
Mean =	45	78	93	60	68	87		
Age 49–60								
1955	38 (293)	77 (108)	89 (37)	63	52	82	***	55
1957	53 (130)	86 (50)	83 (29)	70	–	64	***	47
1959	50 (143)	74 (82)	91 (22)	48	65	82	**	38
1962	58 (109)	74 (72)	100 (20)	38	100	100	**	30
1967	42 (140)	78 (134)	92 (38)	62	64	86	**	53
Mean =	48	78	91	58	59	83		
Age 61–72								
1955	35 (115)	78 (27)	100 (4)	66	100	100	***	53
1957	43 (113)	85 (41)	100 (6)	74	100	100	***	58
1959	55 (145)	87 (27)	92 (12)	75	27	82	***	56
1962	48 (109)	87 (23)	92 (13)	75	38	85	***	50
1967	44 (169)	80 (40)	89 (27)	64	45	80	***	57
Mean =	45	83	95	69	71	91		

SOURCES: 1955, NORC 367; 1957, Gallup, 582; 1959, NORC 423; 1962, NORC 447; 1967, NORC 4018.
[a]Reads one or more regularly, except for 1962 survey, which is, reads at least one magazine a week.

TABLE 31. Book Reading

	Percentage Who Read Books			Index of Effectiveness			Relationship over Full Range on Variables	
	Elem. School	High Sch. Grad.	College Grad.	High Elem.	Col. High	Col. Elem.	Chi-Sq. (P)	Assoc. (γ)
Age 25–36								
1952[a]	5 (75)	17 (85)	40 (30)	13	28	37	***	48
1953[a]	5 (59)	21 (159)	47 (51)	17	33	44	***	48
1957[a]	17 (47)	23 (80)	60 (30)	07	48	52	***	32
Mean =	9	20	49	12	36	44		
1962[b]	32 (44)	65 (145)	98 (47)	48	94	97	***	45
1963[b c]	28 (101)	65 (230)	90 (111)	51	71	86	***	52
Mean =	30	65	94	50	83	91		
Age 37–48								
1952	3 (97)	12 (57)	59 (27)	09	53	58	***	64
1953	6 (100)	21 (112)	39 (33)	16	23	35	***	45
1957	15 (100)	25 (131)	41 (27)	12	21	30	***	38
Mean =	8	19	46	12	33	41		
1962	32 (85)	68 (132)	92 (40)	53	75	88	***	44
1963	31 (152)	57 (197)	89 (54)	38	74	84	***	53
Mean =	32	63	91	46	76	87		
Age 49–60								
1952	6 (127)	34 (44)	71 (17)	30	56	69	***	65
1953	6 (113)	18 (44)	47 (17)	13	35	44	***	60
1957	8 (127)	27 (55)	61 (18)	21	46	58	***	48
Mean =	7	26	60	20	46	57		
1962	29 (104)	52 (71)	90 (20)	32	79	86	NS	39
1963	14 (188)	58 (101)	80 (54)	51	52	77	NS	61
Mean =	22	55	85	42	67	81		
Age 61–72								
1952	7 (85)	20 (20)	83 (6)	14	79	82	***	68
1953	5 (78)	20 (20)	33 (6)	16	16	29	*	42
1957	17 (86)	36 (25)	50 (6)	23	22	40	NS	35
Mean =	10	25	55	17	40	50		
1962	28 (99)	59 (22)	100 (13)	43	100	100	***	65
1963	27 (207)	58 (67)	43 (14)	42	–	22	NS	39
Mean =	28	59	72	43	32	61		

SOURCES: 1952, Gallup 505 TPS; 1953, Gallup 521K; 1957, Gallup 580K; 1962, NORC 447; 1963, Gallup 667K.
[a]Reading a book now. [b]Read a book during past year. [c]Grade school limited to grades 5–8.

TABLE 32. Moviegoing

	Percentages			Index of Effectiveness			Relationship over Full Range on Variables	
	Elem. School	High Sch. Grad.	College Grad.	High Elem.	Col. High	Col. Elem.	Chi-Sq. (P)	Assoc. (γ)
Age 25–36								
1955[a]	64 (67)	76 (166)	93 (45)	33	70	80	*	15
1962[b]	72 (46)	83 (149)	92 (48)	39	53	71	***	24
1963[b c]	24 (101)	82 (230)	96 (111)	76	78	95	NS	72
Mean =	53	80	94	57	70	87		
Age 37–48								
1955	53 (108)	57 (108)	92 (38)	08	81	83	*	24
1962	33 (90)	66 (134)	80 (40)	49	41	70	***	38
1963	36 (152)	71 (197)	96 (54)	55	86	94	***	52
Mean =	41	65	89	41	69	81		
Age 49–60								
1955	38 (117)	60 (47)	58 (19)	35	—	32	NS	22
1962	29 (108)	54 (69)	55 (20)	35	02	37	*	32
1963	32 (188)	51 (104)	50 (54)	28	—	26	***	28
Mean =	33	55	54	33	—	31		
Age 61–72								
1955	32 (109)	45 (29)	60 (10)	19	27	41	NS	25
1962	23 (106)	48 (23)	46 (13)	32	—	30	*	35
1963	16 (207)	52 (67)	36 (14)	43	—	24	***	50
Mean =	24	48	47	32	—	30		

SOURCES: 1955, Gallup 549K; 1962, NORC 447; 1963, Gallup 667K.
[a]Attended movie within past 6 months. [b]Attended movie within past year. [c]Grade school limited to grades 5–8.

TABLE 33. Daily Television Viewing

	Percentage Viewing TV			Index of Effectiveness			Relationship over Full Range on Variables	
	Elem. School	High Sch. Grad.	College Grad.	High Elem.	Col. High	Col. Elem.	Chi-Sq. (P)	Assoc. (γ)
Age 25–36								
1956	82 (62)	90 (136)	78 (37)	44	—	—	*	−05
1962	63 (46)	71 (150)	60 (48)	22	—	—	*	−10
1967	90 (39)	99 (228)	91 (79)	90	—	10	***	−20
Mean =	78	87	76	41	—	—		
Age 37–48								
1956	71 (100)	87 (124)	69 (45)	55	—	—	**	−06
1962	61 (90)	55 (135)	44 (41)	—	—	—	NS	−13
1967	98 (94)	96 (194)	100 (47)	—	100	100	***	−24
Mean =	77	79	71	09	—	—		
Age 49–60								
1956	77 (93)	78 (37)	68 (19)	0	—	—	NS	−18
1962	67 (109)	67 (72)	25 (20)	0	—	—	**	−13
1967	94 (140)	97 (134)	100 (38)	50	100	100	***	−01
Mean =	79	81	64	10	—	—		
Age 61–72								
1956	70 (115)	60 (20)	67 (15)	—	18	—	NS	−05
1962	70 (109)	65 (23)	62 (13)	—	—	—	NS	08
1967	95 (169)	97 (40)	100 (27)	40	100	100	NS	−02
Mean =	78	74	76	—	08	—		

SOURCES: 1956, Gallup 576K; 1962, NORC 447; 1967, NORC 4018.

TABLE 34. Daily Radio Listening

| | Percentage Listening | | | Index of Effectiveness | | | Relationship over Full Range on Variables | |
	Elem. School	High Sch. Grad.	College Grad.	High Elem.	Col. High	Col. Elem.	Chi-Sq. (P)	Assoc. (γ)
Age 25–36								
1956	62 (62)	57 (136)	40 (37)	—	—	—	NS	−02
1962	72 (46)	65 (149)	72 (47)	—	20	—	NS	07
Mean =	67	61	56	—	—	—		
Age 37–48								
1956	53 (100)	48 (124)	38 (45)	—	—	—	NS	−13
1962	69 (90)	72 (135)	71 (41)	10	—	06	NS	02
Mean =	61	60	55	—	—	—		
Age 49–60								
1956	38 (93)	49 (37)	32 (19)	18	—	—	NS	00
1962	60 (108)	63 (72)	70 (20)	07	19	25	NS	15
Mean =	49	56	51	14	—	04		
Age 61–72								
1956	49 (115)	40 (20)	33 (15)	—	—	—	NS	−06
1962	59 (109)	48 (23)	54 (13)	—	11	—	*	−18
Mean =	54	44	42	—	—	—		

SOURCES: 1956, Gallup 576K; 1962, NORC 447.

TABLE 35. Reading about Election Campaign in Newspapers

	Percentage Reading among			Index of Effectiveness			Relationship over Full Range on Variables	
	Elem. School	High Sch. Grad.	College Grad.	High Elem.	Col. High	Col. Elem.	Chi-Sq. (P)	Assoc. (γ)
Age 25–36								
1952[a][c]	23 (39)	38 (77)	61 (23)	19	37	49	***	40
1960[b]	14 (21)	28 (79)	53 (30)	16	35	45	NS	31
1964[b]	21 (28)	32 (99)	48 (46)	14	23	34	***	33
1968[b]	46 (11)	42 (48)	39 (23)	–	–	–	NS	12
Mean =	26	35	50	12	23	32		
Age 37–48								
1952[a][d]	25 (91)	53 (74)	66 (41)	37	28	55	***	43
1960	20 (60)	44 (86)	55 (29)	30	20	44	NS	25
1964	22 (60)	40 (102)	69 (32)	23	48	60	***	31
1968	9 (35)	33 (88)	56 (34)	26	34	52	***	40
Mean =	19	43	62	30	33	53		
Age 49–60								
1952[a][e]	40 (58)	65 (26)	80 (15)	42	43	67	***	46
1960	36 (87)	49 (39)	56 (27)	20	14	31	***	19
1964	20 (91)	37 (46)	63 (27)	21	41	54	***	37
1968	31 (52)	46 (46)	60 (15)	22	26	42	*	29
Mean =	32	49	65	35	31	49		
Age 61–72								
1952[a][f]	37 (81)	50 (26)	100 (12)	21	100	100	***	42
1960	44 (75)	56 (18)	57 (14)	21	02	02	NS	19
1964	41 (76)	25 (16)	40 (15)	–	20	–	NS	14
1968	33 (76)	47 (19)	57 (14)	21	19	36	*	25
Mean =	39	45	64	10	35	41		

SOURCE: SRC.
[a] "Much."
[b] "Regularly."
[c] Age 25–34.
[d] Age 35–49.
[e] Age 50–59.
[f] Age 60 and over.

TABLE 36. Reading about Election Campaigns in Magazines

	Percentage Reading			Index of Effectiveness			Relationship over Full Range on Variables	
	Elem. School	High Sch. Grad.	College Grad.	High Elem.	Col. High	Col. Elem.	Chi-Sq. (P)	Assoc. (γ)
Age 25–36								
1952[a][c]	5 (39)	17 (77)	38 (24)	13	25	35	***	45
1960[b]	0 (21)	6 (79)	30 (30)	06	25	30	***	42
1964[b]	0 (28)	6 (100)	20 (46)	06	15	20	***	47
1968[b]	0 (11)	2 (48)	13 (23)	02	11	13	***	41
Mean =	1	8	25	07	18	24		
Age 37–48								
1952[a][d]	4 (91)	15 (72)	35 (40)	11	23	32	***	48
1960	2 (60)	6 (86)	38 (29)	04	34	37	***	37
1964	3 (60)	8 (104)	30 (33)	05	24	28	***	49
1968	0 (35)	7 (88)	11 (35)	07	04	11	***	52
Mean =	2	9	29	07	22	28		
Age 49–60								
1952[a][e]	10 (58)	23 (26)	47 (15)	14	31	41	***	49
1960	3 (87)	5 (39)	26 (27)	02	22	24	***	33
1964	2 (91)	4 (45)	28 (29)	02	25	26	***	50
1968	4 (52)	7 (46)	33 (15)	03	28	30	***	53
Mean =	5	10	34	05	27	31		
Age 61–72								
1952[a][f]	11 (81)	19 (26)	33 (12)	09	17	25	**	41
1960	5 (75)	6 (18)	50 (14)	01	47	47	***	43
1964	8 (77)	0 (16)	33 (15)	–	33	27	**	31
1968	1 (74)	32 (19)	29 (14)	31	–	28	***	58
Mean =	6	14	36	09	26	32		

SOURCE: SRC.
[a]"Much."
[b]"Regularly."
[c]Age 25–34.
[d]Age 35–49.
[e]Age 50–59.
[f]Age 60 and above.

TABLE 37. Watching Election Campaigns on Television

	Percentage Watching			Index of Effectiveness			Relationship over Full Range on Variables	
	Elem. School	High Sch. Grad.	College Grad.	High Elem.	Col. High	Col. Elem.	Chi-Sq. (P)	Assoc. (γ)
Age 25–36								
1952a c	25 (36)	44 (73)	39 (23)	25	—	19	NS	09
1960b	29 (21)	42 (79)	53 (30)	18	19	34	NS	23
1964b	32 (28)	26 (100)	39 (46)	—	17	10	NS	11
1968b	55 (11)	29 (48)	35 (23)	—	08	—	NS	03
Mean =	35	35	42	0	11	11		
Age 37–48								
1952a d	35 (88)	57 (70)	47 (38)	34	—	18	***	28
1960	38 (60)	42 (86)	45 (29)	06	05	11	NS	12
1964	32 (60)	36 (104)	42 (33)	06	09	15	NS	06
1968	40 (35)	40 (88)	54 (35)	0	23	23	NS	15
Mean =	36	44	47	13	05	17		
Age 49–60								
1952a e	24 (55)	42 (26)	67 (15)	24	43	56	NS	12
1960	45 (87)	28 (39)	37 (27)	—	12	—	**	06
1964	39 (91)	33 (46)	41 (29)	—	12	03	NS	02
1968	35 (52)	44 (46)	60 (15)	14	28	38	NS	20
Mean =	36	37	51	02	22	23		
Age 61–72								
1952a f	21 (75)	28 (25)	33 (12)	09	07	15	**	28
1960	53 (75)	67 (18)	43 (14)	30	—	—	NS	04
1964	53 (77)	69 (16)	53 (15)	34	—	0	NS	−05
1968	53 (76)	68 (19)	46 (13)	32	—	—	NS	−08
Mean =	45	58	44	24	—	—		

SOURCE: SRC.
a"Much."
b"Many."
cAge 25–34.
dAge 35–49.
eAge 50–59.
fAge 60 and over.

TABLE 38. Listening to Election Campaigns on Radio

	Percentage Listening			Index of Effectiveness			Relationship over Full Range on Variables	
	Elem. School	High Sch. Grad.	College Grad.	High Elem.	Col. High	Col. Elem.	Chi-Sq. (P)	Assoc. (γ)
Age 25–36								
1952[a] [c]	18 (39)	27 (77)	46 (22)	11	26	34	NS	17
1960[b]	0 (21)	6 (79)	13 (30)	06	07	13	NS	11
1964[b]	7 (28)	5 (100)	9 (46)	–	04	02	NS	25
1968[b]	9 (11)	2 (48)	13 (23)	–	11	04	NS	15
Mean =	9	10	20	01	11	12		
Age 37–48								
1952[a] [d]	24 (91)	32 (73)	56 (41)	10	35	42	NS	17
1960	12 (60)	8 (86)	10 (29)	–	02	–	NS	12
1964	7 (60)	8 (104)	9 (33)	01	01	02	NS	08
1968	6 (35)	7 (88)	9 (34)	01	02	03	NS	15
Mean =	12	14	21	02	08	10		
Age 49–60								
1952[a] [e]	29 (58)	46 (26)	53 (15)	24	13	34	*	21
1960	16 (87)	18 (39)	15 (27)	02	–	–	NS	15
1964	9 (91)	4 (45)	14 (29)	–	10	05	NS	07
1968	10 (51)	13 (46)	27 (15)	03	16	19	NS	13
Mean =	16	20	27	05	09	13		
Age 61–72								
1952[a] [f]	43 (80)	39 (26)	33 (12)	–	–	–	NS	09
1960	21 (75)	17 (18)	14 (14)	–	–	–	NS	16
1964	21 (76)	0 (16)	7 (15)	–	07	–	NS	–09
1968	19 (75)	11 (19)	14 (14)	–	03	–	NS	–14
Mean =	26	17	17	–	00	–		

SOURCE: SRC.
[a] "Much."
[b] "Many."
[c] Age 25–34.
[d] Age 35–49.
[e] Age 50–59.
[f] Age 60 and over.

TABLE 39. Interest in Politics

	Percentage Interested			Index of Effectiveness			Relationship over Full Range on Variables	
	Elem. School	High Sch. Grad.	College Grad.	High Elem.	Col. High	Col. Elem.	Chi-Sq. (P)	Assoc. (γ)
Age 25–36								
1952[a]	10 (41)	34 (85)	70 (27)	27	54	67	***	45
1960[b]	48 (21)	66 (79)	83 (30)	35	50	67	*	36
1966[b]	13 (24)	18 (63)	52 (27)	06	41	45	***	52
1967[b]	19 (32)	27 (219)	44 (79)	10	23	31	***	32
1968[b]	30 (10)	43 (47)	74 (23)	18	54	63	**	44
1970[b]	23 (13)	34 (106)	82 (50)	14	73	77	***	49
1971[a]	21 (19)	18 (115)	50 (38)	–	39	37	***	32
Mean =	23	34	65	14	47	55		
Age 37–48								
1952[a]	24 (100)	38 (82)	59 (41)	18	34	46	***	41
1960[b]	43 (60)	64 (86)	86 (29)	37	61	75	**	35
1966[b]	12 (42)	31 (85)	74 (23)	21	62	70	***	53
1967[b]	28 (83)	35 (190)	63 (46)	10	43	49	***	26
1968[b]	27 (34)	48 (88)	77 (34)	29	56	68	***	46
1970[b]	28 (53)	40 (63)	86 (21)	17	77	80	***	49
1971[a]	29 (35)	30 (104)	54 (26)	01	34	35	*	24
Mean =	27	41	71	19	51	60		
Age 49–60								
1952[a]	36 (67)	61 (28)	83 (18)	39	56	73	***	41
1960[b]	54 (87)	67 (39)	70 (27)	28	09	35	NS	23
1966[b]	13 (55)	32 (38)	69 (16)	22	54	64	***	49
1967[b]	26 (121)	30 (129)	51 (37)	05	30	34	**	22
1968[b]	25 (52)	52 (46)	93 (14)	36	85	91	***	49
1970[b]	18 (67)	57 (51)	87 (15)	47	70	84	***	53
1971[a]	19 (53)	35 (69)	20 (10)	20	–	01	***	26
Mean =	27	48	68	29	38	56		

Age 61–72

1952[a]	39 (87)	46 (26)	80 (15)	11	63	67	***	38
1960[b]	59 (75)	83 (18)	64 (14)	58	–	12	NS	23
1966[b]	27 (78)	43 (21)	75 (8)	22	56	66	*	42
1967[b]	34 (137)	35 (37)	67 (27)	01	49	50	***	31
1968[b]	17 (75)	53 (19)	64 (14)	43	23	57	***	46
1970[b]	28 (86)	62 (29)	73 (15)	47	29	62	***	42
1971[a]	20 (87)	36 (44)	27 (11)	20	–	09	NS	25
Mean =	32	51	64	28	27	47		

SOURCES: 1952, SRC; 1960, SRC; 1966, SRC; 1967, NORC 4018; 1968, SRC; 1970, SRC; 1971, NORC 4119.
[a]"Very Interested."
[b]"High Interest."

TABLE 40. Following Public Affairs (1960) and Vietnam War (1968, 1970)

	Percentages			Index of Effectiveness			Relationship over Full Range on Variables	
	Elem. School	High Sch. Grad.	College Grad.	High Elem.	Col. High	Col. Elem.	Chi-Sq. (P)	Assoc. (γ)
A. Follow them regularly								
Age 26–35	17 (18)	20 (59)	40 (20)	04	25	28	*	40
36–50	22 (55)	28 (79)	50 (24)	08	30	36	***	36
51–60	20 (70)	52 (23)	46 (13)	40	–	32	**	43
60 and over	31 (131)	52 (31)	67 (12)	30	31	52	NS	43
B. Follow them in newspapers, every day								
Age 26–35	17 (18)	37 (59)	60 (20)	24	36	52	*	03
36–50	24 (54)	48 (79)	67 (24)	31	36	56	**	09
51–60	36 (70)	70 (23)	69 (13)	53	–	51	*	04
60 and over	46 (131)	55 (32)	83 (12)	17	62	68	*	23
C. Follow them on radio or TV, every day								
Age 26–35	39 (18)	51 (59)	60 (20)	20	18	34	NS	04
36–50	41 (54)	54 (79)	58 (24)	22	09	29	**	29
51–60	37 (70)	61 (23)	54 (13)	38	–	27	NS	06
60 and over	44 (131)	48 (31)	83 (12)	07	67	70	**	32
D. Follow them in magazines, weekly								
Age 26–35	6 (18)	22 (59)	65 (20)	17	55	63	***	19
36–50	7 (54)	25 (79)	42 (24)	19	23	38	***	01
51–60	14 (70)	39 (23)	69 (13)	29	49	64	***	24
60 and over	15 (131)	23 (31)	64 (11)	09	53	58	***	03

E. Talk about them, every day

Age 26–35	0 (18)	14 (59)	35 (20)	14	24	35	**	45
36–50	4 (55)	13 (79)	42 (24)	09	33	39	***	41
51–60	11 (70)	22 (23)	15 (13)	12	–	04	**	48
60 and over	11 (131)	23 (31)	17 (12)	13	–	07	*	31

F. Pay much attention to Vietnam War (1968)

Age 25–36	55 (11)	46 (48)	55 (22)	–	17	0	NS	16
37–48	46 (35)	54 (87)	54 (35)	15	0	15	NS	09
49–60	55 (53)	59 (46)	93 (15)	09	83	84	NS	25
61–72	45 (75)	63 (19)	57 (14)	33	–	22	NS	27

G. Pay good deal of attention to Vietnam War (1970)

Age 25–36	15 (13)	32 (106)	48 (50)	20	23	39	***	37
37–48	40 (53)	33 (63)	48 (21)	–	22	13	**	22
49–60	53 (68)	60 (52)	73 (15)	15	32	42	NS	18
61–72	50 (88)	63 (30)	56 (16)	26	–	12	NS	14

SOURCES: 1960, Almond-Verba; 1968, 1970, SRC.

TABLE 41. Information Seeking about Health (1955)

	Percentages			Index of Effectiveness			Relationship over Full Range on Variables	
	Elem. School	High Sch. Grad.	College Grad.	High Elem.	Col. High	Col. Elem.	Chi-Sq. (P)	Assoc. (γ)
A. Read health columns in newspapers, frequently								
Age 25–34	15 (76)	31 (197)	15 (55)	19	—	0	**	17
35–44	18 (124)	29 (133)	10 (41)	13	—	—	*	07
45–54	17 (154)	35 (72)	28 (25)	22	—	13	***	26
55–64	24 (140)	24 (37)	36 (14)	0	16	16	NS	18
65–74	20 (117)	35 (29)	0 (5)	19	—	—	NS	26
B. Read health columns in magazines, frequently								
Age 25–34	16 (76)	47 (197)	64 (55)	37	32	57	***	43
35–44	23 (124)	44 (133)	42 (41)	27	—	25	***	26
45–54	20 (154)	39 (72)	64 (25)	24	41	55	***	44
55–64	21 (140)	32 (37)	57 (14)	14	37	45	***	46
65–74	16 (117)	41 (29)	60 (5)	30	32	52	**	45
C. Listen to health programs on radio or TV								
Age 25–34	25 (76)	22 (197)	15 (55)	—	—	—	NS	02
35–44	15 (124)	20 (133)	15 (41)	06	—	0	NS	−01
45–54	20 (154)	17 (72)	12 (25)	—	—	—	NS	−01
55–64	19 (140)	11 (37)	7 (14)	—	—	—	NS	−13
65–74	18 (117)	21 (29)	0 (5)	04	—	100	NS	06

SOURCE: NORC 367.

TABLE 42. Information Seeking about Dental Health (1959)

	Percentages			Index of Effectiveness			Relationship over Full Range on Variables	
	Elem. School	High Sch. Grad.	College Grad.	High Elem.	Col. High	Col. Elem.	Chi-Sq. (P)	Assoc. (γ)
See dental ads								
Age 25–36	23 (40)	57 (162)	86 (49)	44	67	82	***	37
37–48	42 (77)	66 (143)	72 (25)	41	18	52	**	33
49–60	39 (139)	63 (82)	82 (22)	39	51	70	**	35
61–72	29 (140)	67 (27)	75 (12)	53	24	65	**	46
Read dental articles, frequently								
Age 25–36	7 (43)	9 (162)	18 (49)	02	10	12	***	33
37–48	4 (85)	8 (144)	15 (26)	04	08	11	***	31
49–60	6 (145)	11 (83)	14 (22)	05	03	08	***	32
61–72	3 (146)	26 (27)	0 (12)	24	–	–	***	46
Ask dentist for advice								
Age 25–36	14 (42)	44 (160)	51 (49)	35	12	43	**	31
37–48	29 (85)	37 (143)	54 (26)	11	27	35	NS	13
49–60	25 (139)	29 (82)	38 (21)	05	13	17	NS	15
61–72	25 (137)	39 (26)	50 (12)	19	18	33	*	29

SOURCE: NORC 423.

TABLE 43. Adult Education and Self-Instruction

	Percentages			Index of Effectiveness			Relationship over Full Range on Variables	
	Elem. School	High Sch. Grad.	College Grad.	High Elem.	Col. High	Col. Elem.	Chi-Sq. (P)	Assoc. (γ)
Age 25–36								
1950 ever taken course	7 (76)	32 (114)	52 (25)	27	29	48	***	47
1962 ever taken course	24 (46)	51 (150)	77 (44)	35	53	70	***	59
1963 taken in past year[a]	0 (101)	11 (230)	26 (110)	11	17	26	***	18
1962 tried self-study	39 (46)	37 (150)	56 (48)	–	30	28	NS	
Age 37–48								
1950 ever taken course	17 (105)	37 (54)	59 (27)	24	35	51	***	50
1962 ever taken course	26 (90)	58 (136)	83 (41)	43	59	77	***	50
1963 taken in past year	5 (152)	17 (197)	46 (54)	13	35	43	***	33
1962 tried self-study	24 (90)	39 (136)	61 (41)	20	36	49	***	
Age 49–60								
1950 ever taken course	10 (108)	32 (28)	67 (12)	24	51	63	***	56
1962 ever taken course	25 (109)	49 (70)	90 (20)	32	80	87	***	59
1963 taken in past year	6 (188)	7 (101)	54 (54)	01	50	51	***	28
1962 tried self-study	28 (109)	40 (72)	50 (20)	17	17	30	*	
Age 61–72								
1950 ever taken course	7 (61)	14 (14)	38 (8)	07	27	32	***	58
1962 ever taken course	24 (109)	57 (23)	75 (12)	43	42	67	***	59
1963 taken in past year	3 (207)	0 (67)	21 (14)	–	21	18	***	43
1962 tried self-study	17 (109)	52 (23)	15 (13)	42	–	–	***	

SOURCES: 1950, Gallup 452 TPS; 1962, NORC 447; 1963, Gallup 667K.
[a]Grade school limited to grades 5–8.

TABLE 44. Effects of Education on Media Exposure, with Social Origins Controlled

(Survey) Item	RItem and Education	RItem and Education with Origins Controlled	RItem and Origins
(NORC 4018—1967)			
Watch TV	.14	.14	.07
Watch TV news	.08	.07	.05
Read paper	.28	.26	.18
No. magazines read	.40	.37	.19
No. newsmagazines read	.41	.38	.19
(Average)	.26	.24	
(NORC 447—1962)			
Try teach self	.17	.11	.20
Read paper	.19	.15	.21
Books read	.36	.26	.41
Movies seen	.29	.22	.34
Read magazines	.29	.23	.31
Watch TV	.14	.12	.18
Listen radio	.05	.04	.13
Adult education	.32	.25	.36
(Average)	.22	.17	

TABLE 45. Two Relatively "Easy" Items, "Learned at Different Stages"

	Elementary School	High School	College
Know where Leaning Tower is (1957)	32%	72%	87%
Know (vaguely, at least) where Suez Canal is (1951)	30	48	84

TABLE 46. Two "Difficult" Items, "Learned at Different Stages"

	Elementary School	High School	College
Can name four cancer symptoms (1955)	3%	14%	16%
Can name planet nearest sun (1955)	4	6	21

TABLE 47. Four Items of Similar "Difficulty," "Learned at Different Stages"

	Elementary School	High School	College
Know author of **Tom Sawyer** (1957)	12%	54%	76%
Know author of **Midsummer Night's Dream** (1955)	8	44	76
Identify Tolstoy correctly (1952)	9	32	72
Identify Freud correctly (1952)	4	27	79

TABLE 48. Eight Items Ordered by "Index of Placement" (P)

	P
Can name four cancer symptoms	11
Know where Leaning Tower is	28
Know author of **Tom Sawyer**	34
Know author of **Midsummer Night's Dream**	36
Identify Tolstoy correctly	63
Know (vaguely, at least) where Suez Canal is	68
Identify Freud correctly	69
Can name planet nearest sun	84

TABLE 49. "Placement" Indexes (P) for Answers of Varying Difficulty to Four "Compound" Items

"Will you please tell me the number on this map which locates each of the following countries? France. Spain. Yugoslavia. England. Bulgaria. Romania. Poland. Austria." (1955)

	Elementary School	College	P
Can locate at least **one**.	64%	96%	20
Can locate at least **three**.	39	90	41
Can locate at least **four**.	22	73	56
Can locate at least **five**.	11	54	71
Can locate all eight	1	13	75

"Will you tell me the names of any of the first four books of the New Testament of the Bible—that is, the first four Gospels?" (1950)

Named at least **one**.	37	73	54
Named all four.	27	65	69

Cabinet positions—1960

Named at least **one**.	55	96	24
Named at least **five**.	15	80	57

Symptoms of Cancer—1955

Named at least **one**.	46	86	23
Named at least **four**.	3	16	11

TABLE 50. "Placement" Indexes (P) for Partly and Entirely Correct Answers to Nine Items

	Elementary School	College	P
Define "monopoly" (1949)			
At least partly correct	40%	92%	20
Correct	20	73	35
Define "electoral college" (1951)			
At least partly correct	22	75	49
Correct	9	61	60
Define "foreign policy" (1951)			
At least partly correct	41	90	42
Correct	21	78	46
Identify Plato (1952)			
At least partly correct	10	88	51
Correct	7	69	59
Identify Bach (1952)			
At least partly correct	26	91	30
Correct	16	60	37
Locate Iran (1951)			
At least partly correct	21	81	39
Correct	12	52	54
Locate Formosa (1951)			
At least partly correct	28	75	36
Correct	17	68	57
Locate Suez Canal (1951)			
At least partly correct	30	84	68
Correct	22	68	74
Locate Manchuria (1951)			
At least partly correct	43	87	18
Correct	38	75	12

TABLE 51. Academic Knowledge of the Humanities

	Elementary School	College	P
Identify Shakespeare (1952)	64%	99%	08
Identify Beethoven (1952)	39	98	19
Name author of **Macbeth** (1957)	11	87	29
Identify Bach—at least partly correct (1952)	26	91	30
Name author of **Tom Sawyer** (1957)	12	76	34
Name author of **Midsummer Night's Dream** (1955)	8	76	36
Identify Bach—correct (1952)	16	60	37
Name author of **Huckleberry Finn** (1953)	14	82	40
Identify Raphael (1952)	9	82	47
Identify Aristotle (1952)	7	91	51
Identify Plato—at least partly correct (1952)	10	88	51
Name a painter (1952)	9	61	52
Identify Plato—correct (1952)	7	69	59
Name author of **Tale of Two Cities** (1953)	4	71	59
Identify Karl Marx (1952)	12	91	59
Identify Tolstoy (1952)	9	72	63
Name composer of **The Messiah** (1955)	5	54	67
Name author of **War and Peace** (1952)	1	41	68
Name the four Gospels (1950)	27	65	69
Identify Freud (1952)	4	79	69
Identify Rubens (1952)	3	56	73
Identify Thackery (1957)	6	65	79
Identify Rubens (1957)	6	45	86

	P .5 or less	**P greater than .5**	**Total**
Average percentage elementary school	22	8	13
Average percentage college	83	68	74
Average P	—	—	52

TABLE 52. Academic Knowledge of History

	Elementary School	College	P
Identify Columbus (1952)	83%	99%	04
Name inventor of telephone (1955)	59	97	11
Give Florence Nightingale's profession (1955)	44	92	18
Identify Napoleon (1952)	46	99	23
Identify Lindbergh (1955)	71	96	32
Know war Battle of the Bulge was in (1957)[a]	38	88	34
Know country Waterloo is in (1955)	18	60	38
Know war Gettysburg was in (1957)	43	93	43
Know war Bunker Hill was in (1957)	22	83	50
Know war Waterloo was in (1957)	19	75	54
Identify Gutenberg (1952)	10	75	68

	P .5 or less	P greater than .5	Total
Average percentage elementary school	48	14	40
Average percentage college	90	75	87
Average P	—	—	34

[a]Not included in computation of averages.

TABLE 53. Academic Knowledge of Civics and Government

	Elementary School	College	P
Know that all states elect congressmen this year (1952)	33%	43%	(0)[a]
Know name of national anthem (1947)	64	91	12
Know term of president (1952)	90	98	14[b]
Know month of presidential election (1952)	82	98	19
Can name at least one cabinet position (1960)	55	96	24
Know number of senators per state (1951)	46	93	32
Can define "filibuster" (1949-AT)	28	88	34
Can define "monopoly" (1949)[c]	20	73	35
Can define "filibuster" (1949-AK)	33	85	36
Can define "filibuster" (1949-B)	30	87	36
Can define "filibuster" (1949-C)	36	89	38
Can define "electoral college" (1954)	15	75	42
Can define "foreign policy" (1951)[c]	21	78	46
Can define "filibuster" (1963)	34	93	49
Can define "electoral college" (1961)	20	88	50
Can name **five** cabinet positions	15	80	57
Can define "electoral college" (1951)[c]	9	61	60
Know "job of State Department" (1951)	26	89	61
Know length of congressional term (1970)	25	66	62
Name the three branches of the federal government (1952)	7	61	63
Can define "electoral college" (1950)	16	88	65
Know length of Senate term (1970)	15	58	68
Know meaning of "GOP" (1952)	20	66	68

	P .5 or less	P greater than .5	Total
Average percentage elementary school	40	17	32
Average percentage college	85	71	80
Average P	—	—	42

[a]High school percentage is somewhat **higher** than college percentage.

[b]Small difference between elementary school and college percentages means that P is subject to extreme sampling variation.

[c]Only "correct" answers entered in this table, although "partly correct" was also coded.

TABLE 54. Academic Knowledge of Geography

	Elementary School	College	P
Know ocean between U.S. and Britain (1951)	82%	98%	09
Knows Michigan borders Canada (1955)	60	89	12
Can locate Manchuria (1951)[a]	38	75	12
Can locate at least 1 (of 8) countries (1955)	64	96	20
Know location of Pyramids (1957)	46	96	21
Know location of Eiffel Tower (1957)	37	94	28
Know location of Leaning Tower (1957)	32	87	28
Know location of Kremlin (1957)	11	03	29
Know Minnesota borders Canada (1955)	45	75	33
Know what nation New Delhi capital of (1955)	33	90	35
Know ocean Midway Islands in (1955)	52	98	38
Can locate Spain (on map) (1947)	47	94	38
Know state named for president (1955)	66	90	39
Know capital of Spain (1955)	37	86	40
Can name highest mountain in world (1955)	23	78	44
Know location of Mount Vernon (1957)	27	57	48
Can locate France (on map) (1947)	55	95	48
Can locate Poland (on map) (1947)	30	74	48
Know Montana borders Canada (1955)	44	71	50
Know Maine borders Canada (1955)	59	78	51
Can locate Iran (1951)[a]	12	52	54
Knows location of Parthenon (1957)	8	73	55
Can locate Formosa (1951)[a]	17	68	57
Know population of U.S. (1951)	32	65	62
Can locate Yugoslavia (on map) (1947)	16	52	65
Can locate Bulgaria (on map) (1947)	8	32	68
Can locate Romania (on map) (1947)	11	38	68
Can locate at least 5 (of 8) countries	11	54	71
Locate Suez Canal (1951)[a]	22	68	74
Know what language spoken in Brazil (1955)	9	51	80

	P .5 or less	P greater than .5	Total
Average percentage elementary school	45	19	36
Average percentage college	86	57	76
Average P	—	—	44

[a]Only "correct" answers entered in this table, although "partly correct" was also coded.

TABLE 55. Academic Knowledge of Science, Health, Mathematics, etc.

	Elementary School	College	P
Know number of pecks in a bushel (1955)	76%	68%	(0)[a]
Can name four cancer symptoms (1955)	3	16	11
Can define "pyorrhea" (1959)	72	91	16
Has heard about fluoridation (1959)	59	97	27
Know person associated with theory of relativity (1955)	44	98	27
Know how many 3¢ stamps for 75¢ (1951)	74	96	34
Know diabetes not contagious (1955)	73	95	35
Know number of feet in a mile (1955)	19	66	37
Know number of inches in a yard (1951)	92	98	63[b]
Know planet nearest sun (1955)	4	21	84

	P 0.5 or less	P greater than 0.5	Total
Average percentage elementary school	52	48	52
Average percentage college	78	60	75
Average P	—	—	33

[a]**Negative** relation to education. Since what learning is done takes place early, P is entered as 0.

[b]Small differences between elementary school and college percentages mean that P is subject to extreme sampling variation.

TABLE 56. "Placement" Indexes (P) for Answers of Varying Difficulty to Three "Compound" Public Affairs Items

	Elementary School	College	P
Can name at least one senator from home state (1951)	43%	83%	45
Can name both senators	23	58	76
Can name at least one senator from home state (1967)	42	84	39
Can name both senators	21	61	73
Can name at least one Supreme Court Justice (1966)	25	85	46
Can name at least two	9	55	54
Can name at least three	3	35	72
Can name at least four.	1	20	93
Can name at least five	—	7	86

TABLE 57. "Placement" Indexes (P) for Partly and Entirely Correct Answers
to Public Affairs Items

	Elementary School	College	P	Difference In value of P
Who Is Chiang (1950)				
At least partly correct	67%	97%	24	
Correct	35	81	52	28
Who Is Chiang (1951)				
At least partly correct	65	100	24	
Correct	32	87	61	37
What is NATO (1951)				
At least partly correct	12	68	63	
Correct	6	43	60	−3
What is Voice of America (1951)				
At least partly correct	28	92	41	
Correct	19	81	49	8
What is trouble in Iran (1951)				
At least partly correct	40	92	48	
Correct	39	91	49	1
What Is 38th Parallel (1951)				
At least partly correct	41	87	38	
Correct	34	68	15	−23
Who is Dean Acheson (1951)				
At least partly correct	51	96	69	
Correct	45	96	64	−5
Who is Rockefeller (1963)				
At least partly correct	79	98	21	
Correct	74	96	37	16
Who Is Nixon (1963)				
At least partly correct	84	97	44	
Correct	77	89	03	−41
Who Is Goldwater (1963)				
At least partly correct	60	98	52	
Correct	45	90	56	4
Who is Romney (1963)				
At least partly correct	17	74	44	
Correct	14	68	46	2
Who is Scranton (1963)				
At least partly correct	21	40	47	
Correct	16	51	43	−4
Who Is Clifford Case (1963)				
At least partly correct	8	24	76	
Correct	7	23	78	2
Who Is Mark Hatfield (1963)				
At least partly correct	4	22	63	
Correct	3	17	76	13
Who Is Harold Stassen (1963)				
At least partly correct	31	75	75	
Correct	12	50	70	−5
Who Is Milton Eisenhower (1963)				
At least partly correct	54	88	44	
Correct	40	73	39	−5
Who is Thruston Morton (1963)				
At least partly correct	7	39	57	
Correct	6	30	60	3

TABLE 57—Continued

	Elementary School	College	P	Difference in value of P
Political Information level (1966)				
High or average	32	89	49	
High	8	58	72	23
Political Information level (1968)				
High or average	48	95	50	
High	18	71	60	10
Political Information level (1970)				
High or average	43	98	49	
High	12	73	73	24
What is automation (1957)				
At least partly correct	10	65	51	
Correct	4	24	31	−20

TABLE 58. "Placement" Indexes (P) for Related Items of Varying Difficulty

	Elementary School	College	P
Heard of Hoover Commission (1950)	24%	84%	47
Knows what it is	18	73	53
Heard of Hoover Commission (1952)	17	79	61
Knows what it is	9	67	67
Heard of J. Edgar Hoover (1950)	74	97	14
Can identify Hoover (1957)	54	94	22
Can identify Hoover (1960)	63	99	29
Can identify FBI head (1955)	64	98	25

TABLE 59. Knowledge of Population of Mainland China at Two Times

	Elementary School	High School	College	P
1951	3%	3%	3%	—
1952	1%	4%	10%	65

TABLE 60. Knowledge of Several Items as They Become "Easier"

	Elementary School	High School	College	d
Heard about NATO				
(March 1949)	33%	50%	90%	70
(June 1949)	46	73	95	45
Heard about Chinese civil war				
(June 1949)	63	85	98	36
(January 1950)	67	91	98	23
Know what "wiretapping" means				
(1949)	32	55	68	35
(1950)	53	82	89	19
Heard about H-bomb				
(January 1950)	64	88	97	29
(February 1950)	80	97	97	03
Heard of Tito				
(1950)	24	47	78	59
(1951)	30	63	87	24
Heard about test ban talks				
(March 1963)	63	77	98	60
Heard about test ban treaty				
(August 1963)	67	88	96	27

TABLE 61. Knowledge of Two Items, Where P Increases as Items Get "Easier"

	Elementary School	High School	College	P
Know Rockefeller				
(March 1963)	63%	93%	95%	09
(August 1963)	74	88	96	37
Know Goldwater				
(March 1963)	27	55	85	52
(August 1963)	45	64	90	56

TABLE 62. Knowledge of Several Items as They Become More "Difficult"

	Elementary School	High School	College	P
Heard of Arab-Israeli trouble				
(May 1967)	83	90	98	54
Heard about Arab-Israeli War				
(1969)	78	89	98	45
Heard about Taft-Hartley				
(1949)	72	93	99	24
(May 1952)	54	77	94	42
(September 1952)	62	82	97	43
(October 1952)	46	78	95	34
Heard of Hoover Commission				
(1950)	24	55	84	47
(1952)	17	42	79	61
Know what Hoover Commission Is				
(1950)	18	44	73	53
(1952)	9	28	67	67
Know mainland China Communist, not in UN				
(1964)	55	80	93	35
(1968)	39	65	91	50

TABLE 63. Public Affairs Items Dealing with Domestic Public Figures (Not Included in Earlier Tables), Ordered by P Value

	Elementary School	College	P
Name county clerk (1966)[a]	31%	26%	(0)[b]
Name mayor (1966)[a]	65	67	(0)[b]
Know Johnson's home state (1964)	84	94	11
Heard of George Marshall (1951)	69	99	19
Know Dean Rusk (1967)	56	90	21
Know vice president (1955)	68	97	22
Have high candidate knowledge (1958)[a]	27	40	25
Know vice president (1952)	52	94	27
Name school board head (1967)[a]	36	63	27
Name state senator (1966)[a]	17	43	28
Know Kennedy's religion (1960)	92	100	30
Know Earl Warren (1952)	39	88	31
Name secretary of state (1971)[a]	6	38	33
Know Goldwater's home state (1964)	61	93	34
Name governor (1967)	84	98	35
Name mayor (1967)[a]	65	76	36
Know Nixon's home state (1960)	35	88	36
Name Republican V.P. nominee (1968)	47	90	36
Name Democratic V.P. nominee (1968)	42	82	37
Know Rockefeller (1967)	71	100	39
Know Kennedy's home state (1960)	33	86	40
Heard of James Petrillo (1957)	28	76	41
Know Kefauver (1952)	18	50	42
Name governor (1971)	80	100	43
Know Eisenhower (1952)	37	72	43
Know Harriman (1952)	4	24	44
Heard of John L. Lewis (1957)	68	87	45
Heard of Dave Beck (1957)	55	95	46
Know Taft (1952)	22	61	50
Know Walter Reuther (1957)	43	75	51
Know George Romney (1963)	12	69	51
Know Goldwater (1963)	27	85	52
Know Stevenson (1952)	12	50	54
Know Charles Percy (1967)	26	69	55
Heard of Harry Bridges (1957)	33	82	56
Know Robert Kerr (1952)	6	22	56
Name congressman (1967)	31	70	57
Know Nixon's religion (1960)	26	61	62
Know William Scranton (1963)	20	60	63
Name congressman (1957)	33	55	70
Know Richard Russell (1952)	6	37	70
Know Harold Stassen (1952)	14	57	75
Heard of George Meany (1957)	28	62	80
Know Frank Stanton (1960)	2	21	83
Know Elmo Roper (1960)	2	34	88
Know Sam Lubell (1960)	—	15	89
Heard of David McDonald (1957)	12	23	(100)[c]

TABLE 63—Continued

	For all Domestic Public Figure Items[d]		
	P .5 or less	P greater than .5	Total
Average percentage elementary school	50	18	37
Average percentage college	79	53	68
Average P	—	—	45

[a]P less than 40; college percentage lower than 80.
[b]High school percentage higher than college percentage.
[c]High school percentage lower than elementary school percentage.
[d]Includes items presented in tables 56–62. For "compound" items and those with a "partly correct" alternative, the most difficult answer was used in this computation (except for question dealing with Supreme Court justices, where ability to name two or more was taken as "correct").

TABLE 64. Public Affairs Items Dealing with Domestic Issues and Events (Not Included in Earlier Tables), Ordered by P Value[a]

	Elementary School	College	P
Heard about government seizing steel Industry (1952)	69%	96%	15
Know month political conventions held (1952)	22	54	29
Heard about congressional investigation of unions (1957)	58	98	34
Heard about mass civil rights rally (1963)	56	85	34
Know city political conventions held in (1952)	29	68	45
Heard about Truman health plan (1949)	48	95	47
Heard criticism of Atomic Energy Commission (1949)	42	93	55
Follow discussion of Taft-Hartley (1953)	23	75	56
Heard about new presidential budget (1957)	55	89	62
Heard discussion of Taft-Hartley (1949)	40	85	65
Heard about fallout (1957)	48	77	71
Had some information on each of eight issues (1958)	49	75	(100)[b]

	For all Domestic Issue and Event Items[c]		
	P .5 or less	P greater than .5	Total
Average percentage elementary school	48	33	41
Average percentage college	83	78	80
Average P	—	—	60

[a]Ten questions asking which party controlled Congress before and after five congressional elections are omitted from this table but included in the averages. There was considerable but not readily interpretable variation in both their difficulty and in the P value for these items. In general, lower values of P were found for the less "difficult" items.

[b]High school percentage is lower than elementary school percentage.

[c]Includes items presented in tables 56–62. For items with a "partly correct" alternative, only the more difficult answer was used in this computation.

TABLE 65. Public Affairs Items Dealing with Foreign Public Figures (Not Included in Earlier Tables), Ordered by P Value

	Elementary School	College	P
Know Kosygin (1967)	49%	92%	20
Know Synghman Rhee (1953)	33	88	37
Know prime minister of U.K. (1953)	42	88	38
Know what country Franco is from (1953)	39	95	42
Know Nehru (1957)	25	78	45
Know Nguyen Cao Ky (1967)	28	75	48
Know Adenauer (1957)	20	64	61
Know Anthony Eden (1951)	11	56	69

	For all Foreign Public Figure Items[a]		
	P .5 or less	P greater than .5	Total
Average percentage elementary school	35	24	31
Average percentage college	86	73	81
Average P	—	—	49

[a]Includes items presented in tables 56–62. For items with a "partly correct" alternative, only the more difficult answer was used in this computation.

TABLE 66. Public Affairs Items Dealing with Foreign Issues and Events (Not Included in Earlier Tables), Ordered by P Value

	Elementary School	College	P
Know size of Chinese Army (1951)	3%	4%	—[a]
Know about Chinese Communists (1954)	60	94	30
Heard of Berlin dispute (1961)	86	100	33
Heard of Vietnam War (1964)	62	96	38
Heard about Korea hearings (1951)	58	97	44
Heard of Nationalist China (1964)	30	77	63
Can define "Isolationism" (1950)	35	78	68

	For all Foreign Issues and Events Items[b]		
	P .5 or less	P greater than .5	Total
Average percentage elementary school	57	36	51
Average percentage college	93	71	86
Average P	—	—	43

[a]Not included in averages below; high school percentage is lower than elementary school percentage.

[b]Includes items presented in tables 56–62. For items with a "partly correct" alternative, only the more difficult answer was used in this computation.

TABLE 67. Knowledge of Public Affairs among Canadians Age 30–39

	Percentage Informed			Index of Effectiveness			Relationship over Full Range on Variables	
	Elem. School	High School	College	High Elem.	Col. High	Col. Elem.	Chi-Sq. (P)	Assoc. (γ)
Domestic								
Know Lester Pearson (1953)	54 (145)	87 (209)	95 (37)	72	62	89	***	71
Heard about St. Lawrence Seaway plan (1954)	64 (203)	94 (257)	100 (60)	83	100	100	***	83
Know a cabinet member (1954)	26 (188)	46 (287)	64 (77)	27	33	51	***	45
Know a member of Diefenbaker cabinet (9/1957)	14 (78)	32 (132)	64 (22)	21	47	58	***	56
Heard about debate trans-Canada pipeline (1956)	63 (172)	83 (222)	93 (45)	54	59	81	***	53
Heard about next federal election (1957)	50 (189)	70 (265)	83 (57)	40	43	66	***	43
Index knowledge provincial premiers "high score" (1956)	32 (148)	65 (250)	80 (54)	49 / 44	43 / 47	71 / 70	***	60 / 59
Mean =	43	68	83					
Foreign								
Know Henry Cabot Lodge (1953)	11 (145)	40 (207)	76 (38)	33	60	73	***	72
Heard proposed summit meeting (1953)	59 (210)	82 (298)	98 (41)	56	89	95	***	59
Heard of Arab-Israel conflict (5/1956)	75 (103)	90 (188)	100 (44)	60	100	100	***	63
Heard of Suez Canal dispute (9/1956)	80 (163)	93 (239)	97 (75)	65 / 45	57 / 71	85 / 84	***	57 / 63
Mean =	56	76	93					

TABLE 68. Knowledge of Public Affairs among Canadians Age 40–49

	Percentage Informed			Index of Effectiveness			Relationship over Full Range on Variables	
	Elem. School	High School	College	High Elem.	Col. High	Col. Elem.	Chi-Sq. (P)	Assoc. (γ)
Domestic								
Know Lester Pearson (1953)	67 (197)	88 (207)	96 (54)	64	67	88	***	63
Heard about St. Lawrence Seaway plan (1954)	80 (237)	93 (187)	96 (50)	65	43	80	***	54
Know a cabinet member (1954)	34 (211)	58 (201)	71 (34)	36	31	56	***	46
Know a member of Diefenbaker cabinet (9/1957)	28 (109)	43 (147)	71 (21)	21	49	60	***	41
Heard about debate trans-Canada pipeline (1956)	62 (157)	88 (182)	96 (26)	68	67	89	***	66
Heard about next federal election (1957)	57 (183)	75 (195)	90 (41)	42	60	77	***	45
Index knowledge provincial premiers "high score" (1956)	43 (148)	72 (186)	77 (35)	51	18	60	***	50
Mean =	53	74	85	45	42	68		52
Foreign								
Know Henry Cabot Lodge (1953)	14 (198)	38 (204)	78 (54)	28	65	74	***	68
Heard proposed summit meeting (1953)	61 (192)	84 (200)	97 (39)	59	81	92	***	61
Heard of Arab-Israel conflict (5/1956)	76 (121)	85 (142)	100 (14)	38	100	100	*	35
Heard of Suez Canal dispute (9/1956)	82 (181)	95 (171)	92 (36)	72	—	56	***	50
Mean =	58	76	92	43	67	81		54

TABLE 69. Knowledge of Public Affairs among Canadians Age 50 or over

	Percentage Informed			Index of Effectiveness			Relationship over Full Range on Variables	
	Elem. School	High School	College	High Elem.	Col. High	Col. Elem.	Chi-Sq. (P)	Assoc. (γ)
Domestic								
Know Lester Pearson (1953)	66 (335)	85 (193)	100 (38)	56	100	100	***	58
Heard about St. Lawrence Seaway plan (1954)	80 (292)	95 (167)	100 (55)	75	100	100	***	75
Know a cabinet member (1954)	38 (192)	54 (151)	88 (33)	26	74	81	***	45
Know a member of Diefenbaker cabinet (9/1957)	33 (197)	45 (104)	79 (19)	18	62	69	***	38
Heard about debate trans-Canada pipeline (1956)	72 (344)	94 (207)	97 (30)	79	50	89	***	73
Heard about next federal election (1957)	69 (340)	77 (234)	95 (38)	26	78	84	**	29
Index knowledge provincial premiers "high score" (1956)	59 (293)	70 (253)	92 (49)	40	73	84	***	48
Mean =	58	74	93	38	73	83		51
Foreign								
Know Henry Cabot Lodge (1953)	20 (334)	52 (194)	72 (39)	40	42	65	***	64
Heard proposed summit meeting (1953)	75 (251)	86 (151)	96 (44)	44	71	84	***	44
Heard of Arab-Israel conflict (5/1956)	83 (223)	97 (169)	100 (23)	82	100	100	***	77
Heard of Suez Canal dispute (9/1956)	81 (331)	99 (215)	100 (67)	95	100	100	***	94
Mean =	65	84	92	54	50	77		69

TABLE 70. Knowledge of Popular Culture among Canadians Age 30–39

	Percentage Informed			Index of Effectiveness			Relationship over Full Range on Variables	
	Elem. School	High School	College	High Elem.	Col. High	Col. Elem.	Chi-Sq. (P)	Assoc. (γ)
Heard of Kinsey's studies on sex (1953)	31 (209)	62 (297)	78 (41)	44	42	68	***	57
Know Grey Cup sport (9/1955)	52 (197)	86 (277)	91 (55)	70	35	81	***	68
Know Grey Cup sport (9/1956)	57 (166)	85 (242)	89 (75)	65	26	74	***	58
Heard of Duke of Windsor (1956)	93 (166)	98 (240)	97 (75)	71	—	57	*	a
Know site of Olympics (1956)	41 (166)	68 (242)	68 (75)	45	0	45	***	40
Mean =	55	80	85	55	25	66		56

aIndeterminate.

TABLE 71. Knowledge of Popular Culture among Canadians Age 40–49

	Percentage Informed			Index of Effectiveness			Relationship over Full Range on Variables	
	Elem. School	High School	College	High Elem.	Col. High	Col. Elem.	Chi-Sq. (P)	Assoc. (γ)
Heard of Kinsey's studies on sex (1953)	19 (192)	57 (200)	80 (39)	46	53	75	***	70
Know Grey Cup sport (9/1955)	47 (173)	73 (236)	100 (30)	49	100	100	***	60
Know Grey Cup sport (9/1956)	62 (184)	73 (175)	89 (36)	28	59	71	**	33
Heard of Duke of Windsor (1956)	95 (184)	100 (174)	100 (36)	100	0	100	**	a
Know site of Olympics (1956)	30 (184)	57 (175)	67 (36)	38	23	52	***	50
Mean =	51	72	87	42	53	73		53

aIndeterminate.

TABLE 72. Knowledge of Popular Culture among Canadians Age 50 or Over

	Percentage Informed			Index of Effectiveness			Relationship over Full Range on Variables	
	Elem. School	High School	College	High Elem.	Col. High	Col. Elem.	Chi-Sq. (P)	Assoc. (γ)
Heard of Kinsey's studies on sex (1953)	27 (251)	50 (151)	66 (44)	31	32	53	***	50
Know Grey Cup sport (9/1955)	51 (195)	75 (151)	76 (25)	48	04	51	***	45
Know Grey Cup sport (9/1956)	48 (337)	79 (218)	85 (67)	59	28	71	***	60
Heard of Duke of Windsor (1956)	94 (337)	100 (218)	100 (67)	100	0	100	***	a
Know site of Olympics (1956)	29 (337)	57 (218)	87 (67)	39	69	81	***	64
Mean =	50	72	83	44	39	66		55

a Indeterminate.

TABLE 73. Spelling Ability for U.S. White Adults and English-Speaking Canadian Adults Mean Number of Words Correctly Spelled on Ten-Item Test[a]

	Whites in U.S. Who Completed				English-Speaking Canadians Who Completed			
	1–8 Years School	9–12 Years School	At Least Some College	Diff. Col. vs. Elem.	1–8 Years School	9–12 Years School	At Least Some College	Diff. Col. vs. Elem.
Age 30–39	3.05	5.65	7.40	4.35	5.06	7.04	7.57	2.51
N =	(72)	(215)	(64)		(71)	(203)	(42)	
Age 40–49	2.94	5.77	6.86	3.92	4.27	7.49	9.15	4.88
N =	(81)	(148)	(72)		(121)	(208)	(47)	
Age 50 or over	3.14	5.55	7.07	3.93	4.58	6.72	8.22	3.64
N =	(263)	(163)	(55)		(157)	(127)	(32)	

a1955 National sample surveys containing following ten words: magazine, sandwich, calamity, deceive, kerosene, cauliflower, parallel, accelerator, picnicking, penitentiary.

Appendix B
Tables Containing
Detailed Findings
on Knowledge

TABLE 1.1. Knowledge of Public Affairs among Individuals Age 25–36 in the Early 1950s

	Percentage Informed			Index of Effectiveness			Relationship over Full Range on Variables	
	Elem. School	High Sch. Grad.	College Grad.	High Elem.	Col. High	Col. Elem.	Chi-Sq. (P)	Assoc. (γ)
Domestic Affairs—Persons								
Heard of J. Edgar Hoover	74 (81)	94 (123)	97 (34)	77	50	89	***	59
Know Dean Acheson	38 (79)	77 (168)	98 (84)	63	91	97	***	64
Heard of George Marshall	59 (73)	91 (115)	100 (27)	78	100	100	***	66
Know own senators	07 (73)	25 (116)	56 (27)	19	41	53	***	27
Know Eisenhower	27 (59)	54 (102)	70 (33)	37	35	59	***	35
Know Harriman	03 (59)	10 (102)	15 (33)	07	05	12	***	37
Know Kefauver	17 (59)	33 (102)	52 (33)	19	28	42	***	37
Know R. Kerr	09 (59)	11 (102)	18 (33)	02	08	10	**	25
Know R. Russell	02 (59)	17 (102)	36 (33)	15	23	35	**	38
Know Taft	22 (59)	38 (102)	67 (33)	21	47	58	***	39
Know Stevenson	14 (59)	23 (102)	55 (33)	13	42	48	**	32
Know Earl Warren	36 (59)	69 (102)	88 (33)	52	61	81	***	53
Know vice president	42 (59)	79 (102)	94 (33)	64	71	90	***	52
Know Stassen	15 (59)	18 (102)	61 (33)	04	52	54	***	38
Mean =	26	46	65	27	35	53		38
Domestic Affairs—Events								
Heard Taft-Hartley Law (3/49)	71 (79)	89 (136)	100 (39)	62	100	100	***	50
Heard Taft-Hartley Law (5/52)	43 (72)	73 (194)	94 (70)	53	78	90	***	49
Heard Taft-Hartley Law (10/52)	41 (76)	73 (95)	97 (30)	54	89	95	***	58
Heard Taft-Hartley Law (9/52)	50 (42)	78 (83)	93 (27)	56	68	86	***	54
Follow Taft-Hartley Law (6/49)	26 (131)	53 (240)	79 (79)	36	55	72	***	43
Follow Taft-Hartley Law (10/53)	20 (59)	39 (158)	61 (51)	24	36	51	***	35
Know wiretapping (6/49)	30 (131)	59 (240)	68 (79)	42	22	55	***	36
Know wiretapping (1/50)	52 (58)	83 (109)	90 (52)	65	41	80	***	45
Heard criticism of AEC	31 (131)	62 (239)	94 (79)	45	84	91	***	51
Heard Hoover Commission (1/50)	07 (58)	49 (109)	84 (51)	45	69	83	***	68
Heard Hoover Commission (5/52)	13 (72)	33 (194)	80 (70)	23	70	77	***	53
Know Hoover Commission (1/50)	05 (58)	36 (109)	71 (52)	33	55	70	***	64
Know Hoover Commission (5/52)	06 (72)	22 (195)	70 (70)	17	62	68	***	42
Heard Truman health insurance plan	38 (80)	61 (137)	97 (39)	37	92	95	***	49

Know date political convention	10 (59)	39 (102)	58 (33)	32	31	53	***	41
Know convention cities	12 (59)	42 (102)	64 (33)	34	38	59	***	32
Know if all states hold congressional elections (1952)	29 (59)	39 (102)	49 (33)	14	16	28	**	31
Heard of government's seizure steel industry	54 (59)	95 (102)	94 (33)	89	—	87	***	58
Information index—"good" score	02 (46)	14 (127)	40 (52)	12	30	39	***	69
Know population of U.S.	25 (76)	35 (105)	73 (41)	13	59	64	***	29
Mean =	28	54	78	36	52	69		
Foreign Affairs—Persons								
Know Tito (10/50)	20 (81)	42 (123)	82 (34)	28	84	78	***	48
Know Tito (4/51)	19 (73)	57 (116)	89 (27)	47	75	86	***	58
Know Chiang Kai-shek (12/50)	38 (40)	53 (154)	80 (40)	24	58	58	***	34
Know Chiang Kai-shek (4/51)	23 (73)	53 (116)	85 (27)	39	68	31	***	51
Know Anthony Eden	07 (76)	21 (105)	63 (41)	15	53	60	***	51
Know Synghman Rhee	29 (59)	60 (159)	88 (51)	44	70	83	***	51
Know Franco	32 (59)	66 (159)	92 (51)	50	76	88	***	52
Mean =	24	50	83	34	66	78		
Foreign Affairs—Events								
Heard NATO (3/49)	28 (80)	41 (137)	90 (38)	18	83	86	***	47
Heard NATO (6/49)	42 (130)	71 (239)	92 (79)	50	73	86	***	52
Heard H-bomb (1/50)	64 (58)	85 (109)	100 (51)	58	100	100	***	58
Heard H-bomb (2/50)	74 (76)	97 (114)	92 (25)	96	—	69	***	70
Heard Chinese civil war (6/49)	59 (130)	84 (240)	100 (79)	61	100	100	***	59
Heard Chinese civil war (1/50)	71 (58)	89 (109)	100 (52)	62	100	100	***	51
Know Atlantic Pact	04 (73)	17 (116)	41 (27)	14	29	39	***	43
Know 38th Parallel	21 (73)	61 (116)	70 (27)	51	23	62	***	45
Know size Chinese Army	03 (76)	04 (105)	07 (41)	01	03	04	**	23
Know population of China (12/51)	04 (76)	03 (105)	05 (41)	—	02	01	NS	22
Know population of China (2/52)	00 (62)	05 (188)	16 (57)	05	09	16	***	51
Heard about hearings on Korea	48 (79)	76 (168)	96 (84)	54	83	92	***	54
Know about trouble in Iran	30 (79)	60 (168)	92 (84)	43	80	89	***	55
Know Voice of America	15 (79)	54 (168)	86 (84)	46	70	84	***	53
Mean =	33	53	71	30	38	57		

TABLE 1.2. Knowledge of Public Affairs among individuals Age 37-48 in the Early 1950s

	Percentage Informed			Index of Effectiveness			Relationship over Full Range on Variables	
	Elem. School	High Sch. Grad.	College Grad.	High Elem.	Col. High	Col. Elem.	Chi-Sq. (P)	Assoc. (γ)
Domestic Affairs—Persons								
Heard of J. Edgar Hoover	73 (118)	92 (62)	97 (35)	70	62	89	***	56
Know Dean Acheson	46 (106)	73 (119)	97 (68)	50	89	94	***	52
Know George Marshall	64 (87)	91 (58)	96 (26)	75	56	89	***	71
Know own senators	24 (88)	40 (58)	57 (28)	21	28	44	***	30
Know Eisenhower	40 (86)	65 (68)	75 (32)	42	31	58	***	38
Know Harriman	02 (86)	25 (68)	28 (32)	24	04	27	***	46
Know Kefauver	16 (86)	43 (68)	50 (32)	32	12	40	***	35
Know R. Kerr	07 (86)	18 (68)	13 (32)	12	–	06	NS	20
Know R. Russell	07 (86)	13 (68)	34 (32)	11	24	29	**	37
Know Taft	15 (86)	41 (68)	56 (32)	31	25	48	**	36
Know Stevenson	14 (86)	31 (68)	38 (32)	20	10	28	**	34
Know Earl Warren	37 (86)	78 (68)	84 (32)	49	27	75	***	52
Know vice president	47 (86)	81 (68)	91 (32)	64	57	83	***	56
Know Stassen	09 (86)	31 (68)	53 (32)	24	32	44	***	43
Mean =	29	52	62	32	21	46		
Domestic Affairs—Events								
Heard Taft-Hartley Law (3/49)	68 (112)	96 (72)	98 (42)	87	50	94	***	57
Heard Taft-Hartley Law (5/52)	55 (145)	79 (116)	96 (67)	53	81	91	***	51
Heard Taft-Hartley Law (10/52)	41 (98)	85 (58)	96 (27)	75	73	93	***	65
Heard Taft-Hartley Law (9/52)	75 (101)	86 (81)	100 (41)	44	100	100	***	41
Follow Taft-Hartley Law (6/49)	42 (202)	54 (144)	90 (87)	21	78	83	***	38
Follow Taft-Hartley Law (10/53)	20 (100)	48 (119)	85 (33)	35	71	81	***	50
Know wiretapping (6/49)	57 (83)	84 (90)	87 (45)	63	19	70	**	41
Know wiretapping (1/50)	29 (202)	52 (144)	68 (87)	32	33	55	***	44
Heard criticism of AEC	46 (202)	64 (143)	95 (87)	33	86	91	***	50
Heard Hoover Commission (1/50)	23 (83)	57 (89)	89 (45)	44	75	85	***	61
Heard Hoover Commission (5/52)	11 (145)	47 (116)	75 (67)	40	53	72	***	62
Know Hoover Commission (1/50)	17 (83)	47 (90)	82 (45)	36	66	78	***	57
Know Hoover Commission (5/52)	05 (146)	31 (116)	61 (67)	27	44	59	***	44
Heard Truman health insurance plan	45 (112)	79 (72)	91 (42)	62	57	84	***	44

Know date political convention	20 (86)	40 (68)	47 (32)	25	11	34	***	35
Know convention cities	23 (86)	54 (68)	72 (32)	40	39	64	***	36
Know if all states hold congressional elections (1952)	36 (86)	46 (68)	38 (32)	17	—	03	NS	11
Heard of government's seizure steel Industry	64 (86)	93 (68)	100 (32)	80	100	100	***	74
Information Index	08 (53)	13 (117)	28 (36)	05	17	22	***	40
Know population of U.S.	31 (81)	53 (75)	68 (37)	32	32	54	***	31
Mean =	36	60	78	38	45	65		
Foreign Affairs—Persons								
Know Tito (10/50)	24 (118)	48 (62)	71 (35)	32	44	62	***	47
Know Tito (4/51)	31 (88)	66 (58)	89 (28)	51	68	84	***	48
Know Chiang Kai-shek (12/50)	35 (85)	53 (79)	75 (40)	28	46	62	***	32
Know Chiang Kai-shek (4/51)	34 (88)	50 (58)	86 (28)	24	72	79	***	48
Know Anthony Eden	11 (81)	29 (75)	54 (37)	20	35	43	***	49
Know Synghman Rhee	29 (100)	71 (112)	94 (33)	59	80	92	***	53
Know Franco	39 (100)	79 (112)	100 (33)	66	100	100	***	58
Mean =	29	57	81	39	56	73		
Foreign Affairs—Events								
Heard NATO (3/49)	28 (112)	56 (71)	83 (42)	39	61	76	***	49
Heard NATO (6/49)	49 (196)	77 (144)	98 (86)	55	91	96	***	52
Heard H-bomb (1/50)	60 (82)	90 (88)	93 (45)	75	30	82	***	51
Heard H-bomb (2/50)	78 (105)	96 (54)	100 (27)	82	100	100	***	70
Heard Chinese civil war (6/49)	65 (196)	89 (144)	100 (86)	69	100	100	***	60
Heard Chinese civil war (1/50)	69 (83)	92 (87)	98 (45)	74	75	94	***	60
Know Atlantic Pact	07 (88)	24 (58)	43 (28)	18	25	39	***	45
Know 38th Parallel	32 (88)	64 (58)	68 (28)	47	11	53	***	38
Know size Chinese Army	04 (81)	01 (75)	03 (37)	—	02	—	NS	23
Know population of China (12/51)	00 (81)	03 (75)	00 (37)	03	—	0	NS	37
Know population of China (2/52)	02 (116)	02 (142)	06 (69)	0	04	04	NS	35
Heard about hearings on Korea	55 (106)	78 (119)	97 (68)	51	86	93	***	50
Know about trouble in Iran	42 (106)	66 (119)	88 (68)	41	65	80	***	46
Know Voice of America	19 (106)	45 (119)	74 (68)	32	53	68	***	51
Mean =	36	56	68	31	27	50		

TABLE 1.3. Knowledge of Public Affairs among Individuals Age 49–60 in the Early 1950s

	Percentage Informed			Index of Effectiveness			Relationship over Full Range on Variables	
	Elem. School	High Sch. Grad.	College Grad.	High Elem.	Col. High	Col. Elem.	Chi-Sq. (P)	Assoc. (γ)
Domestic Affairs—Persons								
Heard of J. Edgar Hoover	76 (111)	100 (24)	94 (16)	100	—	75	**	63
Know Dean Acheson	45 (156)	85 (95)	94 (48)	73	72	89	***	57
Know George Marshall	81 (109)	100 (26)	100 (16)	100	0	100	*	64
Know own senators	32 (110)	31 (26)	69 (16)	—	55	54	**	27
Know Eisenhower	36 (114)	53 (40)	75 (12)	27	47	61	***	46
Know Harriman	04 (114)	18 (40)	33 (12)	15	18	30	***	51
Know Kefauver	21 (114)	40 (40)	50 (12)	24	17	37	***	44
Know R. Kerr	04 (114)	10 (40)	42 (12)	06	36	40	***	54
Know R. Russell	03 (114)	20 (40)	50 (12)	18	38	49	***	46
Know Taft	25 (114)	43 (40)	58 (12)	24	26	44	***	49
Know Stevenson	10 (114)	43 (40)	67 (12)	37	42	64	***	51
Know Earl Warren	39 (114)	78 (40)	92 (12)	64	64	87	***	65
Know vice president	57 (114)	93 (40)	100 (12)	84	100	100	***	67
Know Stassen	14 (114)	28 (40)	67 (12)	16	54	62	***	52
Mean =	32	53	71	31	38	57		52
Domestic Affairs—Events								
Heard Taft-Hartley Law (3/49)	79 (143)	98 (48)	100 (22)	90	100	100	***	51
Heard Taft-Hartley Law (5/52)	57 (172)	79 (72)	91 (42)	51	57	79	***	47
Heard Taft-Hartley Law (10/52)	52 (127)	89 (44)	100 (17)	77	100	100	***	60
Heard Taft-Hartley Law (9/52)	64 (66)	89 (28)	100 (18)	70	100	100	***	56
Follow Taft-Hartley Law (6/49)	40 (181)	63 (95)	85 (53)	38	60	75	***	44
Follow Taft-Hartley Law (10/53)	27 (113)	56 (45)	94 (17)	40	36	92	***	44
Know wiretapping (6/49)	51 (111)	78 (37)	92 (24)	55	64	84	***	35
Know wiretapping (1/50)	33 (181)	51 (95)	70 (53)	27	39	55	***	54
Heard criticism of AEC	41 (181)	70 (95)	93 (53)	49	77	88	***	52
Heard Hoover Commission (1/50)	28 (109)	62 (64)	71 (24)	47	24	60	***	54
Heard Hoover Commission (5/52)	22 (172)	47 (72)	81 (42)	32	64	76	***	54
Know Hoover Commission (1/50)	21 (111)	51 (37)	58 (24)	38	14	47	***	49
Know Hoover Commission (5/52)	11 (172)	32 (72)	67 (42)	21	66	63	***	47
Heard Truman health insurance plan	59 (143)	92 (48)	100 (22)	80	100	100	***	49

Know date political convention	22 (114)	55 (40)	58 (12)	42	07	46	***	48
Know convention cities	36 (114)	60 (40)	67 (12)	38	18	49	***	41
Know if all states hold congressional elections (1952)	29 (114)	50 (40)	42 (12)	30	—	18	NS	21
Heard of government's seizure steel Industry	75 (114)	88 (40)	92 (12)	52	33	68	***	56
Information index	11 (140)	22 (103)	42 (41)	12	28	35	***	41
Know population of U.S.	37 (116)	55 (33)	33 (12)	29	—	—	NS	14
Mean =	40	64	77	40	36	62		
Foreign Affairs—Persons								
Know Tito (10/50)	27 (111)	63 (24)	88 (16)	49	68	84	***	59
Know Tito (4/51)	38 (110)	77 (26)	88 (16)	63	48	81	***	48
Know Chiang Kai-shek (12/50)	29 (94)	71 (52)	87 (37)	59	55	82	***	47
Know Chiang Kai-shek (4/51)	37 (110)	62 (26)	94 (16)	40	84	90	***	51
Know Anthony Eden	14 (116)	24 (33)	33 (12)	13	12	22	***	42
Know Synghman Rhee	39 (113)	71 (45)	38 (17)	52	59	80	***	45
Know Franco	45 (113)	69 (45)	100 (17)	37	100	100	***	51
Mean =	33	62	83	43	55	75		
Foreign Affairs—Events								
Heard NATO (3/49)	43 (143)	65 (48)	100 (21)	39	100	100	***	37
Heard NATO (6/49)	45 (181)	71 (94)	94 (53)	47	79	89	***	55
Heard H-bomb (1/50)	68 (109)	84 (37)	100 (23)	50	100	100	***	59
Heard H-bomb (2/50)	82 (108)	96 (28)	100 (12)	88	100	100	*	72
Heard Chinese civil war (6/49)	64 (180)	82 (94)	94 (53)	50	67	33	***	53
Heard Chinese civil war (1/50)	66 (110)	89 (37)	96 (24)	68	64	38	***	66
Heard Atlantic Pact	07 (110)	27 (26)	50 (16)	22	32	46	*	45
Heard 38th Parallel	44 (110)	65 (26)	75 (16)	38	31	55		30
Heard size Chinese Army	04 (116)	03 (33)	03 (12)	—	—	—	NS	11
Heard population of China (12/51)	03 (116)	06 (33)	03 (12)	03	02	05	NS	31
Heard population of China (2/52)	03 (146)	02 (84)	10 (40)	—	08	07	NS	42
Heard about hearings on Korea	60 (156)	86 (95)	96 (48)	65	78	90	***	60
Know about trouble in Iran	40 (156)	75 (95)	92 (48)	58	68	87	***	57
Know Voice of America	20 (156)	53 (95)	81 (48)	41	60	76	***	54
Mean =	39	57	71	30	33	52		

TABLE 1.4. Knowledge of Public Affairs among Individuals Age 61–72 in the Early 1950s

	Percentage Informed			Index of Effectiveness			Relationship over Full Range on Variables	
	Elem. School	High Sch. Grad.	College Grad.	High Elem.	Col. High	Col. Elem.	Chi-Sq. (P)	Assoc. (γ)
Domestic Affairs—Persons								
Heard of J. Edgar Hoover	75 (95)	93 (14)	100 (8)	72	100	100	NS	68
Know Dean Acheson	49 (128)	79 (28)	87 (15)	30	38	75	*	47
Know George Marshall	66 (68)	100 (13)	100 (6)	100	0	100	*	69
Know own senators	26 (69)	54 (13)	50 (6)	38	—	33	NS	33
Know Eisenhower	44 (71)	56 (25)	60 (5)	21	09	29	NS	25
Know Harriman	09 (71)	12 (25)	40 (5)	03	32	34	*	43
Know Kefauver	17 (71)	28 (25)	40 (5)	13	17	28	*	38
Know R. Kerr	07 (71)	16 (25)	60 (5)	10	52	57	***	41
Know R. Russell	13 (71)	04 (25)	20 (5)	—	17	08	***	38
Know Taft	24 (71)	52 (25)	60 (5)	37	17	47	**	48
Know Stevenson	14 (71)	36 (25)	40 (5)	26	38	54	**	50
Know Earl Warren	45 (71)	68 (25)	100 (5)	35	100	100	***	50
Know vice president	58 (71)	84 (25)	100 (5)	62	100	100	NS	57
Know Stassen	18 (71)	32 (25)	40 (5)	17	12	27	NS	40
Mean =	33	51	64	27	27	46		
Domestic Affairs—Events								
Heard Taft-Hartley Law (3/49)	69 (80)	92 (13)	100 (8)	74	100	100	***	88
Heard Taft-Hartley Law (5/52)	55 (117)	90 (29)	92 (13)	79	20	82	***	48
Heard Taft-Hartley Law (10/52)	48 (85)	65 (20)	67 (6)	33	06	37	**	35
Heard Taft-Hartley Law (9/52)	68 (84)	77 (26)	93 (15)	28	70	78	***	44
Follow Taft-Hartley Law (6/49)	51 (118)	60 (35)	93 (27)	22	83	87	***	37
Follow Taft-Hartley Law (10/53)	23 (78)	75 (20)	83 (6)	68	32	78	***	68
Know wiretapping (6/49)	52 (86)	71 (14)	85 (13)	40	48	69	*	35
Know wiretapping (1/50)	35 (118)	57 (35)	63 (27)	34	14	43	**	53
Heard criticism of AEC	48 (118)	77 (35)	85 (27)	55	35	71	***	54
Heard Hoover Commission (1/50)	33 (86)	79 (14)	85 (13)	69	29	78	***	57
Heard Hoover Commission (5/52)	22 (116)	66 (29)	92 (13)	56	77	90	***	64
Know Hoover Commission (1/50)	24 (86)	71 (14)	77 (13)	62	21	70	***	57
Know Hoover Commission (5/52)	12 (117)	45 (29)	77 (13)	37	58	74	***	49
Heard Truman health insurance plan	43 (80)	85 (13)	88 (8)	74	20	79	***	63

Know date political convention	34 (71)	60 (25)	60 (5)	39	0	39	NS	28
Know convention cities	39 (71)	60 (25)	80 (5)	34	50	67	NS	26
Know if all states hold congressional elections (1952)	41 (71)	48 (25)	40 (5)	18	—	—	NS	19
Heard of government's seizure steel industry	78 (71)	88 (25)	100 (5)	50	100	100	***	42
Information Index	12 (74)	15 (33)	38 (8)	03	27	30	NS	31
Know population of U.S.	33 (73)	50 (10)	60 (5)	25	20	40	NS	32
Mean =	41	67	78	44	33	63		

Foreign Affairs—Persons

Know Tito (10/50)	24 (95)	57 (14)	75 (8)	43	42	67	**	51
Know Tito (4/51)	28 (69)	77 (13)	67 (6)	68	43	54	*	43
Know Chiang Kai-shek (12/50)	43 (75)	79 (14)	92 (12)	63	62	86	***	39
Know Chiang Kai-shek (4/51)	30 (69)	54 (13)	83 (6)	34	63	76	NS	54
Know Anthony Eden	11 (73)	30 (20)	60 (5)	21	43	55	NS	40
Know Synghman Rhee	33 (78)	95 (20)	50 (6)	93	—	25	***	66
Know Franco	37 (78)	85 (20)	83 (6)	76	—	73	**	59
Mean =	29	68	73	55	16	62		

Foreign Affairs—Events

Heard NATO (3/49)	27 (81)	62 (13)	100 (8)	48	100	100	***	64
Heard NATO (6/49)	48 (118)	77 (35)	93 (27)	56	70	87	***	63
Heard H-bomb (1/50)	63 (86)	100 (14)	92 (13)	100	—	79	***	68
Heard H-bomb (2/50)	87 (61)	100 (14)	100 (8)	100	0	100	NS	53
Heard Chinese civil war (6/49)	65 (117)	89 (35)	93 (27)	68	36	80	***	56
Heard Chinese civil war (1/50)	63 (86)	100 (14)	92 (13)	100	—	78	**	50
Know Atlantic Pact	04 (69)	23 (13)	33 (6)	20	14	30	***	49
Know 38th Parallel	33 (69)	62 (13)	33 (6)	43	—	0	**	29
Know size Chinese Army	01 (73)	00 (10)	00 (5)	—	—	—	NS	12
Know population of China (12/51)	04 (73)	00 (10)	00 (5)	—	0	—	NS	09
Know population of China (2/52)	00 (131)	14 (28)	06 (16)	14	—	06	NS	26
Heard about hearings on Korea	66 (128)	89 (28)	100 (15)	68	100	100	***	55
Know about trouble in Iran	41 (128)	64 (28)	100 (15)	39	100	100	***	51
Know Voice of America	22 (128)	50 (28)	87 (15)	36	74	83	***	52
Mean =	37	59	66	35	17	62		

TABLE 1.5. Academic Knowledge among Individuals Age 25-36 in the Early 1950s

	Percentage Informed			Index of Effectiveness			Relationship over Full Range on Variables	
	Elem. School	High Sch. Grad.	College Grad.	High Elem.	Col. High	Col. Elem.	Chi-Sq. (P)	Assoc. (γ)
History								
Know Columbus	84 (76)	98 (95)	97 (30)	88	—	81	*	32
Know Napoleon	34 (76)	81 (93)	97 (30)	71	84	95	***	70
Know Karl Marx	07 (76)	35 (95)	90 (30)	30	85	89	***	65
Know Gutenberg	07 (76)	23 (95)	73 (30)	17	65	71	***	56
Mean =	33	59	89	39	73	84		56
Humanities								
Know painter Rubens	01 (76)	10 (95)	43 (30)	09	37	42	***	53
Know Shakespeare	61 (76)	97 (95)	97 (30)	92	0	92	***	78
Know Aristotle	04 (76)	45 (95)	90 (30)	43	82	90	***	68
Know Freud	04 (76)	27 (94)	73 (30)	24	63	72	***	67
Know painter Raphael	03 (76)	43 (95)	80 (30)	41	65	79	***	67
Know Beethoven	41 (76)	86 (75)	97 (30)	76	79	95	***	62
Know Plato	05 (62)	28 (188)	70 (57)	24	58	68	***	51
Know author **War and Peace** (2/52)	02 (62)	11 (188)	53 (57)	09	47	52	***	52
Know Tolstoy (10/52)	04 (76)	23 (95)	70 (30)	20	61	69	***	71
Know Bach	18 (62)	47 (188)	65 (57)	35	34	57	***	39
Name a painter	03 (62)	31 (188)	67 (57)	29	52	66	***	46
Know author **Huckleberry Finn**	19 (59)	55 (159)	80 (51)	44	56	75	***	49
Know author **Tale of Two Cities**	03 (59)	32 (159)	69 (51)	30	54	68	***	56
Mean =	13	41	73	32	54	69		56
Geography								
Know ocean between U.S. and U.K.	71 (62)	96 (188)	97 (57)	86	25	90	***	58
Locate Formosa	16 (73)	35 (116)	67 (27)	23	49	61	***	40
Locate Manchuria	34 (73)	74 (116)	70 (27)	61	—	55	***	44
Locate Iran	15 (79)	29 (168)	45 (84)	16	23	35	***	41
Locate Suez Canal	18 (76)	32 (105)	66 (41)	17	50	59	***	36
Mean =	31	53	69	32	34	55		36

Civics								
Know number of senators	45 (76)	69 (105)	93 (41)	44	77	87	***	46
Know month president elected	75 (59)	93 (102)	97 (33)	72	57	88	*	42
Know 3 branches federal government	07 (59)	26 (102)	61 (33)	20	47	58	***	47
Know term of office of president	85 (59)	97 (102)	97 (33)	74	0	80	NS	49
Know meaning "GOP"	12 (59)	26 (102)	55 (33)	16	39	49	**	31
Know meaning "isolationism"	33 (40)	58 (154)	85 (40)	37	64	78	***	46
Know electoral college	05 (76)	40 (114)	96 (25)	37	93	96	***	75
Know "filibuster" (1/49)	28 (116)	64 (294)	89 (94)	50	69	85	***	56
Know "filibuster" (3/49)	32 (81)	67 (137)	92 (39)	51	76	88	***	57
Mean =	36	60	85	38	63	77		
Miscellaneous								
Know how many inches in yard	88 (76)	93 (105)	98 (41)	87	72	83	NS	33
Know how many 3¢ stamps in 75¢	62 (76)	86 (105)	93 (41)	63	50	81	***	44
Mean =	75	90	96	60	60	84		

TABLE 1.6. Academic Knowledge among Individuals Age 37–48 in the Early 1950s

	Percentage Informed			Index of Effectiveness			Relationship over Full Range on Variables	
	Elem. School	High Sch. Grad.	College Grad.	High Elem.	Col. High	Col. Elem.	Chi-Sq. (P)	Assoc. (γ)
History								
Know Columbus	79 (99)	100 (58)	100 (27)	100	0	100	***	62
Know Napoleon	48 (99)	93 (58)	100 (27)	87	100	100	***	66
Know Karl Marx	09 (99)	50 (58)	85 (27)	45	70	81	***	53
Know Gutenberg	08 (99)	35 (58)	74 (27)	29	60	72	***	51
Mean =	36	70	90	53	67	84		
Humanities								
Know painter Rubens	06 (99)	22 (58)	63 (27)	17	53	61	***	47
Know Shakespeare	64 (99)	97 (58)	100 (27)	92	100	100	***	67
Know Aristotle	06 (99)	52 (58)	93 (27)	49	85	93	***	69
Know Freud	03 (99)	29 (58)	89 (27)	27	85	89	***	75
Know painter Raphael	13 (99)	52 (58)	89 (27)	45	77	87	***	67
Know Beethoven	35 (99)	91 (58)	100 (27)	86	100	100	***	74
Know Plato	04 (116)	35 (142)	67 (69)	30	49	66	***	60
Know author War and Peace (2/52)	01 (116)	20 (142)	44 (69)	19	30	43	***	51
Know Tolstoy (10/52)	04 (99)	33 (58)	74 (27)	30	61	73	***	63
Know Bach	18 (116)	43 (142)	65 (69)	31	39	57	***	46
Name a painter	09 (116)	37 (142)	64 (69)	29	43	61	***	49
Know author Huckleberry Finn	08 (100)	57 (112)	85 (33)	53	65	84	***	65
Know author Tale of Two Cities	03 (100)	32 (112)	76 (33)	20	65	75	***	66
Mean =	13	46	78	38	59	75		
Geography								
Know ocean between U.S. and U.K.	80 (115)	98 (140)	99 (69)	90	50	95	***	70
Locate Formosa	18 (88)	45 (58)	75 (28)	33	55	69	***	43
Locate Manchuria	33 (88)	53 (58)	82 (28)	30	51	73	***	40
Locate Iran	12 (106)	30 (119)	53 (68)	21	33	47	***	44
Locate Suez Canal	22 (81)	39 (75)	78 (37)	22	64	72	***	42
Mean =	33	53	77	30	51	66		

Civics

Know number of senators	44 (81)	87 (75)	97 (37)	77	84	95	***	57
Know month president elected	84 (86)	96 (68)	100 (32)	75	100	–00	***	48
Know 3 branches federal government	06 (86)	32 (68)	59 (32)	28	40	56	***	59
Know term of office of president	90 (86)	94 (68)	100 (32)	40	100	100	***	52
Know meaning "GOP"	20 (86)	44 (68)	66 (32)	30	39	58	***	42
Know meaning "isolationism"	31 (85)	66 (79)	65 (40)	51	–	49	***	43
Know electoral college	13 (105)	44 (54)	78 (27)	36	61	75	***	66
Know "filibuster" (1/49)	24 (201)	72 (191)	88 (93)	63	57	84	***	65
Know "filibuster" (3/49)	34 (112)	68 (72)	88 (42)	52	63	82	***	51
Mean =	38	67	82	47	45	71		

Miscellaneous

Know how many inches in yard	91 (81)	97 (75)	100 (37)	67	100	100	*	32
Know how many 3¢ stamps in 75¢	78 (81)	91 (75)	97 (37)	59	66	86	***	41
Mean =	85	94	99	60	83	93		

TABLE 1.7. Academic Knowledge among Individuals Age 49–60 in the Early 1950s

	Percentage Informed			Index of Effectiveness			Relationship over Full Range on Variables	
	Elem. School	High Sch. Grad.	College Grad.	High Elem.	Col. High	Col. Elem.	Chi-Sq. (P)	Assoc. (γ)
History								
Know Columbus	87 (128)	96 (44)	100 (17)	83	100	100	***	57
Know Napoleon	52 (128)	89 (44)	100 (17)	77	100	100	***	67
Know Karl Marx	16 (128)	57 (44)	100 (17)	49	100	100	***	53
Know Gutenberg	12 (128)	39 (44)	82 (17)	31	70	80	***	62
Mean =	42	70	96	48	80	93		
Humanities								
Know painter Rubens	01 (128)	25 (44)	59 (17)	24	45	59	***	70
Know Shakespeare	69 (128)	93 (44)	100 (17)	87	100	100	***	64
Know Aristotle	09 (128)	50 (44)	88 (17)	45	76	83	***	70
Know Freud	06 (128)	25 (44)	71 (17)	20	61	69	***	65
Know painter Raphael	09 (128)	52 (44)	77 (17)	47	52	75	***	67
Know Beethoven	38 (128)	84 (44)	94 (17)	74	62	90	***	65
Know Plato	05 (146)	36 (84)	73 (40)	33	58	72	***	62
Know author War and Peace (2/52)	01 (146)	12 (84)	23 (40)	11	13	22	***	44
Know Tolstoy (10/52)	13 (128)	43 (44)	65 (17)	23	39	60	***	48
Know Bach	14 (146)	38 (84)	58 (40)	28	32	51	***	52
Name a painter	08 (146)	37 (84)	53 (40)	32	25	49	***	57
Know author Huckleberry Finn	17 (113)	40 (45)	82 (17)	28	70	78	***	60
Know author Tale of Two Cities	04 (113)	22 (45)	71 (17)	19	63	70	***	66
Mean =	15	43	70	33	47	65		
Geography								
Know ocean between U.S. and U.K.	87 (146)	98 (84)	100 (39)	85	100	100	**	68
Locate Formosa	20 (110)	42 (26)	63 (16)	28	36	54	***	47
Locate Manchuria	47 (110)	89 (26)	75 (16)	79	–	53	***	55
Locate Iran	12 (156)	34 (95)	52 (48)	25	27	45	***	48
Locate Suez Canal	28 (116)	36 (33)	50 (12)	15	22	31	*	32
Mean =	39	60	68	34	20	48		

Civics

Know number of senators	52 (116)	85 (33)	83 (12)	69	13	65	NS	33
Know month president elected	85 (114)	98 (40)	100 (12)	93	100	100	**	62
Know 3 branches federal government	05 (114)	25 (40)	75 (12)	21	67	74	***	67
Know term of office of president	92 (114)	100 (40)	100 (12)	100	0	100	***	76
Know meaning "GOP"	23 (114)	43 (40)	83 (12)	26	70	78	***	42
Know meaning "isolationism"	36 (94)	71 (52)	78 (37)	55	24	66	***	50
Know electoral college	19 (108)	36 (28)	100 (12)	21	100	100	***	58
Know "filibuster" (1/49)	37 (223)	68 (123)	82 (56)	49	44	71	***	54
Know "filibuster" (3/49)	44 (145)	75 (48)	86 (22)	55	44	75	***	46
Mean =	44	67	87	41	61	77		

Miscellaneous

Know how many inches in yard	93 (116)	88 (33)	92 (12)	—	33	—	NS	02
Know how many 3¢ stamps in 75¢	78 (116)	91 (33)	100 (12)	59	100	100	***	50
Mean =	86	90	96	29	60	71		

TABLE 1.8. Academic Knowledge among Individuals Age 61–72 in the Early 1950s

	Percentage Informed			Index of Effectiveness			Relationship over Full Range on Variables	
	Elem. School	High Sch. Grad.	College Grad.	High Elem.	Col. High	Col. Elem.	Chi-Sq. (P)	Assoc. (γ)
History								
Know Columbus	80 (85)	100 (20)	100 (6)	100	0	100	NS	62
Know Napoleon	47 (85)	90 (20)	100 (6)	81	100	100	***	59
Know Karl Marx	14 (85)	45 (20)	100 (6)	36	100	100	***	58
Know Gutenberg	11 (85)	35 (20)	67 (6)	27	50	63	***	67
Mean =	38	68	92	48	75	87		
Humanities								
Know painter Rubens	06 (85)	25 (20)	83 (6)	20	77	82	***	59
Know Shakespeare	61 (85)	95 (20)	100 (6)	87	100	100	***	74
Know Aristotle	08 (85)	50 (20)	100 (6)	45	100	100	***	79
Know Freud	01 (85)	25 (20)	83 (6)	24	77	83	***	84
Know painter Raphael	11 (85)	50 (20)	83 (6)	44	46	81	***	68
Know Beethoven	42 (85)	80 (20)	100 (6)	66	100	100	**	64
Know Plato	12 (131)	36 (28)	69 (16)	27	52	65	***	54
Know author **War and Peace** (2/52)	02 (131)	11 (28)	31 (16)	09	22	30	***	34
Know Tolstoy (10/52)	13 (85)	50 (20)	100 (6)	43	100	100	***	71
Know Bach	15 (131)	46 (28)	31 (16)	37	–	19	***	47
Name a painter	13 (131)	36 (28)	50 (16)	27	22	43	***	34
Know author **Huckleberry Finn**	13 (78)	75 (20)	83 (6)	71	32	80	***	74
Know author **Tale of Two Cities**	04 (78)	35 (20)	67 (5)	32	49	66	***	69
Mean =	15	47	75	38	53	71		
Geography								
Know ocean between U.S. and U.K.	85 (131)	93 (28)	100 (16)	53	100	100	NS	34
Locate Formosa	10 (69)	39 (13)	50 (6)	32	18	45	***	55
Locate Manchuria	32 (69)	85 (13)	67 (6)	78	–	51	**	58
Locate Iran	09 (128)	25 (28)	80 (15)	16	73	78	***	57
Locate Suez Canal	15 (73)	10 (10)	60 (5)	29	55	53	***	49
Mean =	30	50	71	29	42	59		

Civics

Know number of senators	40 (73)	80 (10)	80 (5)	67	0	67	*	45
Know month president elected	79 (71)	92 (25)	80 (5)	62	—	52	**	60
Know 3 branches federal government	10 (71)	20 (25)	40 (5)	11	25	33	***	51
Know term of office of president	92 (71)	96 (25)	80 (5)	50	—	—	**	50
Know meaning "GOP"	21 (71)	32 (25)	100 (5)	14	100	100	NS	36
Know meaning "Isolationism"	40 (75)	86 (14)	92 (12)	77	43	87	***	48
Know electoral college	28 (61)	43 (14)	75 (8)	21	56	28	NS	37
Know "filibuster" (1/49)	30 (142)	51 (37)	82 (17)	30	63	74	***	44
Know "filibuster" (3/49)	31 (87)	77 (13)	88 (8)	67	48	83	***	62
Mean =	41	64	80	39	44	63		

Miscellaneous

Know how many inches in yard	95 (73)	100 (10)	100 (5)	100	0	100	NS	92
Know how many 3¢ stamps in 75¢	74 (73)	90 (10)	100 (5)	62	100	100	NS	59
Mean =	85	95	100	67	100	100		

TABLE 2.1. Knowledge of Public Affairs among Individuals Age 25-36 in the Late 1950s

	Percentage Informed			Index of Effectiveness			Relationship over Full Range on Variables	
	Elem. School	High Sch. Grad.	College Grad.	High Elem.	Col. High	Col. Elem.	Chi-Sq. (P)	Assoc. (γ)
Domestic Affairs—Persons								
Name congressman	11 (45)	34 (155)	58 (31)	26	36	53	**	34
Know J. Edgar Hoover (1957)	42 (41)	82 (130)	97 (38)	69	83	95	***	36
Know head of FBI (1955)	52 (68)	88 (164)	96 (45)	75	67	92	***	63
Know vice president of U.S.	62 (68)	90 (164)	98 (45)	74	80	95	***	65
Heard W. Reuther	19 (48)	51 (167)	76 (42)	40	51	70	***	47
Heard G. Meany	19 (48)	28 (167)	62 (42)	11	33	53	***	44
Heard D. Beck	33 (48)	74 (167)	93 (42)	61	73	90	***	49
Heard H. Bridges	17 (48)	51 (167)	81 (42)	41	61	77	***	48
Heard J. L. Lewis	54 (48)	76 (167)	86 (42)	48	42	70	***	31
Heard Petrillo	15 (48)	55 (167)	74 (42)	47	42	70	*	46
Heard D. McDonald	02 (48)	11 (167)	24 (42)	09	15	23		27
Index knowledge of candidates "high" score	16 (19)	32 (72)	32 (22)	19	0	19	NS	21
Mean =	29	56	73	38	39	62		
Domestic Affairs—Events								
Index information "informed" on 8 issues	54 (26)	44 (79)	82 (22)	—	68	61	*	24
Heard about fallout	47 (43)	69 (177)	84 (43)	41	49	70	**	31
Heard about president's new budget	38 (48)	57 (166)	91 (42)	31	79	85	***	36
Heard about Congress investigating unions	44 (48)	81 (167)	98 (42)	66	90	97	***	51
Know party congressional majority before election	23 (26)	47 (79)	77 (22)	31	57	70	**	30
Know party election majority	65 (26)	89 (79)	100 (22)	69	100	100	*	41
Mean =	45	65	89	36	69	80		
Foreign Affairs—Persons								
Know Nehru	18 (45)	54 (155)	84 (31)	44	65	81	***	56
Know Adenauer	11 (45)	32 (155)	65 (31)	24	49	61	***	51
Know prime minister of Britain	32 (68)	67 (164)	89 (45)	52	67	84	***	50
Mean =	20	51	79	39	57	74		

TABLE 2.2. Knowledge of Public Affairs among Individuals Age 37–48 in the Late 1950s

	Percentage Informed			Index of Effectiveness			Relationship over Full Range on Variables	
	Elem. School	High Sch. Grad.	College Grad.	High Elem.	Col. High	Col. Elem.	Chi-Sq. (P)	Assoc. (γ)
Domestic Affairs—Persons								
Name congressman	30 (79)	44 (119)	54 (35)	20	18	34	NS	15
Know J. Edgar Hoover (1957)	57 (100)	90 (107)	94 (35)	77	40	86	***	61
Know head of FBI (1955)	69 (106)	91 (107)	100 (40)	71	100	100	***	59
Know vice president of U.S.	71 (106)	92 (107)	95 (40)	73	38	83	***	59
Heard W. Reuther	27 (85)	57 (136)	57 (28)	41	0	41	**	48
Heard G. Meany	19 (85)	38 (136)	54 (28)	23	26	43	***	31
Heard D. Beck	48 (85)	75 (136)	100 (28)	52	100	100	***	46
Heard H. Bridges	20 (85)	55 (136)	82 (28)	44	38	77	**	49
Heard J. L. Lewis	73 (85)	81 (136)	100 (28)	30	100	-00	**	20
Heard Petrillo	27 (85)	62 (136)	75 (28)	48	34	62	***	46
Heard D. McDonald	14 (85)	11 (136)	14 (28)	—	03	0	NS	27
Index knowledge of candidates: "high" score	14 (43)	38 (61)	37 (27)	28	—	27	**	21
Mean =	39	61	72	36	28	54		
Domestic Affairs—Events								
Index information "informed" on 8 issues	35 (65)	54 (69)	74 (27)	29	44	60	*	33
Heard about fallout	46 (95)	67 (129)	71 (35)	39	12	46	***	35
Heard about president's new budget	48 (84)	73 (136)	86 (28)	48	48	73	***	33
Heard about Congress investigating unions	57 (85)	85 (135)	96 (28)	65	73	91	***	46
Know party congressional majority before election	29 (65)	51 (69)	85 (27)	31	70	79	***	41
Know party electing majority	63 (65)	84 (69)	100 (27)	57	100	100	***	55
Mean =	46	69	85	43	52	72		
Foreign Affairs—Persons								
Know Nehru	23 (79)	51 (119)	71 (35)	23	41	62	***	47
Know Adenauer	13 (79)	37 (119)	60 (35)	28	37	61	***	50
Know prime minister of Britain	47 (106)	74 (107)	93 (40)	51	73	87	***	48
Mean =	28	54	75	36	46	65		

TABLE 2.3. Knowledge of Public Affairs among Individuals Age 49–60 in the Late 1950s

	Percentage Informed			Index of Effectiveness			Relationship over Full Range on Variables	
	Elem. School	High Sch. Grad.	College Grad.	High Elem.	Col. High	Col. Elem.	Chi-Sq. (P)	Assoc. (γ)
Domestic Affairs—Persons								
Name congressman	39 (91)	53 (49)	47 (15)	23	–	13	NS	11
Know J. Edgar Hoover (1957)	54 (105)	84 (38)	86 (22)	65	12	70	***	57
Know head of FBI (1955)	67 (116)	96 (48)	100 (19)	88	100	100	***	68
Know vice president of U.S.	72 (116)	92 (48)	100 (19)	71	100	100	**	63
Heard W. Reuther	37 (123)	57 (68)	94 (16)	32	36	90	***	39
Heard G. Meany	27 (123)	43 (68)	63 (16)	22	35	49	**	33
Heard D. Beck	59 (123)	84 (68)	94 (16)	61	62	85	***	42
Heard H. Bridges	37 (123)	60 (68)	81 (16)	37	53	70	**	37
Heard J. L. Lewis	67 (123)	81 (68)	68 (16)	43	–	03	NS	24
Heard Petrillo	29 (123)	50 (68)	75 (16)	30	50	65	***	43
Heard D. McDonald	10 (123)	15 (68)	19 (16)	06	05	10	NS	18
Index knowledge of candidates "high" score	34 (61)	48 (23)	44 (18)	21	–	15	NS	20
Mean =	44	64	73	36	25	52		
Domestic Affairs—Events								
Index information "informed" on 8 issues	53 (72)	48 (25)	75 (20)	–	52	47	*	17
Heard about fallout	54 (130)	66 (50)	72 (29)	26	18	39	NS	26
Heard about president's new budget	60 (123)	81 (68)	94 (16)	52	68	85	**	42
Heard about Congress investigating unions	58 (121)	90 (67)	100 (16)	76	100	100	***	53
Know party congressional majority before election	51 (72)	56 (25)	80 (20)	10	55	59	NS	29
Know party election majority	79 (72)	88 (25)	90 (20)	43	17	52	***	36
Mean =	59	72	85	32	46	63		
Foreign Affairs—Persons								
Know Nehru	25 (91)	59 (49)	87 (15)	45	68	83	***	48
Know Adenauer	24 (91)	49 (49)	73 (15)	33	47	88	***	48
Know prime minister of Britain	44 (116)	81 (48)	79 (19)	66	–	63	***	56
Mean =	31	63	80	46	46	71		

TABLE 2.4. Knowledge of Public Affairs among Individuals Age 61–72 in the Late 1950s

	Percentage Informed			Index of Effectiveness			Relationship over Full Range on Variables	
	Elem. School	High Sch. Grad.	College Grad.	High Elem.	Col. High	Col. Elem.	Chi-Sq. (P)	Assoc. (γ)
Domestic Affairs—Persons								
Name congressman	41 (92)	35 (20)	75 (4)	—	62	58	***	20
Know J. Edgar Hoover (1957)	57 (92)	82 (22)	100 (9)	58	100	100	**	51
Know head of FBI (1955)	63 (109)	86 (27)	100 (10)	62	100	100	*	55
Know vice president of U.S.	65 (109)	93 (28)	100 (10)	80	100	100	***	78
Heard W. Reuther	43 (109)	52 (25)	86 (14)	16	71	76	**	42
Heard G. Meany	42 (109)	48 (25)	79 (14)	10	60	64	NS	25
Heard D. Beck	65 (109)	84 (25)	93 (14)	54	56	80	NS	37
Heard H. Bridges	47 (109)	60 (25)	86 (14)	25	65	74	*	31
Heard J. L. Lewis	72 (109)	76 (25)	86 (14)	14	42	64	*	25
Heard Petrillo	36 (109)	56 (25)	86 (14)	31	69	78	*	38
Heard D. McDonald	17 (109)	16 (25)	43 (14)	—	32	31	NS	15
Index knowledge of candidates "high" score	33 (54)	40 (15)	63 (8)	10	38	45	NS	22
Mean =	48	61	83	25	56	57		
Domestic Affairs—Events								
Index information "informed" on 8 issues	55 (76)	53 (17)	63 (8)	—	21	18	NS	14
Heard about fallout	44 (113)	76 (41)	83 (6)	57	29	70	NS	41
Heard about president's new budget	64 (109)	80 (25)	86 (14)	44	30	51	*	35
Heard about Congress investigating unions	67 (109)	88 (25)	100 (14)	64	100	100	NS	38
Know party congressional majority before election	47 (75)	65 (17)	100 (8)	34	100	100	**	45
Know party election majority	69 (75)	88 (17)	100 (8)	61	100	100	NS	51
Mean =	58	75	89	40	56	74		
Foreign Affairs—Persons								
Know Nehru	32 (92)	60 (20)	50 (4)	41	—	26	NS	34
Know Adenauer	28 (92)	50 (20)	50 (4)	31	0	31	NS	25
Know prime minister of Britain	41 (109)	64 (28)	80 (10)	39	45	66	**	46
Mean =	34	58	60	36	05	39		

TABLE 2.5. Academic Knowledge among Individuals Age 25–36 in the Late 1950s

	Percentage Informed			Index of Effectiveness			Relationship over Full Range on Variables	
	Elem. School	High Sch. Grad.	College Grad.	High Elem.	Col. High	Col. Elem.	Chi-Sq. (P)	Assoc. (γ)
History								
Know Bunker Hill war	13 (48)	49 (167)	83 (42)	41	67	80	***	57
Know Gettysburg war	27 (48)	70 (167)	95 (42)	59	84	93	***	64
Know Bulge war	27 (48)	68 (167)	91 (42)	56	72	87	***	52
Know Waterloo war	08 (48)	41 (167)	83 (42)	36	71	82	***	62
Know Florence Nightingale's profession	47 (68)	87 (164)	96 (45)	76	69	92	***	64
Know Lindbergh	60 (68)	79 (164)	96 (45)	48	81	90	***	47
Know city U.N. organized in	15 (68)	42 (164)	64 (45)	32	38	58	***	44
Know country Waterloo in	15 (68)	44 (164)	64 (45)	34	36	58	***	43
Mean =	27	60	84	45	60	78		
Geography								
Locate Kremlin	26 (47)	76 (160)	94 (31)	68	75	92	***	54
Locate Leaning Tower	15 (47)	70 (160)	81 (31)	65	37	78	***	52
Locate Eiffel Tower	30 (47)	77 (161)	94 (31)	67	74	91	***	54
Locate Pyramids	40 (47)	86 (160)	97 (31)	77	79	95	***	66
Locate Parthenon	04 (47)	38 (160)	71 (31)	36	53	70	***	56
Locate Mt. Vernon	17 (47)	37 (159)	65 (31)	24	45	58	***	32
Know largest lake in North America	16 (68)	27 (164)	47 (45)	13	27	37	***	39
Know highest mountain in world	16 (68)	51 (164)	78 (45)	42	55	74	***	49
Know ocean Midway Island	54 (68)	78 (164)	96 (45)	52	82	91	***	53
Know whether Montana borders Canada	49 (68)	56 (164)	69 (45)	14	30	39	*	09
Know Maine borders Canada	57 (68)	67 (164)	80 (45)	29	39	54	*	12
Know Michigan borders Canada	54 (68)	86 (164)	91 (45)	70	36	80	***	28
Know Minnesota borders Canada	38 (68)	61 (164)	71 (45)	37	26	53	***	24
Know state named for president	69 (68)	79 (164)	89 (45)	32	48	65	NS	27
Know capital of Spain	24 (68)	61 (164)	89 (45)	49	72	85	***	56
Know New Delhi capital of India	25 (68)	66 (164)	89 (45)	55	68	85	***	62
Mean =	33	64	81	46	47	72		

Humanities

Know author **Tom Sawyer**	12 (43)	61 (177)	74 (43)	56	33	70	***	53
Know author **Macbeth**	14 (43)	64 (177)	86 (43)	58	61	84	***	69
Know painter Rubens	02 (45)	08 (155)	39 (31)	06	34	38	***	71
Know Thackeray	02 (45)	13 (155)	45 (31)	09	37	44	***	67
Know composer **Messiah**	02 (68)	20 (164)	56 (45)	18	45	55	***	67
Know author **Midsummer Night's Dream**	04 (68)	37 (164)	73 (45)	34	57	72	***	65
Mean =	6	34	62	30	42	60		

Miscellaneous

Know planet nearest sun	03 (68)	06 (164)	20 (45)	03	15	18	*	28
Know discoverer relativity	46 (68)	83 (164)	98 (45)	69	88	96	***	68
Know inventor telephone	57 (68)	95 (164)	96 (45)	88	20	91	***	73
Know discoverer polio vaccine	59 (68)	93 (164)	96 (45)	83	43	93	***	70
Knowledge "automation" ("high score")	03 (40)	15 (126)	30 (37)	12	18	28	***	45
Index knowledge cancer:								
Know 4 plus cancer symptoms[a]	01 (76)	12 (197)	15 (55)	11	03	14	***	37
Know 1 plus cancer symptoms	45 (76)	79 (197)	87 (55)	62	38	77		
Know diabetes not contagious	71 (75)	87 (196)	98 (55)	55	85	93	**	09
Heard about fluoridation	44 (43)	82 (162)	98 (49)	68	89	97	***	60
Know "pyorrhea"	56 (43)	89 (162)	90 (49)	75	10	77	***	48
Know feet in mile	19 (68)	42 (164)	58 (45)	28	28	48	***	32
Know pecks in bushel	71 (68)	65 (164)	53 (45)	–	–	–	NS	17
Know language of Brazil	07 (68)	13 (164)	58 (45)	06	52	55	***	59
Know medal for wounded in action	69 (68)	90 (164)	91 (45)	68	10	71	***	49
Mean =	42	65	75	40	29	57		

aNot included in mean score.

TABLE 2.6. Academic Knowledge among Individuals Age 37–48 in the Late 1950s

	Percentage Informed			Index of Effectiveness			Relationship over Full Range on Variables	
	Elem. School	High Sch. Grad.	College Grad.	High Elem.	Col. High	Col. Elem.	Chi-Sq. (P)	Assoc. (γ)
History								
Know Bunker Hill war	11 (85)	56 (136)	79 (28)	50	52	76	***	56
Know Gettysburg war	37 (85)	74 (136)	89 (28)	59	58	83	***	51
Know Bulge war	46 (85)	77 (136)	89 (28)	57	52	80	***	54
Know Waterloo war	12 (85)	48 (135)	68 (28)	41	39	64	***	52
Know Florence Nightingale's profession	52 (106)	86 (107)	90 (40)	71	29	79	***	58
Know Lindbergh	77 (106)	96 (107)	95 (40)	83	—	79	***	54
Know city U.N. organized in	19 (106)	49 (107)	58 (40)	37	18	48	***	47
Know country Waterloo in	21 (106)	41 (107)	58 (40)	25	29	47	***	41
Mean =	34	66	78	48	35	67		
Geography								
Locate Kremlin	40 (102)	81 (129)	85 (27)	68	21	75	***	50
Locate Leaning Tower	33 (102)	72 (130)	85 (27)	58	47	78	***	51
Locate Eiffel Tower	34 (102)	79 (131)	96 (27)	67	81	94	***	54
Locate Pyramids	42 (102)	86 (129)	93 (27)	76	50	83	***	61
Locate Parthenon	03 (102)	36 (128)	74 (27)	34	60	73	***	64
Locate Mt. Vernon	26 (102)	46 (129)	52 (27)	27	11	35	***	25
Know largest lake in North America	23 (106)	44 (107)	55 (40)	27	20	42	**	27
Know highest mountain in world	27 (106)	55 (107)	75 (40)	38	45	66	***	50
Know ocean Midway Island	59 (106)	85 (107)	100 (40)	64	100	100	***	57
Know whether Montana borders Canada	44 (106)	61 (107)	73 (40)	30	31	52	NS	29
Know Maine borders Canada	59 (106)	65 (107)	73 (40)	15	23	34	NS	16
Know Michigan borders Canada	61 (106)	81 (107)	85 (40)	51	21	62	*	34
Know Minnesota borders Canada	48 (106)	63 (107)	75 (40)	29	33	52	NS	24
Know state named for president	70 (106)	81 (107)	90 (40)	37	47	67	NS	26
Know capital of Spain	41 (106)	65 (107)	73 (40)	41	23	54	***	43
Know New Delhi capital of India	34 (106)	73 (107)	93 (40)	59	74	90	***	60
Mean =	40	67	80	45	39	67		

Humanities

	(1)	Sig.	(2)	(3)	(4)	(5) (N)	(6) (N)	(7) (N)
Know author **Tom Sawyer**	61	***	71	63	51	83 (35)	54 (129)	06 (95)
Know author **Macbeth**	75	***	86	52	70	86 (35)	71 (129)	03 (95)
Know painter **Rubens**	49	***	38	31	10	40 (35)	13 (119)	03 (79)
Know **Thackeray**	69	***	73	67	19	74 (35)	21 (119)	03 (79)
Know composer **Messiah**	64	***	53	42	19	55 (40)	22 (107)	04 (106)
Know author **Midsummer Night's Dream**	73	***	76	49	53	78 (40)	57 (107)	09 (106)
Mean =	67		67	48	37	69	40	05

Miscellaneous

	(1)	Sig.	(2)	(3)	(4)	(5) (N)	(6) (N)	(7) (N)
Know planet nearest sun	42	**	26	24	03	30 (40)	08 (107)	05 (106)
Know discoverer relativity	76	***	100	100	74	100 (40)	85 (107)	42 (106)
Know inventor telephone	65	***	100	100	79	100 (40)	92 (107)	62 (106)
Know discoverer polio vaccine	68	***	100	100	79	100 (40)	93 (107)	67 (106)
Knowledge "automation" ("high score")	46	***	16	–	18	20 (35)	22 (105)	05 (107)
Index knowledge cancer:								
Know 4 plus cancer symptoms[a]	39	***	14	–	21	17 (41)	23 (133)	03 (124)
Know 1 plus cancer symptoms			74	43	54	88 (41)	79 (133)	54 (124)
Know diabetes not contagious	05	NS	61	42	33	93 (41)	88 (133)	82 (124)
Heard about fluoridation	60	***	91	56	79	96 (26)	91 (144)	58 (85)
Know "pyorrhea"	46	**	65	–	68	89 (26)	90 (144)	69 (85)
Know feet in mile	41	***	58	39	32	70 (40)	51 (107)	28 (106)
Know pecks in bushel	08	NS	–	–	0	75 (40)	76 (107)	76 (106)
Know language of Brazil	45	***	37	26	15	43 (40)	23 (107)	09 (106)
Know medal for wounded in action			86	64	61	95 (40)	86 (107)	64 (106)
Mean =	47		56	28	38	77	68	48

[a] Not included in mean score.

TABLE 2.7. Academic Knowledge among Individuals Age 49–60 in the Late 1950s

	Percentage Informed			Index of Effectiveness			Relationship over Full Range on Variables	
	Elem. School	High Sch. Grad.	College Grad.	High Elem.	Col. High	Col. Elem.	Chi-Sq. (P)	Assoc. (γ)
History								
Know Bunker Hill war	24 (122)	52 (68)	81 (16)	37	60	75	***	49
Know Gettysburg war	49 (122)	66 (68)	94 (16)	33	83	89	***	38
Know Bulge war	41 (123)	62 (68)	75 (16)	36	34	58	***	38
Know Waterloo war	24 (123)	41 (68)	56 (16)	22	25	42	***	38
Know Florence Nightingale's profession	44 (116)	83 (48)	90 (19)	70	41	82	***	65
Know Lindbergh	78 (116)	96 (48)	100 (19)	82	100	100	*	60
Know city U.N. organized in	27 (116)	46 (48)	90 (19)	26	82	82	***	52
Know country Waterloo in	17 (116)	48 (48)	47 (19)	37	45	36	***	48
Mean =	38	62	79	39	45	66		
Geography								
Locate Kremlin	50 (127)	82 (54)	100 (18)	64	100	100	***	55
Locate Leaning Tower	38 (127)	72 (54)	100 (18)	55	100	100	***	57
Locate Eiffel Tower	46 (127)	78 (55)	89 (18)	59	50	80	**	48
Locate Pyramids	56 (126)	87 (54)	100 (18)	70	100	100	***	59
Locate Parthenon	15 (124)	39 (54)	72 (18)	28	54	67	***	53
Locate Mt. Vernon	32 (127)	54 (54)	50 (18)	32	—	26	***	27
Know largest lake in North America	22 (116)	40 (48)	63 (19)	23	38	52	***	45
Know highest mountain in world	27 (116)	60 (48)	74 (19)	45	35	65	***	48
Know ocean Midway Island	53 (116)	85 (48)	100 (19)	68	100	100	***	63
Know whether Montana borders Canada	38 (116)	52 (48)	58 (19)	23	13	32	***	19
Know Maine borders Canada	62 (116)	77 (48)	74 (19)	40	—	32	***	01
Know Michigan borders Canada	65 (116)	81 (48)	95 (19)	45	74	86	***	31
Know Minnesota borders Canada	47 (116)	71 (48)	68 (19)	45	—	40	***	26
Know state named for president	68 (116)	79 (48)	84 (19)	34	24	50	NS	21
Know capital of Spain	41 (116)	75 (48)	100 (19)	58	100	100	***	56
Know New Delhi capital of India	37 (116)	77 (48)	90 (19)	64	57	84	***	62
Mean =	44	69	82	45	42	68		

Humanities

Know author **Tom Sawyer**	15 (130)	44 (50)	72 (29)	34	50	67	***	59
Know author **Macbeth**	16 (130)	50 (50)	90 (29)	40	80	88	***	71
Know painter **Rubens**	07 (91)	18 (49)	67 (15)	12	60	65	***	59
Know **Thackeray**	07 (91)	27 (49)	87 (15)	22	82	36	***	57
Know composer **Messiah**	09 (116)	25 (48)	58 (19)	18	44	54	***	59
Know author **Midsummer Night's Dream**	12 (116)	46 (48)	74 (19)	39	52	70	***	66
Mean =	11	35	75	27	62	72		51

Science and Miscellaneous

Know planet nearest sun	03 (116)	04 (48)	11 (19)	01	73	08	NS	18
Know discoverer relativity	51 (116)	88 (48)	95 (19)	76	58	90	***	62
Know inventor telephone	60 (116)	92 (48)	95 (19)	80	38	88	***	66
Know discoverer polio vaccine	73 (116)	96 (48)	100 (19)	85	100	100	***	78
Knowledge "automation" ("high score")	04 (104)	11 (37)	14 (22)	07	03	10	***	51
Index knowledge cancer:								
Know 4 plus cancer symptoms[a]	04 (141)	08 (37)	21 (14)	04	14	18	**	31
Know 1 plus cancer symptoms	45 (141)	51 (37)	79 (14)	11	57	62		
Know diabetes not contagious	74 (140)	87 (37)	93 (14)	50	46	73	NS	12
Heard about fluoridation	63 (145)	92 (83)	96 (22)	79	50	90	***	63
Know "pyorrhea"	83 (145)	86 (83)	86 (22)	18	0	18	NS	06
Know feet in mile	17 (116)	58 (48)	68 (19)	50	24	62	***	57
Know pecks in bushel	79 (116)	85 (48)	84 (19)	29	–	24	NS	10
Know language of Brazil	09 (116)	17 (48)	42 (19)	09	30	36	**	46
Know medal for wounded in action	60 (116)	73 (48)	95 (19)	33	81	83	NS	29
Mean =	48	65	74	33	26	50		

[a]Not included in mean score.

TABLE 2.8. Academic Knowledge among Individuals Age 61–72 in the Late 1950s

	Percentage Informed			Index of Effectiveness			Relationship over Full Range on Variables	
	Elem. School	High Sch. Grad.	College Grad.	High Elem.	Col. High	Col. Elem.	Chi-Sq. (P)	Assoc. (γ)
History								
Know Bunker Hill war	34 (108)	64 (25)	93 (14)	45	81	90	***	44
Know Gettysburg war	49 (108)	88 (25)	93 (14)	76	42	86	**	52
Know Bulge war	33 (109)	80 (25)	93 (14)	70	65	90	***	54
Know Waterloo war	22 (109)	60 (25)	86 (14)	49	65	82	***	55
Know Florence Nightingale's profession	36 (109)	50 (28)	90 (10)	22	80	84	**	47
Know Lindbergh	64 (109)	100 (28)	100 (10)	100	–	100	***	78
Know city U.N. organized in	27 (109)	54 (28)	80 (10)	37	56	73	***	52
Know country Waterloo in	19 (109)	46 (28)	70 (10)	33	45	63	***	55
Mean =	36	68	88	50	63	81		
Geography								
Locate Kremlin	52 (86)	80 (25)	100 (6)	58	100	100	NS	42
Locate Leaning Tower	33 (86)	76 (25)	83 (6)	64	34	75	***	47
Locate Eiffel Tower	31 (86)	76 (25)	100 (6)	65	100	100	***	67
Locate Pyramids	40 (86)	80 (25)	100 (6)	67	100	100	***	66
Locate Parthenon	04 (86)	32 (25)	83 (6)	29	75	82	***	76
Locate Mt. Vernon	27 (86)	44 (25)	67 (6)	23	41	55	*	29
Know largest lake in North America	15 (109)	61 (28)	80 (10)	54	49	76	***	55
Know highest mountain in world	18 (109)	54 (28)	100 (10)	44	100	100	***	72
Know ocean Midway Island	41 (109)	68 (28)	100 (10)	46	100	100	***	59
Know whether Montana borders Canada	47 (109)	64 (28)	100 (10)	32	100	100	*	10
Know Maine borders Canada	59 (109)	79 (28)	100 (10)	49	100	100	**	13
Know Michigan borders Canada	56 (109)	100 (28)	80 (10)	100	–	55	**	12
Know Minnesota borders Canada	45 (109)	89 (28)	100 (10)	80	100	100	***	26
Know state named for president	59 (109)	89 (28)	100 (10)	74	100	100	**	54
Know capital of Spain	36 (109)	86 (28)	100 (10)	78	100	100	**	68
Know New Delhi capital of India	32 (109)	75 (28)	90 (10)	63	60	85	***	55
Mean =	37	72	93	56	75	89		

Humanities

Know author **Tom Sawyer**	13 (113)	42 (41)	57 (6)	33	61	62	***	54
Know author **Macbeth**	10 (113)	68 (41)	83 (6)	65	47	81	***	76
Know painter Rubens	09 (92)	10 (20)	50 (4)	01	45	45	**	43
Know Thackerey	10 (92)	25 (20)	50 (4)	17	33	45	***	51
Know composer **Messiah**	05 (109)	18 (28)	30 (10)	14	15	26	*	56
Know author of **Midsummer Night's Dream**	06 (109)	25 (28)	90 (10)	20	87	90	***	66
Mean =	09	31	62	24	45	58		

Science and Miscellaneous

Know planet nearest Sun	04 (109)	04 (28)	10 (10)	0	06	06	NS	19
Know discoverer relativity	37 (109)	75 (28)	100 (10)	60	100	100	***	75
Know inventor telephone	56 (109)	89 (28)	100 (10)	75	100	100	***	76
Know discoverer polio vaccine	62 (109)	100 (28)	100 (10)	100	0	100	***	74
Knowledge "automation" ("high score")	02 (92)	19 (21)	38 (8)	17	23	37	**	48
Index knowledge cancer:								
Know 4 plus cancer symptoms[a]	01 (117)	03 (29)	0 (5)	02	—	—		
Know 1 plus cancer symptoms	38 (117)	69 (29)	60 (5)	50	—	36	**	50
Heard about fluoridation	64 (115)	83 (29)	80 (5)	53	—	45	NS	22
Know "pyorrhea"	63 (146)	93 (27)	100 (12)	81	100	100	***	70
Know feet in mile	75 (146)	89 (27)	100 (12)	56	100	100	*	48
Know pecks in bushel	12 (109)	61 (28)	80 (10)	56	49	77	***	72
Know language of Brazil	77 (109)	86 (28)	70 (10)	39	—	—	NS	07
Know medal for wounded in action	11 (109)	21 (28)	70 (10)	11	62	67	***	49
Mean =	44 (109)	50 (28)	80 (10)	40	31	59	NS	26

[a]Not included in mean score.

TABLE 3.1. Knowledge of Public Affairs among Individuals Age 25–36 in the Early 1960s

	Percentage Informed			Index of Effectiveness			Relationship over Full Range on Variables	
	Elem. School	High Sch. Grad.	College Grad.	High Elem.	Col. High	Col. Elem.	Chi-Sq. (P)	Assoc. (γ)
Domestic Affairs—Persons								
Know Goldwater (3/63)	34 (99)	57 (289)	86 (113)	35	66	79	***	49
Know Goldwater (8/63)	26 (91)	59 (252)	92 (97)	45	81	89	***	58
Know Nixon	77 (91)	92 (252)	91 (97)	65	—	61	***	37
Know Wm. Scranton (3/63)	05 (99)	35 (289)	62 (113)	32	42	60	***	50
Know Wm. Scranton (8/63)	06 (91)	26 (252)	59 (97)	21	45	56	***	51
Know Romney (3/63)	03 (99)	37 (289)	67 (113)	37	46	66	***	66
Know Romney (8/63)	02 (91)	39 (252)	68 (97)	28	31	67	***	63
Know Milton Eisenhower	36 (91)	55 (252)	65 (97)	30	22	45	***	23
Know Mark Hatfield	00 (91)	02 (252)	17 (97)	02	15	17	***	65
Know Harold Stassen	02 (91)	13 (252)	38 (97)	09	29	37	***	29
Know Thruston Morton	00 (91)	13 (252)	31 (97)	13	21	31	***	53
Know Rockefeller (3/63)	77 (99)	93 (289)	98 (113)	70	71	91	***	51
Know Rockefeller (8/63)	76 (91)	92 (252)	95 (97)	67	33	79	***	39
Know Clifford Case	00 (91)	09 (252)	17 (97)	09	09	17	***	57
Know Johnson home state	68 (28)	91 (100)	98 (46)	72	78	94	**	40
Know Goldwater home state	57 (28)	80 (100)	98 (46)	54	90	95	***	51
Know Kennedy's religion	86 (21)	97 (77)	100 (30)	79	100	100	*	64
Know Kennedy home state	29 (21)	58 (79)	87 (30)	41	69	82	***	47
Know Nixon's religion	29 (21)	29 (76)	63 (30)	0	48	48	***	02
Know Nixon home state	14 (21)	58 (79)	87 (30)	51	69	85	***	58
Know J. Edgar Hoover	38 (16)	89 (243)	100 (75)	82	100	100	***	61
Know Elmo Roper	0 (76)	04 (243)	33 (75)	4	30	33	***	82
Know Frank Stanton	05 (76)	06 (243)	21 (75)	1	16	17	***	38
Know Sam Lubell	0 (76)	01 (243)	16 (75)	1	15	16	***	58
Mean =	28	47	66	26	36	39		

Domestic Affairs—Events

Heard about civil rights rally	31 (91)	65 (252)	80 (97)	49	43	71	***	53
Know party with election majority (fall 1964)	46 (24)	83 (94)	98 (45)	69	56	96	**	57
Know party with congressional majority before election (fall 1964)	39 (23)	59 (94)	91 (45)	33	78	85	**	43
Know party with election majority (fall 1960)	58 (19)	63 (73)	80 (30)	12	46	52	NS	20
Know party with congressional majority before election (fall 1960)	53 (19)	73 (74)	90 (30)	43	63	79	**	43
Mean =	45	69	88	44	61	78		

Foreign Affairs—Events

Index knowledge of mainland China	42 (24)	77 (94)	96 (45)	60	83	93	***	54
Heard about nuclear test ban (3/63)	65 (99)	72 (289)	99 (113)	20	96	97	***	41
Heard about nuclear test ban (8/63)	56 (91)	83 (252)	93 (97)	61	59	84	***	46
Heard about Berlin dispute	89 (75)	92 (207)	100 (70)	27	100	100	**	47
Mean =	63	81	97	49	84	92		

TABLE 3.2. Knowledge of Public Affairs among Individuals Age 37–48 in the Early 1960s

Domestic Affairs—Persons	Percentage Informed			Index of Effectiveness			Relationship over Full Range on Variables	
	Elem. School	High Sch. Grad.	College Grad.	High Elem.	Col. High	Col. Elem.	Chi-Sq. (P)	Assoc. (γ)
Know Goldwater (3/63)	23 (254)	59 (341)	94 (103)	47	85	92	***	62
Know Goldwater (8/63)	40 (218)	72 (274)	90 (92)	53	64	84	***	50
Know Nixon	85 (218)	86 (274)	86 (92)	07	0	07	***	17
Know Wm. Scranton (3/63)	19 (254)	34 (341)	62 (103)	19	42	53	***	35
Know Wm. Scranton (8/63)	16 (218)	42 (274)	48 (92)	31	10	38	***	46
Know Romney (3/63)	10 (254)	36 (341)	70 (103)	29	53	67	***	61
Know Romney (8/63)	10 (218)	42 (274)	65 (92)	36	40	61	***	59
Know Milton Eisenhower	39 (218)	64 (274)	79 (92)	41	42	65	***	43
Know Mark Hatfield	02 (218)	10 (274)	22 (92)	08	13	20	***	52
Know Harold Stassen	10 (218)	35 (274)	50 (92)	28	23	45	***	44
Know Thruston Morton	06 (218)	19 (274)	28 (92)	14	11	23	***	52
Know Rockefeller (3/63)	72 (254)	95 (341)	96 (103)	82	20	86	***	59
Know Rockefeller (8/63)	71 (218)	89 (274)	96 (92)	62	64	86	***	57
Know Clifford Case	10 (218)	13 (274)	32 (92)	03	22	24	NS	38
Know Johnson home state	87 (60)	92 (104)	91 (33)	39	–	31	**	11
Know Goldwater home state	60 (60)	81 (104)	88 (33)	53	37	70	**	35
Know Kennedy's religion	86 (58)	98 (55)	100 (29)	86	100	100	***	47
Know Kennedy home state	25 (60)	65 (86)	100 (29)	53	100	100	***	51
Know Nixon's religion	16 (55)	40 (85)	72 (29)	29	53	67	***	10
Know Nixon home state	32 (60)	74 (86)	97 (29)	62	89	96	***	54
Know J. Edgar Hoover	64 (240)	84 (191)	100 (81)	55	100	100	***	65
Know Elmo Roper	03 (240)	06 (191)	41 (81)	3	37	39	***	69
Know Frank Stanton	05 (240)	07 (191)	24 (81)	2	18	20	***	36
Know Sam Lubell	00 (240)	02 (191)	21 (81)	2	19	21	***	80
Mean =	33	52	69	28	35	54		

Domestic Affairs—Events								
Heard about civil rights rally	50 (216)	77 (270)	85 (92)	54	35	70	***	45
Know party with election majority (fall 1964)	61 (56)	91 (98)	97 (30)	77	67	93	***	65
Know party with congressional majority before election (fall 1964)	39 (56)	67 (98)	93 (30)	46	49	89	***	46
Know party with election majority (fall 1960)	40 (55)	60 (79)	86 (28)	33	65	77	**	28
Know party with congressional majority before election (fall 1960)	44 (54)	70 (79)	100 (28)	46	100	100	***	48
Mean =	47	73	92	49	70	85		
Foreign Affairs—Events								
Index knowledge mainland China	47 (57)	77 (98)	90 (30)	56	57	81	**	33
Heard about nuclear test ban (3/63)	71 (254)	81 (341)	98 (103)	34	89	93	***	41
Heard about nuclear test ban (8/63)	63 (218)	90 (274)	98 (92)	73	90	95	***	63
Heard about Berlin dispute	78 (157)	98 (204)	100 (68)	91	100	100	***	81
Mean =	65	87	97	63	77	91		

TABLE 3.3. Knowledge of Public Affairs among Individuals Age 49–60 in the Early 1960s

Domestic Affairs—Persons	Percentage Informed			Index of Effectiveness			Relationship over Full Range on Variables	
	Elem. School	High Sch. Grad.	College Grad.	High Elem.	Col. High	Col. Elem.	Chi-Sq. (P)	Assoc. (γ)
Know Goldwater (3/63)	27 (415)	44 (214)	79 (72)	23	62	71	***	44
Know Goldwater (8/63)	59 (212)	58 (155)	86 (58)	—	67	66	***	31
Know Nixon	80 (212)	91 (155)	95 (58)	55	45	75	***	49
Know Wm. Scranton (3/63)	22 (415)	35 (214)	61 (72)	17	40	50	***	38
Know Wm. Scranton (8/63)	12 (212)	36 (155)	47 (58)	27	17	40	***	38
Know Romney (3/63)	13 (415)	40 (214)	76 (72)	31	60	72	***	64
Know Romney (8/63)	11 (212)	39 (155)	78 (58)	32	64	75	***	55
Know Milton Eisenhower	48 (212)	61 (155)	62 (58)	25	03	27	***	35
Know Mark Hatfield	06 (212)	07 (155)	16 (58)	01	10	10	***	32
Know Harold Stassen	16 (212)	19 (155)	74 (58)	04	68	69	***	51
Know Thruston Morton	05 (212)	17 (155)	31 (58)	13	17	27	***	40
Know Rockefeller (3/63)	61 (415)	91 (214)	94 (72)	77	33	85	***	69
Know Rockefeller (8/63)	87 (212)	79 (155)	100 (58)	—	100	100	***	28
Know Clifford Case	09 (212)	13 (155)	22 (58)	04	09	14	***	26
Know Johnson home state	86 (91)	94 (46)	97 (29)	52	50	79	***	13
Know Goldwater home state	57 (91)	85 (46)	97 (29)	65	80	93	***	34
Know Kennedy's religion	93 (84)	97 (39)	100 (27)	57	100	100	NS	62
Know Kennedy home state	35 (87)	69 (39)	89 (27)	52	65	83	***	55
Know Nixon home state	27 (84)	49 (39)	50 (26)	30	02	32	***	24
Know Nixon's religion	37 (87)	80 (39)	82 (27)	68	10	71	***	50
Know J. Edgar Hoover	63 (291)	94 (108)	94 (51)	84	0	84	***	75
Know Elmo Roper	00 (291)	06 (108)	22 (51)	06	17	22	***	64
Know Frank Stanton	01 (291)	01 (108)	20 (51)	0	19	19	***	73
Know Sam Lubell	00 (291)	03 (108)	04 (51)	03	01	04	*	57
Mean =	36	50	66	22	32	48		

Domestic Affairs—Events

Heard about civil rights rally	57 (212)	83 (155)	88 (58)	60	29	72	***	49
Know party with election majority (fall 1964)	77 (83)	84 (43)	100 (28)	30	100	100	NS	37
Know party with congressional majority before election (fall 1964)	61 (84)	70 (43)	96 (27)	23	87	90	*	35
Know party with election majority (fall 1960)	51 (86)	64 (33)	73 (26)	27	25	45	NS	26
Know party with congressional majority before election (fall 1960)	56 (86)	79 (33)	85 (26)	52	29	66	**	37
Mean =	60	76	88	40	50	70		

Foreign Affairs—Events

Index knowledge mainland China	59 (85)	88 (43)	93 (28)	71	42	83	***	60
Heard about nuclear test ban (3/63)	59 (415)	80 (214)	99 (72)	51	95	88	***	53
Heard about nuclear test ban (8/63)	68 (212)	88 (155)	97 (58)	63	75	91	***	50
Heard about Berlin dispute	87 (269)	97 (143)	100 (44)	77	100	100	**	47
Mean =	68	88	97	63	75	91		

TABLE 3.4. Knowledge of Public Affairs among Individuals Age 61–72 in the Early 1960s

	Percentage Informed			Index of Effectiveness			Relationship over Full Range on Variables	
	Elem. School	High Sch. Grad.	College Grad.	High Elem.	Col. High	Col. Elem.	Chi-Sq. (P)	Assoc. (γ)
Domestic Affairs—Persons								
Know Goldwater (3/63)	29 (312)	58 (134)	64 (36)	41	14	49	***	50
Know Goldwater (8/63)	49 (241)	68 (77)	87 (31)	37	59	75	***	25
Know Nixon	78 (241)	84 (77)	84 (31)	27	0	27	***	25
Know Wm. Scranton (3/63)	21 (312)	34 (134)	47 (36)	16	20	33	***	36
Know Wm. Scranton (8/63)	27 (241)	51 (77)	45 (31)	33	—	25	*	18
Know Romney (3/63)	15 (312)	55 (134)	56 (36)	47	02	48	***	62
Know Romney (8/63)	28 (241)	70 (77)	61 (31)	58	—	46	***	47
Know Milton Eisenhower	46 (241)	64 (77)	98 (31)	33	95	96	***	27
Know Mark Hatfield	02 (241)	08 (77)	10 (31)	06	02	08	***	24
Know Harold Stassen	17 (241)	29 (77)	39 (31)	14	14	27	***	22
Know Thruston Morton	08 (241)	09 (77)	32 (31)	01	25	26	***	16
Know Rockefeller (3/63)	55 (312)	88 (134)	86 (36)	73	—	69	***	67
Know Rockefeller (8/63)	77 (241)	88 (77)	94 (31)	48	50	74	***	37
Know Clifford Case	05 (241)	00 (77)	19 (31)	—	19	15	*	01
Know Johnson home state	86 (77)	100 (16)	80 (15)	100	—	—	NS	09
Know Goldwater home state	69 (77)	94 (16)	80 (15)	81	—	35	*	25
Know Kennedy's religion	96 (75)	95 (18)	93 (14)	—	—	—	NS	0
Know Kennedy home state	39 (75)	83 (18)	50 (14)	72	—	18	***	44
Know Nixon's religion	30 (73)	56 (18)	50 (14)	37	—	29	**	01
Know Nixon home state	40 (75)	67 (18)	86 (14)	45	58	77	***	55
Know J. Edgar Hoover	69 (212)	88 (73)	100 (14)	61	100	100	***	53
Know Elmo Roper	02 (212)	10 (73)	50 (14)	08	44	49	***	73
Know Frank Stanton	00 (212)	06 (73)	14 (14)	06	09	14	**	69
Know Sam Lubell	00 (212)	01 (73)	14 (14)	01	13	14	***	79
Mean =	37	54	60	27	13	37		

Domestic Affairs—Events

Heard about civil rights rally	73 (240)	83 (77)	94 (31)	40	65	78	**	30
Know party with election majority (fall 1964)	74 (73)	81 (16)	67 (12)	41	—	—	*	28
Know party with congressional majority before election (fall 1964)	53 (73)	50 (16)	83 (12)	—	66	64	NS	36
Know party with election majority (fall 1960)	44 (70)	63 (16)	77 (13)	34	38	59	*	28
Know party with congressional majority before election (fall 1960)	59 (71)	81 (16)	92 (13)	54	58	81	NS	55
Mean =	61	72	83	28	39	56		

Foreign Affairs—Events

Index knowledge mainland China	60 (73)	94 (16)	92 (12)	85	—	80	NS	40
Heard about nuclear test ban (3/63)	61 (312)	72 (134)	92 (36)	28	71	79	***	32
Heard about nuclear test ban (8/63)	76 (241)	94 (77)	100 (31)	75	100	100	***	52
Heard about Berlin dispute	89 (263)	97 (86)	100 (34)	73	100	100	***	30
Mean =	72	89	96	61	64	86		

TABLE 3.5 Academic Knowledge in the Early 1960s

	Percentage Informed			Index of Effectiveness			Relationship over Full Range on Variables	
	Elem. School	High Sch. Grad.	College Grad.	High Elem.	Col. High	Col. Elem.	Chi-Sq. (P)	Assoc. (γ)
Age 25–36								
Know 5 plus cabinet positions	00 (18)	31 (59)	80 (20)	31	61	80	***	67
Know electoral college	03 (75)	46 (207)	83 (70)	44	69	83	***	73
Know "filibuster"	11 (94)	58 (258)	80 (60)	53	52	78	***	62
Mean =	05	45	81	42	65	80		
Age 37–48								
Know 5 plus cabinet positions	09 (54)	52 (79)	75 (24)	47	48	73	***	60
Know electoral college	08 (157)	60 (204)	94 (68)	56	85	93	***	79
Know "filibuster"	26 (200)	72 (237)	99 (76)	62	97	99	***	73
Mean =	14	61	89	55	72	87		
Age 49–60								
Know 5 plus cabinet positions	20 (70)	61 (23)	92 (13)	51	80	90	***	54
Know electoral college	22 (269)	64 (143)	91 (44)	54	75	88	***	65
Know "filibuster"	40 (216)	67 (144)	98 (40)	45	94	97	***	60
Mean =	27	64	94	51	83	92		
Age 61–72								
Know 5 plus cabinet positions	16 (129)	29 (31)	75 (12)	15	65	70	***	42
Know electoral college	31 (263)	45 (86)	85 (34)	20	73	78	***	36
Know "filibuster"	39 (246)	49 (63)	97 (32)	18	94	95	***	46
Mean =	29	41	86	17	76	80		

TABLE 4.1. Knowledge of Public Affairs among Individuals Age 25–36 in the Late 1960s

	Percentage Informed			Index of Effectiveness			Relationship over Full Range on Variables	
	Elem. School	High Sch. Grad.	College Grad.	High Elem.	Col. High	Col. Elem.	Chi-Sq. (P)	Assoc. (γ)
Domestic Affairs—Persons								
Know 2 plus Supreme Court justices	04 (24)	27 (64)	56 (27)	24	40	54	***	46
Know secretary of state	00 (19)	13 (114)	34 (38)	13	24	34	***	63
Know governor of state (3/71)	68 (19)	84 (115)	100 (38)	50	100	100	***	61
Know governor (2/67)	80 (39)	93 (228)	99 (79)	65	86	95	***	54
Know school board head	23 (39)	49 (228)	63 (79)	34	28	52	***	26
Know mayor (11/66)	75 (59)	68 (278)	72 (102)	–	13	–	***	17
Know mayor (2/67)	54 (39)	66 (228)	72 (79)	26	18	39	NS	12
Know congressman	08 (39)	42 (228)	66 (79)	37	41	63	***	39
Know two senators	10 (39)	31 (228)	65 (79)	23	49	61	***	15
Know GOP vice presidential candidate	27 (22)	70 (147)	93 (55)	59	77	90	***	61
Know Democratic vice presidential candidate	18 (22)	56 (147)	80 (55)	46	55	76	***	46
Know Charles Percy	10 (67)	41 (321)	74 (109)	35	56	71	***	53
Know Nelson Rockefeller	57 (67)	87 (321)	100 (109)	70	100	100	****	42
Know county clerk	09 (59)	32 (278)	28 (102)	25	–	21	**	12
Know state senator	15 (59)	28 (278)	32 (102)	15	06	20	**	21
Mean =	31	52	69	30	35	55		
Domestic Affairs—Events								
High score Index political information (fall 1966)	00 (24)	13 (64)	56 (27)	13	50	56	***	58
High score Index political information (fall 1968)	27 (11)	34 (47)	57 (23)	07	35	41	***	42
Know party with election majority (fall 1968)	36 (11)	53 (47)	65 (23)	27	26	45	NS	24

TABLE 4.1—Continued

	Percentage Informed			Index of Effectiveness			Relationship over Full Range on Variables	
	Elem. School	High Sch. Grad.	College Grad.	High Elem.	Col. High	Col. Elem.	Chi-Sq. (P)	Assoc. (γ)
Know party with congressional majority before election (fall 1968)	64 (11)	62 (47)	74 (23)	—	32	28	NS	18
Know party with election majority (fall 1970)	39 (13)	49 (106)	84 (50)	16	69	74	***	38
Know party with congressional majority before election (fall 1970)	54 (13)	45 (106)	76 (50)	—	56	48	***	38
High score index political information (fall 1970)	15 (13)	25 (106)	74 (50)	12	65	69	***	51
				09	48	53		
Mean =	34	40	69					
Foreign Affairs—Persons								
Know Dean Rusk	37 (38)	82 (317)	92 (106)	72	56	87	***	45
Know Kosygin	26 (38)	81 (317)	96 (106)	74	79	95	***	52
Know Nguyen Cao Ky	26 (38)	52 (317)	85 (106)	35	69	80	***	39
			91	60	67	87		
Mean =	30	72						
Foreign Affairs—Events								
Index knowledge mainland China	46 (11)	65 (48)	83 (23)	35	51	68	NS	36
Heard about Vietnam War	67 (27)	79 (67)	95 (74)	36	76	85	*	44
Heard about Nationalist China	22 (27)	37 (65)	74 (74)	19	59	67	***	01
Know Chinese communism	63 (27)	76 (66)	93 (72)	35	71	81	***	47
Heard about Arab-Israeli conflict (5/67)	78 (67)	89 (321)	100 (109)	50	100	100	***	35
Heard about Arab-Israeli conflict (9/69)	68 (19)	90 (115)	96 (70)	69	60	88	**	46
			91	37	67	79		
Mean =	57	73						

TABLE 4.2. Knowledge of Public Affairs among Individuals Age 37–48 in the Late 1960s

	Percentage Informed			Index of Effectiveness			Relationship over Full Range on Variables	
	Elem. School	High Sch. Grad.	College Grad.	High Elem.	Col. High	Col. Elem.	Chi-Sq. (P)	Assoc. (γ)
Domestic Affairs—Persons								
Know 2 plus Supreme Court justices	02 (44)	31 (85)	65 (23)	30	49	64	***	48
Know secretary of state	06 (35)	14 (104)	42 (26)	09	33	38	***	48
Know governor of state (3/71)	80 (35)	92 (104)	100 (26)	60	100	100	*	53
Know governor (2/67)	81 (94)	92 (194)	96 (47)	58	50	79	**	40
Know school board head	39 (94)	64 (194)	62 (47)	41	–	38	***	35
Know mayor (11/66)	64 (141)	83 (267)	66 (67)	53	–	06	***	13
Know mayor (2/67)	62 (94)	77 (194)	77 (47)	40	0	40	***	27
Know congressman	30 (94)	47 (194)	72 (47)	24	47	60	***	38
Know two senators	21 (94)	34 (194)	51 (47)	16	26	38	***	21
Know GOP vice presidential candidate	49 (45)	81 (134)	95 (40)	63	74	90	***	52
Know Democratic vice presidential candidate	40 (45)	77 (135)	90 (40)	62	57	33	***	35
Know Charles Percy	08 (155)	45 (274)	63 (100)	40	33	60	***	58
Know Nelson Rockefeller	65 (155)	89 (274)	99 (99)	69	91	97	***	65
Know county clerk	36 (141)	35 (267)	18 (67)	–	–	–	**	02
Know state senator	07 (141)	40 (267)	48 (67)	36	13	44	***	36
Mean =	39	60	70	34	25	51		
Domestic Affairs—Events								
High score index political information (fall 1966)	07 (43)	25 (85)	16 (23)	19	–	10	***	52
High score index political information (fall 1968)	14 (35)	37 (86)	74 (34)	27	59	70	***	52
Know party with election majority (fall 1968)	37 (35)	53 (88)	63 (35)	26	21	41	*	24

TABLE 4.2—Continued

	Percentage Informed			Index of Effectiveness			Relationship over Full Range on Variables	
	Elem. School	High Sch. Grad.	College Grad.	High Elem.	Col. High	Col. Elem.	Chi-Sq. (P)	Assoc. (γ)
Know party with congressional majority before election (fall 1968)	43 (35)	78 (88)	86 (35)	61	33	76	***	48
Know party with election majority (fall 1970)	45 (53)	48 (63)	71 (21)	05	44	47	**	30
Know party with congressional majority before election (fall 1970)	40 (53)	52 (63)	67 (21)	20	31	45	***	31
High score index political information (fall 1970)	19 (53)	23 (62)	76 (21)	05	69	70	***	56
Mean =	29	45	65	23	36	51		
Foreign Affairs—Persons								
Know Dean Rusk	47 (108)	89 (347)	86 (117)	79	—	74	***	53
Know Kosygin	48 (108)	86 (347)	92 (117)	73	43	85	***	57
Know Nguyen Cao Ky	29 (108)	57 (347)	75 (117)	•40	42	65	***	44
Mean =	41	77	84	61	30	73		
Foreign Affairs—Events								
Index knowledge mainland China	38 (34)	65 (88)	100 (35)	44	100	100	***	49
Heard about Vietnam War	67 (58)	82 (66)	97 (61)	45	83	91	***	54
Heard about Nationalist China	26 (58)	47 (66)	79 (61)	28	60	72	***	11
Know Chinese communism	62 (58)	92 (66)	97 (61)	79	62	92	***	67
Heard about Arab-Israeli conflict (5/67)	76 (155)	88 (274)	99 (100)	50	92	96	***	49
Heard about Arab-Israeli conflict (9/69)	73 (44)	88 (158)	100 (49)	56	100	100	***	54
Mean =	57	77	95	47	78	88		

TABLE 4.3. Knowledge of Public Affairs among Individuals Age 49–60 in the Late 1960s

	Percentage Informed			Index of Effectiveness			Relationship over Full Range on Variables	
	Elem. School	High Sch. Grad.	College Grad.	High Elem.	Col. High	Col. Elem.	Chi-Sq. (P)	Assoc. (γ)
Domestic Affairs—Persons								
Know 2 plus Supreme Court justices	16 (55)	32 (38)	44 (16)	19	18	33	**	41
Know secretary of state	02 (53)	26 (69)	30 (10)	25	05	29	***	63
Know governor of state (3/71)	79 (53)	88 (69)	100 (10)	43	100	100	*	44
Know governor (2/67)	87 (140)	96 (134)	97 (38)	69	25	77	*	46
Know school board head	41 (140)	60 (134)	63 (38)	32	08	56	***	23
Know mayor (11/66)	61 (266)	81 (216)	67 (52)	51	—	15	***	33
Know mayor (2/67)	64 (140)	77 (134)	82 (38)	36	22	50	*	23
Know congressman	38 (140)	58 (134)	74 (38)	32	38	58	***	37
Know two senators	22 (140)	43 (134)	66 (38)	24	40	50	***	21
Know GOP vice presidential candidate	40 (65)	71 (94)	93 (27)	52	76	89	***	44
Know Democratic vice presidential candidate	40 (65)	68 (94)	82 (27)	47	44	70	***	34
Know Charles Percy	30 (230)	46 (175)	71 (61)	23	46	59	***	40
Know Nelson Rockefeller	74 (230)	88 (175)	100 (61)	54	100	100	***	48
Know county clerk	35 (266)	34 (216)	23 (52)	—	—	—	NS	07
Know state senator	21 (266)	36 (216)	56 (52)	19	31	44	***	30
Mean =	43	60	70	30	25	47		
Domestic Affairs—Events								
High score index political information (fall 1966)	07 (55)	29 (38)	63 (16)	24	48	60	***	53
High score index political information (fall 1968)	19 (52)	44 (46)	93 (14)	31	88	92	***	53
Know party with election majority (fall 1968)	28 (53)	61 (46)	60 (15)	45	—	44	*	29

TABLE 4.3—Continued

	Percentage Informed			Index of Effectiveness			Relationship over Full Range on Variables	
	Elem. School	High Sch. Grad.	Grad. College	High Elem.	Col. High	Col. Elem.	Chi-Sq. (P)	Assoc. (γ)
Know party with congressional majority before election (fall 1968)	60 (53)	85 (46)	93 (15)	62	53	83	**	46
Know party with election majority (fall 1970)	42 (69)	67 (52)	80 (15)	43	40	66	*	37
Know party with congressional majority before election (fall 1970)	38 (69)	58 (52)	80 (15)	32	52	68	***	37
High score index political information (fall 1970)	09 (67)	48 (50)	73 (15)	43	48	70	***	53
Mean =	29	56	77	41	48	68		
Foreign Affairs—Persons								
Know Dean Rusk	51 (222)	83 (230)	97 (90)	65	82	94	***	56
Know Kosygin	50 (222)	85 (230)	89 (90)	70	27	78	***	52
Know Nguyen Cao Ky	33 (222)	55 (230)	72 (90)	33	38	58	***	42
Mean =	45	74	86	53	46	75		
Foreign Affairs—Events								
Index knowledge mainland China	42 (53)	70 (46)	100 (15)	48	100	100	**	52
Heard about Vietnam War	56 (88)	84 (57)	97 (30)	64	81	93	***	62
Heard about Nationalist China	26 (88)	58 (57)	83 (30)	43	60	77	***	24
Know Chinese communism	50 (88)	81 (57)	97 (30)	62	84	94	***	58
Heard about Arab-Israeli conflict (5/67)	84 (230)	93 (175)	100 (61)	56	100	100	***	51
Heard about Arab-Israeli conflict (9/69)	81 (62)	92 (76)	100 (31)	58	100	100	**	54
Mean =	57	80	96	53	80	91		

TABLE 4.4 Knowledge of Public Affairs among Individuals Age 61–72 in the Late 1960s

	Percentage Informed			Index of Effectiveness			Relationship over Full Range on Variables	
	Elem. School	High Sch. Grad.	College Grad.	High Elem.	Col. High	Col. Elem.	Chi-Sq. (P)	Assoc. (γ)
Domestic Affairs—Persons								
Know 2 plus Supreme Court justices	09 (76)	38 (21)	50 (8)	21	19	45	***	56
Know secretary of state	09 (86)	14 (44)	46 (11)	06	37	41	***	37
Know governor of state (3/71)	84 (87)	93 (44)	100 (11)	56	100	100	NS	27
Know governor (2/67)	85 (169)	93 (40)	100 (27)	53	100	100	*	48
Know school board head	32 (169)	43 (40)	67 (27)	16	42	52	**	34
Know mayor (11/66)	66 (217)	94 (82)	57 (30)	82	—	—	***	35
Know mayor (2/67)	71 (169)	68 (40)	78 (27)	—	31	24	NS	05
Know congressman	32 (169)	50 (40)	74 (27)	27	48	62	***	42
Know two senators	21 (169)	45 (40)	63 (27)	30	33	53	***	27
Know GOP vice presidential candidate	57 (90)	77 (31)	67 (21)	47	—	23	**	32
Know Democratic vice presidential candidate	51 (90)	84 (31)	76 (21)	67	—	51	**	37
Know Charles Percy	43 (197)	68 (72)	70 (33)	44	06	47	***	30
Know Nelson Rockefeller	79 (197)	94 (72)	100 (33)	72	100	100	***	42
Know county clerk	30 (217)	28 (82)	43 (30)	—	21	19	*	10
Know state senator	18 (217)	46 (82)	47 (30)	34	02	35	***	40
Mean =	46	62	69	30	18	43		
Domestic Affairs—Events								
High score index political information (fall 1966)	13 (78)	33 (21)	50 (8)	23	25	43	**	49
High score index political information (fall 1968)	11 (76)	53 (19)	50 (14)	47	—	44	***	48
Know party with election majority (fall 1968)	37 (75)	47 (19)	57 (14)	16	19	32	NS	24

TABLE 4.4—Continued

	Percentage Informed			Index of Effectiveness			Relationship over Full Range on Variables	
	Elem. School	High Sch. Grad.	College Grad.	High Elem.	Col. High	Col. Elem.	Chi-Sq. (P)	Assoc. (γ)
Know party with congressional majority before election (fall 1968)	63 (75)	63 (19)	93 (14)	0	81	81	NS	33
Know party with election majority (fall 1970)	48 (87)	77 (30)	63 (16)	56	—	29	***	34
Know party with congressional majority before election (fall 1970)	40 (87)	70 (30)	75 (16)	50	17	58	**	45
High score index political information (fall 1970)	09 (86)	52 (29)	67 (15)	47	31	64	***	47
Mean =	32	56	65	35	20	49		
Foreign Affairs—Persons								
Know Dean Rusk	68 (225)	65 (93)	87 (54)	—	63	60	***	23
Know Kosygin	53 (225)	76 (93)	85 (54)	49	38	68	***	46
Know Nguyen Cao Ky	24 (225)	34 (93)	61 (54)	13	41	49	***	40
Mean =	48	58	78	19	48	58		
Foreign Affairs—Events								
Index knowledge mainland China	37 (75)	63 (19)	79 (14)	41	43	67	***	55
Heard about Vietnam War	63 (112)	92 (26)	93 (15)	78	12	81	*	42
Heard about Nationalist China	38 (112)	54 (26)	67 (15)	26	28	47	**	20
Know Chinese communism	66 (112)	92 (26)	87 (15)	77	—	62	**	49
Heard about Arab-Israeli conflict (5/67)	91 (197)	97 (72)	88 (33)	67	—	—	NS	11
Heard about Arab-Israeli conflict (9/69)	81 (99)	88 (48)	100 (13)	37	100	100	*	28
Mean =	63	81	86	49	26	62		

TABLE 4.5. Academic Knowledge in the Late 1960s

	Percentage Informed			Index of Effectiveness			Relationship over Full Range on Variables	
	Elem. School	High Sch. Grad.	College Grad.	High Elem.	Col. High	Col. Elem.	Chi-Sq. (P)	Assoc. (γ)
Age 25–36								
Know no. terms president serves	54 (13)	63 (106)	86 (50)	20	62	70	***	40
Know length of Senate term	08 (13)	23 (106)	56 (50)	16	43	52	***	42
Know length of term in House	46 (13)	39 (106)	70 (50)	—	51	45	***	32
Mean =	36	42	71	09	50	55		
Age 37–48								
Know no. terms president serves	47 (53)	64 (63)	86 (21)	32	33	74	**	33
Know length of Senate term	19 (53)	27 (63)	67 (21)	10	55	59	***	52
Know length of term in House	28 (53)	32 (63)	71 (21)	06	57	60	***	41
Mean =	31	41	75	14	58	64		
Age 49–60								
Know no. terms president serves	46 (69)	71 (52)	80 (15)	46	31	63	**	32
Know length of Senate term	16 (69)	37 (52)	60 (15)	25	37	52	**	38
Know length of term in House	22 (69)	52 (52)	53 (15)	34	02	35	***	41
Mean =	28	53	64	35	23	50		
Age 61–72								
Know no. terms president serves	59 (88)	77 (30)	81 (16)	44	17	54	NS	19
Know length of Senate term	14 (88)	40 (30)	50 (16)	30	17	42	***	47
Know length of term in House	23 (88)	47 (30)	56 (16)	31	17	43	***	47
Mean =	32	55	62	34	16	44		

TABLE 5.1. Academic Knowledge in the 1970s

	Percentage Informed			Index of Effectiveness			Relationship over Full Range on Variables	
	Elem. School	High Sch. Grad.	College Grad.	High Elem.	Col. High	Col. Elem.	Chi-Sq. (P)	Assoc. (γ)
Age 25–36								
Know Inventor telephone	71 (17)	87 (115)	96 (66)	55	69	86	***	51
Know Florence Nightingale's profession	35 (17)	71 (115)	94 (66)	55	79	91	***	46
Know Bunker Hill war	24 (17)	27 (115)	59 (66)	04	44	46	***	46
Locate Mt. Vernon	41 (17)	63 (115)	85 (66)	37	59	75	***	46
Mean =	43	62	84	33	58	72		
Age 37–48								
Know Inventor telephone	63 (30)	88 (80)	100 (56)	68	100	100	***	63
Know Florence Nightingale's profession	57 (30)	84 (80)	93 (56)	63	56	84	***	46
Know Bunker Hill war	0 (30)	29 (80)	75 (56)	29	65	75	***	71
Locate Mt. Vernon	47 (30)	63 (80)	86 (56)	30	62	74	***	47
Mean =	42	66	89	41	68	81		
Age 49–60								
Know Inventor telephone	61 (41)	96 (92)	92 (36)	90	—	80	***	54
Know Florence Nightingale's profession	49 (41)	87 (92)	97 (36)	74	77	94	***	51
Know Bunker Hill war	15 (41)	37 (92)	78 (36)	26	65	74	***	61
Locate Mt. Vernon	51 (41)	69 (92)	75 (36)	37	19	49	**	24
Mean =	44	72	86	50	50	75		
Age 61–72								
Know Inventor telephone	57 (56)	86 (44)	100 (23)	67	100	100	***	56
Know Florence Nightingale's profession	38 (56)	68 (44)	91 (23)	48	72	85	***	58
Know Bunker Hill war	20 (56)	48 (44)	78 (23)	35	58	72	***	62
Locate Mt. Vernon	59 (56)	68 (44)	87 (23)	22	59	68	NS	20
Mean =	44	68	89	43	66	80		

Appendix C
Surveys and Questions Used

Surveys Used

Gallup Poll Surveys

399*	1947	June	549		June
436	1949	January	552		September
438		March	576	1957	January
443		June	580		March
452K	1950	January	581		April
452TPS		February	582		April
453*		February	584		June
463		October	587		August
469		December	626	1960	March
474	1951	April	649	1961	August
475		May	667	1963	January
478*		August	669		March
483		December	674		June
486	1952	February	676		August
491		April	737	1966	November
492		May	746	1967	May
505		October	747		July
521	1953	October	767	1968	August
541*	1954	February	788	1969	September
546*	1955	April			

National Opinion Research Center Surveys

303*	1951	June	160	1963	May
367	1955	June	857	1965	June
423	1959	October	868		October
Almond-			889	1966	June
Verba			4018	1967	February
study	1960	March	4119	1971	March
447	1962	April			

Survey Research Center Surveys

"Minor Study"	1951
"China Study"	1965
"Election Studies"	1952, 1958, 1960, 1964, 1966, 1968, 1970.

*Used only for the special analysis reported in chapter 5.

Canadian Gallup Poll Surveys

227	1953	May	248	1956	May
231		August	250		July
238	1954	September	251		September
239		November	252		October
244	1955	September	256	1957	March
245		November	260		September

Questions Used as Indicators of Knowledge
Time 1
Gallup Poll Surveys

399T*—6/18/47   Will you please tell me the number on this map
which locates each of the following countries?
(*a*) France (*b*) Yugoslavia (*c*) Spain (*d*) Bulgaria
(*e*) Romania (*f*) Poland
Will you tell me the name of the song which is our
national anthem?

436 K—1/20/49   Will you tell me what the term "filibuster" in Congress means to you?

438 K—3/4/49   Will you tell me what the term "filibuster" means to
you?
Have you heard or read about the North Atlantic
Security Pact?
Have you heard or read about the Truman Admin-
istration's plan for compulsory health insurance?

443 K—6/9/49   Have you heard or read about the recent marriage
of Rita Hayworth to Aly Khan?
Have you followed any of the discussions about the
Taft-Hartley Law?
Will you tell me what your understanding is of the
term "wiretapping?"
Have you heard or read about recent criticisms of
David Lilienthal and the Atomic Energy Com-
mission?
Have you heard or read about the North Atlantic
Security Pact?
Have you heard or read about the civil war in China?

452 K—1/26/50   Will you tell me what your understanding is of the
term "wiretapping?"
Have you heard or read anything about the Herbert
Hoover Commission Reports?
I don't need to know the details, but what is your
understanding, in general, of the purpose of the
(Herbert) Hoover Commission?
Have you heard or read anything about the new
hydrogen bomb?
Have you heard or read about the civil war in China?

452 TPS—   Will you tell me what is meant by the "electoral
2/3/50   college"?
Have you heard or read anything about the new
hydrogen bomb?

453 K*—   Will you please tell me what is meant by a "mo-
2/24/50   nopoly"?
Will you tell me the names of any of the first four
books of the New Testament of the Bible—that is,
the first four Gospels?

463 TPS—   Here are some public figures who have been in the
10/6/50   news recently. Have you ever heard of any of
them?
J. Edgar Hoover
Marshal Tito

*Used only for the special analysis reported in chapter 5.

469—12/30/50   Just in your own words, when a person is described
                    as an "isolationist," what does that mean to you?
                    Will you tell me the name of Bob Hope's latest pic-
                    ture?
                    Will you tell me the name of Loretta Young's latest
                    picture?
                    Will you tell me who Chiang Kai-shek is?

474 TPS—   Here are some public figures who have been in the
   4/14/51   news recently. Have you ever heard of any of
                    them?
                    George C. Marshall
                    Do you happen to know the names of the two U.S.
                    senators from this state?
                    Will you tell me who Marshal Tito is?
                    Will you tell me who Chiang Kai-shek is?
                    Will you tell me what is meant by the term "At-
                    lantic Pact"?
                    Will you tell me what is meant when people refer
                    to the 38th Parallel in Korea?
                    Will you tell me where Formosa is?
                    Will you tell me where Manchuria is?

475 K—5/17/51   Will you tell me who Mr. Dean Acheson is?
                    Have you heard or read anything about the hearings
                    in Washington at which MacArthur, Marshall, and
                    Bradley gave their views on what we should do
                    about Korea?
                    Will you tell me what the trouble is in Iran at pres-
                    ent?
                    Do you happen to know what the "Voice of Amer-
                    ica" is?
                    Do you happen to know where Iran is?

478 K*—8/1/51   Just in your own words, when someone mentions the
                    term "foreign policy," what does that mean to you?
                    Will you tell me what is meant by the "electoral
                    college"?

483 TPS—   Will you tell me who Anthony Eden is?
   12/7/51   What is the population of the United States?
                    What is your guess as to the number of men Com-
                    munist China now has in its armed forces?
                    Just your best guess—what is the population of Com-
                    munist China?
                    Will you tell me where the Suez Canal is?
                    How many senators are there from each state?
                    How many inches are there in a yard?
                    How many 3-cent stamps can you buy for 75 cents?

486 K—2/7/52   Just your best guess—what is the population of Com-
                    munist China?
                    Will you tell me who Plato was?
                    What author wrote *War and Peace*?
                    Will you tell me who Johann Sebastian Bach was?
                    Will you name one of the better known artists, or
                    painters, in the last 50 years?
                    What ocean would you cross in going from the
                    United States to England?

*Used only for the special analysis reported in chapter 5.

491 TPS—   I'm going to read you a list of people in the news.
4/25/52   Will you tell me who each one is—or what he
             does?

Dwight D. Eisenhower	Richard B. Russell
Joan Bennett	Robert A. Taft
W. Averill Harriman	Harold Stassen
Estes Kefauver	Adlai Stevenson
Robert Kerr	Earl Warren
Casey Stengel	

Will you tell me who the vice president of the
United States is?

In what month will the national Republican and
Democratic party conventions be held?

In what city will the conventions be held?

Will each of the 48 states elect members of the
House of Representatives this fall or not?

Have you heard or read anything about the government's seizure, or taking over, of the steel
companies?

In what month will the presidential election be
held?

There are three major branches of the federal government in Washington. Will you tell me what
the three branches of the government are called?

Will you tell me what the initials GOP stand for?

For how many years is a president of the United
States elected—that is, how many years are
there in one term of office?

492 K—5/9/52   Have you heard or read anything about the Taft-
                Hartley Law which deals with labor unions?

Have you heard or read anything about the Herbert
Hoover Commission Reports?

I don't need to know the details, but what is your
understanding, in general, of the purpose of the
(Herbert) Hoover Commission?

505 TPS—   Have you heard or read anything about the Taft-
10/3/52   Hartley Law which deals with labor unions?

Who was:

Columbus	Shakespeare
Napoleon	Aristotle
Karl Marx	Freud
Gutenberg	Tolstoy
Rubens	Raphael
	Beethoven

521 K—10/7/53   I'm going to read you the titles of some books and
                I'd like you to tell me who wrote them.

Huckleberry Finn

A Tale of Two Cities

From Here to Eternity

Have you followed any of the discussions about the
Taft-Hartley Law?

Will you tell me who Syngman Rhee is?

With what country do you associate General Franco?

541—12/29/54   Will you tell me what is meant by the "electoral
                college"?

---

*Used only for the special analysis reported in chapter 5.

National Opinion Research Center Survey

303*—6/51   Can you tell me what is the main job of the State
                 Department, in Washington? (What are they
                 mainly supposed to do at the State Department?)

Survey Research Center Surveys

"Minor" Study   Information Index
  1951
Election Survey   Have you heard anything about the Taft-Hartley
  —9/10/52   Law?

Questions Used as Indicators of Knowledge
Time 2
Gallup Poll Surveys

546 K*—   Will you please tell me the number on this map
  4/12/55   which locates each of the following countries?
                 (a) France (b) Yugoslavia (c) Spain (d) England
                 (e) Bulgaria (f) Romania (g) Poland (h) Aus-
                 tria

549 6/22/55   Who is the head of the FBI?
                 Who is the vice president of the United States?
                 Who is the prime minister of Great Britain?
                 What profession do you associate with Florence
                   Nightingale?
                 Who made the first nonstop solo trans-Atlantic flight?
                 In which city was the United Nations first organized?
                 In what country was the battle of Waterloo fought?
                 Which is the largest lake in North America?
                 What is the name of the highest mountain in the
                   world?
                 In what ocean is the island of Midway?
                 Which of the following states border on Canada?
                   Montana?   Michigan?
                   Maine?   Minnesota?
                 Which state is named for a president of the United
                   States?
                 What is the capital city of Spain?
                 Of what country is New Delhi the capital?
                 What composer wrote the *Messiah*?
                 Who wrote the play titled *A Midsummer Night's
                   Dream*?
                 Which planet is nearest the sun?
                 What great scientist, who died recently, do you as-
                   sociate with the Theory of Relativity?
                 Who invented the telephone?
                 What doctor discovered the antipolio vaccine?
                 How many feet are there in a mile?
                 How many pecks in a bushel?
                 What is the national language of Brazil?
                 What is the name of the decoration given to those in
                   the armed forces who are wounded in action
                   against an enemy?

*Used only for the special analysis reported in chapter 5.

Which baseball team won the last world series?

What is the name of the present heavyweight boxing champion?

What is an "Oscar"?

580 K—3/13/57 Here is another in the Gallup Poll quiz series. This one has to do with famous buildings. Will you tell me in what country or city the following buildings are found?

The Kremlin	The Pyramids
The Leaning Tower	The Parthenon
The Eiffel Tower	Mount Vernon

581 K—4/4/57 Will you tell me if you have ever heard of:

Walter Reuther	David McDonald
George Meany	John L. Lewis
Dave Beck	James Petrillo
Harry Bridges	

Have you heard or read anything about the president's new budget for the next year?

Have you heard or read anything about the congressional investigation of labor unions?

This is another in the series of Gallup Poll quizzes. This one is on famous battles. See if you can tell me in what war these battles were fought. The battle of:

Bunker Hill	The Bulge
Gettysburg	Waterloo

582 K—4/23/57 Here is another in the Gallup Poll quiz series. This one is on famous authors. See if you can tell me who wrote the following:

Tom Sawyer

Macbeth

Have you heard or read anything about the "fall-out" of radio-active matter in H-bomb tests?

584 K—6/4/57 Do you happen to know the name of the congressman for your district?

Please tell me who these people are:

Nehru	Thackeray
Adenauer	Rubens

587 K—8/6/57 Can you tell me what is meant by the word "automation," or haven't you ever heard of it before?

I am going to read you the names of some people. Will you tell me who each is—that is, what he does?

J. Edgar Hoover

National Opinion Research Center Surveys

367 6/55 I'd like to ask you some questions now about particular illnesses. First, do you happen to know any of the signs or symptoms of cancer? (What are they?) Any other ways a person would know he might have cancer?

Do you think it is possible or not possible to catch (illness) from someone else? Diabetes?

423—10/59 Do you happen to know what pyorrhea is?

Have you heard or read about fluoridating public water supplies?

Survey Research Center Surveys

SRC—1958   Knowledge of candidate's characteristics — religion, nationality, class (3-item scale)
       No knowledge of candidate
       Didn't know any characteristics
       Classified candidate on one characteristic
       Classified candidate on two characteristics
       Classified candidate on all three characteristics
     Knowledge of candidate's stand on issues
       Never heard of him
       Heard, but knows no stand on issue areas
       Heard and knows stand on one issue area
       Heard and knows stand on two . . . eight issue areas
     Do you happen to know which party elected the most congressmen in the election (this) (last) month? (Which one?)
     Do you happen to know which party had the most congressmen in Washington before the election (this) (last) month? (Which one?)

QUESTIONS USED AS INDICATORS OF KNOWLEDGE
TIME 3
Gallup Poll Surveys

626 K—3/28/60   I am going to read you the names of some people. Will you tell me who each is—that is, what he does?
       J. Edgar Hoover
       Elmo Roper
       Samuel Lubell
       Frank Stanton

649 K—8/22/61   Have you heard or read about the dispute between the Western allies and Russia over Berlin?
     Will you tell me what is meant by the "electoral college"?

669 K—3/6/63   On the next subject. . . . Can you tell me who the following men are or what they do?
       Nelson Rockefeller
       Barry Goldwater
       George Romney
       William Scranton
     Have you heard or read about the discussions regarding the banning or prohibiting of nuclear weapon tests?

674 K—6/19/63   Will you tell me what the term "filibuster" means to you?

676 K—8/13/63   Can you tell me who the following persons are or what they do?
       Barry Goldwater
       Richard Nixon
       William Scranton
       George Romney
       Milton Eisenhower
       Mark Hatfield
       Harold Stassen

Thruston Morton
Nelson Rockefeller
Clifford Case
Elizabeth Taylor
John Glenn

Have you heard or read about the proposed mass
civil rights rally to be held in Washington, D.C.
on August 28?

Have you heard or read about the agreement with
Russia to have a partial ban on the testing of
nuclear weapons?

National Opinion Research Center Survey

Almond-Verba
Study—3/60

When a new President comes into office, one of the
first things he must do is appoint people to cabinet
positions. Could you tell me what some of the
cabinet positions are? Can you name any others?
(*Probe until respondent names five cabinet positions or until he knows no more.*)

Survey Research Center Surveys

1960 Election
Study

Speaking of Kennedy and Nixon, we're interested in
some of the things that people may have learned
about these candidates recently. Take Vice President Nixon, for instance:

Do you happen to remember what part of the
country he comes from? (Where is that?)
(What state?)

Do you happen to know what Nixon's religion is?
(What is that?)

Now take Senator Kennedy. Do you happen to
know what part of the country he comes from?
(Where is that?) (What state?)

Do you happen to know what Kennedy's religion
is? (What is that?)

Do you happen to know which party elected the
most congressmen in the elections (this) (last)
month? (Which one?)

Do you happen to know which party had the most
congressmen in Washington before the election
(this) (last) month? (Which one?)

1964 Election
Study

Speaking of candidates and voting, we're interested
in what sorts of things people notice about the
candidates. Take Senator Goldwater for instance:

Have you heard what part of the country he comes
from? (Where is that?) (What state?)

Now take President Johnson. Have you heard
what part of the country he comes from? (Where
is that?) (What state?)

Have you paid any attention to what kind of government most of China has right now, that is,
do you remember whether it is democratic, Communist, or something else? (*If necessary*) Which
kind?

(*Communist*) As far as you know, is Communist China a member of the United Nations?

Do you happen to know which party elected the most congressmen in the election (this) (last) month? (Which one?)

Do you happen to know which party had the most congressmen in Washington before the election (this) (last) month? (Which one?)

QUESTIONS USED AS INDICATORS OF KNOWLEDGE
TIME 4
Gallup Poll Surveys

737 K—11/8/66   Do you happen to know the name of the Mayor of this town (or top-ranking official)?

Do you happen to know the name of the person who fills the position of clerk in this county or locality? He may not be called the county clerk here, but I'm interested in finding out who the person is who fills that particular post.

Do you happen to know who will represent this district or locality in the *state* senate next year? I'm not talking about the United States Senator, but the *state senator.*

746 K—5/31/67   Have you heard or read about the troubles between Israel and the Arab nations in the Middle East?

Can you tell me who Charles Percy is or what he does?

Can you tell me who Nelson Rockefeller is or what he does?

747 K—7/20/67   Can you tell me who these people are, or what they do?

Dean Rusk
Alexei Kosygin
Nguyen Cao Ky

767 K—8/30/68   Can you recall the name of the man who was nominated as the vice presidential candidate on the Republican ticket?

Can you recall the name of the man who was nominated as the vice presidential candidate on the Democratic ticket?

788—9/15/69   Have you heard or read about the troubles between Israel and the Arab nations in the Middle East?

NORC Surveys

868—10/65   Now I'd like to ask you some questions about particular jobs.

Would a *metal caster* in a foundry be likely to use any of these tools? Would he be likely to use:
a cold chisel? .
a pair of tongs?
a blowtorch?

Which of the following does a *newspaper proofreader* do?
investigate the accuracy of rumors?
rewrite newspaper stories?
check the work of typesetters?

Does a *personnel director* do either of these things?
administer psychological tests?
tell workers how to do their jobs?

Which of the following tools would a *boilermaker* be likely to use? Would he use a
   jackhammer?
   rivet gun?
   welding torch?

889—6/66   We would like to know something about how people go about guessing words they do not know. On this card are listed some words—you may know some of them and you may not know quite a few of them.

On each line there is a word in capital letters—like BEAST. Then there are five other words. Tell me the number of the word that comes closest to the meaning of the word in capital letters. For example, the first word in capital letters is BEAST. You would say "4," since "animal" comes closer to "beast" than any of the other words. If you wish I will read the words to you. These words are difficult for almost everyone—give me your best guess if you're not sure of the answer.
   ACCUSTOM
   EDIBLE
   CLOISTERED
   PACT
   ALLUSION
   EMANATE

4018—2/67   We are interested in how well known the community leaders are in different places. What is the name of the (Mention the name of the position of the head of the local government unit, such as mayor) of this community?

What is the name of the head of the local school system? (Correct answers include the name of the head of the local school board or the name of the superintendent of schools.)

We want to know how well the different governmental leaders are known around here. Could you tell me the name of the governor of this state?

And what are the names of the senators from this state?

What about the congressman from this district. Do you happen to know his name?

4119—3/71   What about the governor of this state? Do you happen to know his name?

And what is the name of President Nixon's secretary of state?

Survey Research Center Surveys

China Study   Do you happen to know what kind of government
6/65   most of China has right now — whether it's democratic, or Communist, or what? (*If answer unclear*) Do you happen to know if there is any Communist government in China now?

Have you happened to hear anything about another Chinese government besides the Communist one? Do you happen to remember anything about this other Chinese government — like what it is called, or who its leader is, or where it is located?

Have you happened to hear anything about the fighting in Vietnam?

Election Study 66   Now I want to ask you about the justices of the Supreme Court in Washington. Do you happen to know the names of any of the justices? (*If necessary*) Who? Any others?

Election Study 68   Have you paid any attention to what kind of government most of China has right now, that is, do you remember whether it is democratic, Communist, or something else?
(*If necessary*) Which kind?
(*Communist*) As far as you know, is Communist China a member of the United Nations?

Election Studies 68, 70   Do you happen to know which party elected the most congressmen in the elections (this) (last) month? Which one?
Do you happen to know which party had the most congressmen in Washington before the election (this) (last) month? Which one?

Election Studies 66, 68, 70   Respondent's general level of information about politics and public affairs seemed:
Very high
Fairly high
Average
Fairly low
Very low

Election Study 70   How many times can an individual be elected president of the United States?
How long is the term of office for a United States senator?
How long is the term for a member of the House of Representatives in Washington, D.C.?

Canadian Gallup Poll Surveys

227 T—5/29/53   Here are the names of public figures who have been in the news recently. Do you happen to have heard of any of them?
Henry Cabot Lodge
Lester B. Pearson

231—8/19/53   Have you heard or read anything about Dr. Kinsey and his studies on sex?
Have you heard or read anything about the suggestion that United States, Britain, France, and Russia should have a meeting to discuss world problems?

238—9/9/54   Have you heard or read anything about the St. Lawrence Seaway plan?

239—11/54   Do you happen to recall the name of a Cabinet Member in Ottawa?

244—9/55	Do you happen to know what sport the Grey Cup is connected with?
245—11/55	We're conducting a nationwide "spelling bee"—some of the words are pretty hard, but let's see how many you can spell.†

magazine	acceleration
sandwich	parallel
deceive	picnicking
kerosene	cauliflower
calamity	penitentiary

248 K—5/56	Have you heard or read about the trouble between Israel and the Arab countries?
	Have you heard or read anything about the fluoridation of water?
250 K—7/56	Did you happen to hear or read about the debate in the House of Commons over the trans-Canada pipeline?
251 K—9/56	Have you heard or read anything about the Suez Canal dispute?
	Do you happen to have heard of the Duke of Windsor—that is, the former King of England?
	Can you tell me where the Olympic Games are being held this year?
	Do you happen to know what sport the Grey Cup is connected with?
252—10/56	This is a sort of quiz. Here are the names of the premiers of the ten provinces. As I read them, would you tell me if you happen to know the province each one heads:

Leslie M. Frost	Douglas L. Campbell
J. R. Smallwood	T. C. Douglas
H. Hicks	Ernest C. Manning
Hugh John Flemming	William A. C. Bennett
Maurice Duplessis	J. Walter Jones (or Matheson)

256—3/57	Have you heard or read anything about the coming federal election?
260—9/57	Can you recall the names of any cabinet ministers appointed by Mr. Diefenbaker?

†This ten-word spelling test was also included in U.S. Gallup Poll 552 in September 1955.

Appendix D
Tables on the Effects
of Education When Other
Variables are Controlled

TABLE D.1. Knowledge of Public Affairs When Sex Is Controlled, for the Early 1950s

	Male Respondents		Female Respondents	
	Chi-Sq.	γ	Chi-Sq.	γ
Domestic Affairs—Persons				
Heard J. Edgar Hoover		Control not needed		
Know Dean Acheson	S	57	S	57
Know George Marshall	S	80	S	62
Know own senators	S	21	S	33
Know Eisenhower				
Know Harriman				
Know Kefauver				
Know R. Kerr				
Know R. Russell		Control not needed		
Know Taft				
Know Stevenson				
Know Earl Warren				
Know vice president				
Know Stassen				
Domestic Affairs—Events				
Heard Taft-Hartley Law (3/49)		Control not needed		
Heard Taft-Hartley Law (6/49)	S	41	S	42
Heard Taft-Hartley Law (5/52)	S	43	S	53
Heard Taft-Hartley Law (10/52)	S	52	S	65
Heard Taft-Hartley Law (9/52)		Control not needed		
Follow Taft-Hartley Law (10/53)		Control not needed		
Know wiretapping (6/49)	S	38	S	39
Know wiretapping (1/50)	S	48	S	52
Heard criticism of AEC	S	52	S	49
Heard Hoover Commission (1/50)	S	59	S	59
Heard Hoover Commission (5/52)	S	58	S	65
Know Hoover Commission (1/50)	S	52	S	61
Know Hoover Commission (5/52)	S	51	S	32
Heard Truman health insurance plan		Control not needed		
Know date political convention				
Know convention cities				
Know if all states hold				
congressional elections 1952		Control not needed		
Heard government's seizure steel industry				
Information Index				
Know population of U.S.				
Foreign Affairs—Persons				
Know Tito (10/50)		Control not needed		
Know Tito (4/51)	S	55	S	52
Know Chiang Kai-shek (12/50)	S	35	S	40
Know Chiang Kai-shek (4/51)	S	51	S	53
Know Anthony Eden				
Know Synghman Rhee		Control not needed		
Know Franco				

TABLE D.1—Continued

	Male Respondents		Female Respondents	
	Chi-Sq.	γ	Chi-Sq.	γ
Foreign Affairs—Events				
Heard NATO (3/49)		Control not needed		
Heard NATO (6/49)	S	57	S	51
Heard H-bomb (1/50)	S	60	S	55
Heard H-bomb (2/50)	S	69	S	65
Heard Chinese civil war (6/49)	S	58	S	58
Heard Chinese civil war (1/50)	S	50	S	69
Know Atlantic Pact	S	45	S	53
Know 38th Parallel	S	38	S	45
Know size Chinese Army		Control not needed		
Know population of China (12/51)				
Know population of China (2/52)	S	43	S	37
Heard aboout hearings on Korea	S	54	S	49
Know about trouble in Iran	S	57	S	49
Know Voice of America	S	54	S	55

TABLE D.2. Knowledge of Public Affairs When Sex Is Controlled, for the Late 1950s

	Male Respondents		Female Respondents	
	Chi-Sq.	γ	Chi-Sq.	γ
Domestic Affairs—Persons				
Name Congressman		Control not needed		
Know J. Edgar Hoover (1957)	S	66	S	59
Know head of FBI (1955)	}	Control not needed		
Know vice president of U.S.				
Heard W. Reuther	S	46	S	42
Heard G. Meany	S	35	S	30
Heard D. Beck	S	55	S	38
Heard H. Bridges	S	45	S	39
Heard J. L. Lewis	S	27	S	24
Heard Petrillo	S	44	S	48
Heard D. McDonald	NS	16	NS	06
Index Knowledge of candidate "high" score	S	17	S	21
Domestic Affairs—Events				
Index Information "informed" on 8 issues	NS	13	S	30
Heard about fallout	S	36	S	34
Heard about president's new budget	S	37	S	24
Heard about Congress investigating unions	S	64	S	43
Know party with election majority		Control not needed		
Know party with congressional majority before election	S	33	S	35
Foreign Affairs—Persons				
Know Nehru	}	Control not needed		
Know Adenauer				
Know prime minister of Britain				

TABLE D.3. Knowledge of Public Affairs When Sex Is Controlled, for the Early 1960s

	Male Respondents		Female Respondents	
	Chi-Sq.	γ	Chi-Sq.	γ
Domestic Affairs—Persons				
Know Goldwater (3/63)	S	50	S	56
Know Goldwater (8/63)	S	41	S	43
Know Nixon	S	41	S	23
Know Wm. Scranton (3/63)	S	39	S	41
Know Wm. Scranton (8/63)	S	34	S	39
Know Romney (3/63)	S	68	S	57
Know Romney (8/63)	S	55	S	52
Know Milton Eisenhower	S	24	S	36
Know Mark Hatfield	S	44	S	37
Know Harold Stassen	S	26	S	39
Know Thruston Morton	S	39	S	41
Know Rockefeller (3/63)	S	70	S	66
Know Rockefeller (8/63)	S	45	S	43
Know Clifford Case	S	32	S	24
Know Johnson home state	Control not needed			
Know Goldwater home state	Control not needed			
Know Kennedy's religion	NS	32	S	57
Know Kennedy home state	S	50	S	48
Know Nixon's religion	Control not needed			
Know Nixon home state	S	49	S	54
Know J. Edgar Hoover	S	70	S	63
Know Elmo Roper	S	63	S	85
Know Frank Stanton	S	50	S	49
Know Sam Lubell	S	73	S	69
Domestic Affairs—Events				
Heard about civil rights rally	S	41	S	38
Know party with election majority (fall 1960)	S	25	S	30
Know party with election majority (fall 1964)	S	57	S	43
Know party with congressional majority before election (fall 1960)	S	40	S	47
Know party with congressional majority before election (fall 1964)	S	38	S	41
Foreign Affairs—Events				
Index knowledge of mainland China	S	49	S	42
Heard about nuclear test ban treaty (3/63)	S	39	S	48
Heard about nuclear test ban treaty (8/63)	S	53	S	50
Heard about Berlin dispute	S	70	S	47

TABLE D.4. Knowledge of Public Affairs When Sex Is Controlled, for the Late 1960s

	Male Respondents		Female Respondents	
	Chi-Sq.	γ	Chi-Sq.	γ
Domestic Affairs—Persons				
Know 2 plus Supreme Court Justices	S	42	S	49
Know secretary of state	S	47	S	56
Name governor of state (3/71)	S	37	S	45
Know governor (2/67)	Control not needed			
Know school board head	S	24	S	36
Know mayor (11/66)	S	11	S	21
Know mayor (2/67)	Control not needed			
Know congressman	S	32	S	39
Know two senators	S	23	S	20
Know GOP vice presidential candidate	S	42	S	53
Know Democratic vice presidential candidate	S	27	S	40
Know Charles Percy	Control not needed			
Know Nelson Rockefeller	Control not needed			
Know county clerk	S	04	NS	02
Know state senator	S	14	S	41
Domestic Affairs—Events				
High score index political information (fall 1966)	S	50	S	52
High score index political information (fall 1968)	S	51	S	49
Know party with election majority (fall 1968)	S	31	S	28
Know party with congressional majority before election (fall 1968)	S	45	S	35
Know party with election majority (fall 1970)	S	30	S	36
Know party with congressional majority before election (fall 1970)	S	36	S	39
High score index political information (fall 1970)	S	54	S	51
Foreign Affairs—Persons				
Know Dean Rusk	S	61	S	41
Know Kosygin	S	63	S	45
Know Nguyen Cao Ky	S	42	S	46
Foreign Affairs—Events				
Know facts about mainland China	S	52	S	48
Heard about Vietnam War				
Heard about Nationalist China	Control not needed			
Know Chinese communism				
Heard about Arab-Israeli conflict (5/67)				
Heard about Arab-Israeli conflict (9/69)	S	50	S	47

TABLE D.5. Academic Knowledge When Sex Is Controlled, for the Early 1950s

	Male Respondents		Female Respondents	
	Chi-Sq.	γ	Chi-Sq.	γ
History				
Know Columbus		Control not needed		
Know Napoleon	S	62	S	73
Know Karl Marx	S	56	S	60
Know Gutenberg	S	52	S	63
Humanities				
Know Rubens		Control not needed		
Know Shakespeare	S	68	S	78
Know Aristotle	S	67	S	74
Know Freud		Control not needed		
Know Raphael	S	63	S	72
Know Beethoven	S	71	S	74
Know Plato				
Know author **War and Peace** (2/52)				
Know Tolstoy (10/52)				
Know Bach		Control not needed		
Name a painter				
Know author **Huckleberry Finn**				
Know author **Tale of Two Cities**				
Geography				
Know ocean between U.S. and U.K.	S	68	S	52
Locate Formosa	S	51	S	46
Locate Manchuria	S	55	S	45
Locate Iran	S	45	S	50
Locate Suez Canal		Control not needed		
Civics				
Know number of senators				
Know month president elected				
Know 3 branches federal government		Control not needed		
Know term office of president				
Know meaning "GOP"				
Know meaning "isolationism"				
Know electoral college	S	59	S	73
Know "filibuster" (1/49)	S	58	S	57
Know "filibuster" (3/49)	S	49	S	58
Miscellaneous				
Know how many inches in yard		Control not needed		
Know how many 3¢ stamps in 75¢				

TABLE D.6. Academic Knowledge When Sex Is Controlled, for the Late 1950s

	Male Respondents		Female Respondents	
	Chi-Sq.	γ	Chi-Sq.	γ
History				
Know Bunker Hill war	S	44	S	48
Know Gettysburg war	S	54	S	44
Know Bulge war	S	58	S	49
Know Waterloo war	S	50	S	51
Know Florence Nightingale's profession				
Know Lindbergh				
Know city U.N. organized in		Control not needed		
Know country Waterloo in				
Geography				
Locate Kremlin	S	53	S	52
Locate Leaning Tower	S	52	S	53
Locate Eiffel Tower	S	60	S	55
Locate Pyramids				
Locate Parthenon				
Locate Mt. Vernon				
Know largest lake in North America				
Know highest mountain in world				
Know ocean Midway Island				
Know whether Montana borders Canada		Control not needed		
Know Maine borders Canada				
Know Minnesota borders Canada				
Know state named for president				
Know Michigan borders Canada				
Know capital of Spain				
Know New Dehli capital of India				
Humanities				
Know author **Tom Sawyer**		Control not needed		
Know author **Macbeth**	S	74	S	72
Know painter Rubens				
Know Thackeray		Control not needed		
Know composer **Messiah**				
Know author **Midsummer Night's Dream**		Control not needed		
Science and Miscellaneous				
Know planet nearest sun				
Know discoverer relativity				
Know inventor telephone		Control not needed		
Know discoverer polio vaccine				
Knowledge "automation" ("high score")	S	51	S	49
Index knowledge cancer:				
Know 4 plus cancer symptoms	S	39	S	50
Know 1 plus cancer symptoms				
Know diabetes not contagious		Control not needed		
Heard about fluoridation		Control not needed		
Know "pyorrhea"	S	35	S	39
Know feet in mile				
Know pecks in bushel		Control not needed		
Know language of Brazil				
Know medal for wounded in action		Control not needed		

TABLE D.7. Academic Knowledge When Sex Is Controlled, for the 1960s

	Male Respondents		Female Respondents	
	Chi-Sq.	γ	Chi-Sq.	γ
Know cabinet positions	S	60	S	51
Know electoral college	S	62	S	65
Know "filibuster"	S	60	S	62
Know no. terms president serves	S	32	S	34
Know length of Senate term	S	44	S	44
Know length term in House	S	41	S	38

TABLE D.8. Knowledge of Public Affairs When Religion Is Controlled, for the 1950s

	Protestant Respondents		Catholic Respondents	
	Chi-Sq.	γ	Chi-Sq.	γ
Domestic Affairs—Persons				
Heard J. Edgar Hoover (10/50)	Control not needed			
Know head of FBI (1955)	Control not needed			
Know vice president	Control not needed			
Domestic Affairs—Events				
Heard Taft-Hartley Law (10/52)	Control not needed			
Follow Taft-Hartley Law (10/53)	S	42	S	41
Heard Truman health insurance plan	Control not needed			
Foreign Affairs—Persons				
Know Franco	S	52	S	52
Know Synghman Rhee	S	46	S	57
Know Tito	Control not needed			
Know prime minister of Britain	Control not needed			
Foreign Affairs—Events				
Heard H-bomb	Control not needed			

TABLE D.9. Knowledge of Public Affairs When Religion Is Controlled, for the Early 1960s

	Protestant Respondents		Catholic Respondents	
	Chi-Sq.	γ	Chi-Sq.	γ
Domestic Affairs—Persons				
Know Goldwater (3/63)	S	56	S	38
Know Goldwater (8/63)	S	39	S	40
Know Nixon	S	35	S	26
Know Wm. Scranton (3/63)	S	45	S	23
Know Wm. Scranton (8/63)	S	39	S	31
Know Romney (3/63)	S	62	S	62
Know Romney (8/63)	S	49	S	49
Know Milton Eisenhower	S	34	S	14
Know Mark Hatfield	S	39	S	38
Know Harold Stassen	S	33	S	28
Know Thruston Morton	S	41	S	28
Know Rockefeller (3/63)	S	68	S	55
Know Rockefeller (8/63)	S	45	S	40
Know Clifford Case	S	24	S	32
Know Johnson home state	⎱			
Know Goldwater home state	⎰ Control not needed			
Know Kennedy's religion	⎱			
Know Kennedy home state	S	50	S	42
Know Nixon's religion	Control not needed			
Know Nixon home state	S	51	S	57
Know J. Edgar Hoover	S	61	S	61
Know Elmo Roper	S	64	S	68
Know Frank Stanton	S	37	S	45
Know Sam Lubell	S	83	S	32
Domestic Affairs—Events				
Heard about civil rights rally	S	38	S	38
Know party with election majority (fall 1960)	S	31	NS	11
Know party with election majority (fall 1964)	Control not needed			
Know party with congressional majority before election (fall 1960)	Control not needed			
Know party with congressional majority before election (fall 1964)	Control not needed			
Foreign Affairs—Events				
Index knowledge mainland China	Control not needed			
Heard about nuclear test ban treaty (3/63)	S	44	S	37
Heard about nuclear test ban treaty (8/63)	S	46	S	57
Heard about Berlin dispute	S	52	S	52

TABLE D.10. Knowledge of Public Affairs When Religion Is Controlled, for the Late 1960s

	Protestant Respondents		Catholic Respondents	
	Chi-Sq.	γ	Chi-Sq.	γ
Domestic Affairs—Persons				
Know 2 plus Supreme Court justices	S	45	S	45
Know secretary of state	S	44	S	44
Name governor of state (3/71)	Control not needed			
Know governor (2/67)	Control not needed			
Know school board head	S	33	S	34
Know mayor (11/66)	S	15	S	18
Know mayor (2/67)	S	18	NS	07
Know congressman	Control not needed			
Know two senators				
Know GOP vice presidential candidate				
Know Democratic vice presidential candidate	S	31	S	35
Know Charles Percy	S	49	S	31
Know Nelson Rockefeller	S	47	S	42
Know county clerk	S	04	S	13
Know state senator	S	25	S	41
Domestic Affairs—Events				
High score index political information (fall 1966)	S	49	S	52
High score index political information (fall 1968)	S	47	S	55
Know party with election majority (fall 1968)	Control not needed			
Know party with congressional majority before election (fall 1968)				
Know party with election majority (fall 1970)	S	31	NS	24
Know party with congressional majority before election (fall 1970)	S	30	S	44
High score index political information (fall 1970)	S	48	S	54
Foreign Affairs—Persons				
Know Dean Rusk	S	45	S	60
Know Kosygin	S	55	S	34
Know Nguyen Cao Ky	S	44	S	34
Foreign Affairs—Events				
Know facts about mainland China	Control not needed			
Heard about Vietnam War				
Heard about Nationalist China	S	12	S	09
Know Chinese communism	S	54	NS	27
Heard about Arab-Israeli conflict (5/67)	Control not needed			
Heard about Arab-Israeli conflict (9/69)	S	47	S	47

TABLE D.11. Academic Knowledge When Religion Is Controlled, for the 1950s

	Protestant Respondents		Catholic Respondents	
	Chi-Sq.	γ	Chi-Sq.	γ
History				
Know Columbus	S	58	NS	51
Know Napoleon	S	70	S	49
Know Karl Marx	S	58	S	49
Know Gutenberg	S	56	S	52
Know Florence Nightingale's profession	Control not needed			
Know Lindbergh				
Know city U.N. organized in	S	43	S	45
Know country Waterloo in	Control not needed			
Geography				
Know largest lake in North America	S	35	S	35
Know highest mountain in world	Control not needed			
Know ocean Midway Island	S	60	S	47
Know whether Montana borders Canada	S	16	NS	13
Know Maine borders Canada	S	06	NS	10
Know Michigan borders Canada	S	24	S	34
Know Minnesota borders Canada	S	21	NS	14
Know state named for president	Control not needed			
Know capital of Spain	S	53	S	42
Know New Delhi Capital of India	Control not needed			
Locate Kremlin	S	48	S	47
Locate Leaning Tower	S	50	S	56
Locate Eiffel Tower	S	52	S	62
Locate Pyramids	S	62	S	66
Locate Parthenon	S	60	S	59
Locate Mt. Vernon	Control not needed			
Humanities				
Know Rubens	S	58	S	46
Know Shakespeare	S	66	S	87
Know Aristotle	S	73	S	62
Know Freud	S	72	S	71
Know Tolstoy	S	61	S	50
Know Raphael	S	69	S	64
Know Beethoven	S	68	S	74
Know author **Huckleberry Finn**	S	61	S	58
Know author **Tale of Two Cities**	S	64	S	62
Know composer of **Messiah**	S	65	S	52
Know author **Midsummer Night's Dream**	S	71	S	71

TABLE D.11—Continued

	Protestant Respondents		Catholic Respondents	
	Chi-Sq.	γ	Chi-Sq.	γ
Science and Miscellaneous				
Know planet nearest sun	Control not needed			
Know discoverer of relativity	S	69	S	67
Know inventor telephone	Control not needed			
Know discoverer of polio vaccine	S	69	S	73
Index knowledge cancer:				
Know 4 plus cancer symptoms				
Know 1 plus cancer symptoms	Control not needed			
Know diabetes not contagious				
Heard about fluoridation				
Know "pyorrhea"				
Know how many feet in mile	S	51	S	39
Know how many pecks in bushel	S	21	NS	16
Know language of Brazil	S	54	S	24
Know medal for wounded in action	Control not needed			
Know electoral college	S	65	S	57

TABLE D.12. Academic Knowledge When Religion Is Controlled, for the 1960s

	Protestant Respondents		Catholic Respondents	
	Chi-Sq.	γ	Chi-Sq.	γ
Know cabinet positions	Control not needed			
Know electoral college	S	61	S	67
Know "filibuster"	S	62	S	52
Know no. terms president serves	S	33	NS	23
Know length of Senate term	S	44	S	43
Know length term in House	S	36	S	49

TABLE D.13. Knowledge of Public Affairs Among Native-Born Individuals

	Chi-Sq.	γ
Domestic Affairs—Persons		
Know Johnson home state	Control not needed	
Know Goldwater home state	NS	21
Know Kennedy's religion		
Know Kennedy home state		
Know Nixon's religion	Control not needed	
Know Nixon home state		
Domestic Affairs—Events		
Know party with election majority ('60)	Control not needed	
Know party with election majority ('64)	NS	51
Know party with election majority ('70)	S	32
Know party with congressional majority before election ('58)	S	42
Know party with congressional majority before election ('60)	Control not needed	
Know party with congressional majority before election ('64)	NS	21
Know party with congressional majority before election ('70)	S	35
Index: Knowledge of candidates (1958)	S	21
Index information: "Informed" on eight issues (1958)	S	24
Index political information (1970)	S	47
Know governor	Control not needed	
Know school board head	S	32
Know mayor	S	20
Know congressman	Control not needed	
Know two senators		
Index knowledge mainland China (1968)	S	54
Index knowledge mainland China (1964)	NS	34

TABLE D.14. Academic Knowledge Among Native-Born Individuals

	Chi-Sq.	γ
History		
Know Columbus	Control not needed	
Know Napoleon	S	73
Know Karl Marx	S	60
Know Gutenberg	S	57
Humanities		
Know Rubens	S	55
Know Shakespeare	S	72
Know Aristotle	Control not needed	
Know Freud	S	74
Know Tolstoy	S	66
Know Raphael	S	70
Know Beethoven	S	71
Civics		
Know length term in House	S	38
Know length Senate term	S	39
Know maximum term for president	S	33
Heard about fluoridation	S	63

TABLE D.15. Knowledge of Public Affairs When Class Origins Are Controlled

	Professional Fathers		Blue-Collar Fathers	
	Chi-Sq.	γ	Chi-Sq.	γ
Domestic Affairs—Persons				
Know Kennedy's religion	NS	00	NS	24
Know Kennedy home state	**	41	**	36
Know Nixon's religion	*	05	**	05
Know Nixon home state	**	42	**	47
Know Johnson home state	NS	09	NS	17
Know Goldwater home state	**	38	**	26
Know own two senators	*	16	***	20
Know own congressman	*	47	***	30
Know mayor own town	NS	27	NS	01
Know own governor	NS	11	NS	31
Know head of local school board	NS	08	**	25
Know two or more Supreme Court justices	*	28	**	47
Index of knowledge, candidates (1958)	NS	26	NS	23
Domestic Affairs—Events				
Index of political information (1966)	*	43	**	47
Index of political information (1970)	*	62	**	41
Index of information: "Informed" on eight issues (1958)	**	28	NS	14
Index of knowledge, mainland China (1964)	*	32	**	42
Heard of Taft-Hartley Law (1952)	**	58	*	30
Know party with congressional majority before election (1958)	*	41	**	31
Know party with congressional majority before election (1960)	NS	27	**	37
Know party with congressional majority before election (1964)	*	37	**	28
Know party with congressional majority before election (1970)	NS	06	**	32
Know party with election majority (1958)	NS	54	**	45
Know party with election majority (1960)	NS	19	**	27
Know party with election majority (1964)	NS	26	*	39
Know party with election majority (1970)	NS	04	**	32

TABLE D.16. Academic Knowledge When Class Origins Are Controlled

| | Professional Fathers | | Blue-Collar Fathers | |
	Chi-Sq.	γ	Chi-Sq.	γ
Know number of terms president can serve	NS	25	*	25
Know length of Senate term	NS	23	*	37
Know length of term in House	NS	23	**	41
Heard of fluoridation (1966)	NS	72	**	54
Heard of fluoridation (1959)	***	56	***	42
Know meaning of "pyorrhea"	NS	28	**	32
Index of Knowledge of Cancer	***	43	***	41
Know diabetes not contagious	**	30	NS	12
Vocabulary Test—1966:				
Can define "accustom"	NS	09	NS	24
Can define "edible"	**	77	**	63
Can define "pact"	**	51	**	48
Can define "cloistered"	**	44	**	39
Can define "allusion"	***	61	***	46
Can define "emanate"	**	45	**	59

TABLE D.17. Knowledge of Public Affairs When the Opportunities Provided by Class Position Are Equated, for the Early 1950s

	Within Professional Families		Within Blue-Collar Families	
	Chi-Sq.	γ	Chi-Sq.	γ
Domestic Affairs—Persons				
Heard J. Edgar Hoover			Control not needed	
Know Dean Acheson	S	61	S	40
Know George Marshall	S	50	S	55
Know own senators	S	15	S	14
Know Eisenhower	NS	25	S	34
Know Harriman	S	35	S	33
Know Kefauver	S	36	S	32
Know R. Kerr	NS	19	S	34
Know R. Russell	S	31	NS	17
Know Taft	S	27	S	35
Know Stevenson	NS	25	S	32
Know Earl Warren	S	32	S	49
Know vice president	S	47	S	48
Know Stassen	S	29	S	31
Domestic Affairs—Events				
Heard Taft-Hartley Law (3/49)	NS	56	S	39
Heard Taft-Hartley Law (6/49)	S	29	S	23
Heard Taft-Hartley Law (5/52)	S	48	S	36
Heard Taft-Hartley Law (10/52)	S	62	S	47
Heard Taft-Hartley Law (9/52)	S	48	S	32
Follow Taft-Hartley Law (10/53)	S	34	S	33
Know wiretapping (6/49)	NS	25	S	32
Know wiretapping (1/50)	S	50	NS	25
Heard criticism of AEC	S	43	S	32
Heard Hoover Commission (1/50)	S	41	S	54
Heard Hoover Commission (5/52)	S	38	S	38
Know Hoover Commission (1/50)	S	48	S	56
Know Hoover Commission (5/52)	S	28	S	25
Heard Truman health insurance plan	S	49	S	22
Know date political convention	S	29	S	26
Know convention cities	S	25	S	10
Know if all states hold congressional elections (1952)	NS	13	NS	20
Heard government's seizure steel industry	S	68	S	54
Information index	S	36	S	47
Know population of U.S.	NS	21	S	24
Foreign Affairs—Persons				
Know Tito (10/50)			Control not needed	
Know Tito (4/51)	S	43	S	43
Know Chiang Kai-shek (12/50)	S	40	S	28
Know Chiang Kai-shek (4/51)	S	44	S	42
Know Anthony Eden	S	40	S	31
Know Synghman Rhee	S	45	S	41
Know Franco	S	58	S	38

TABLE D.17—Continued

	Within Professional Families Chi-Sq. γ		Within Blue-Collar Families Chi-Sq. γ	
Foreign Affairs—Events				
Heard NATO (3/49)	S	53	S	19
Heard NATO (6/49)	S	54	S	32
Heard H-bomb (1/50)	S	62	S	45
Heard H-bomb (2/50)	S	85	S	65
Heard Chinese civil war (6/49)	S	64	S	38
Heard Chinese civil war (1/50)	NS	19	S	47
Know Atlantic Pact	S	43	S	41
Know 38th Parallel	S	31	S	34
Know Size Chinese Army	NS	35	NS	14
Know population of China (12/51)	Control not needed			
Know population of China (2/52)	S	27	S	33
Heard about hearings on Korea	NS	49	S	43
Know about trouble in Iran	S	56	S	39
Know Voice of America	S	48	S	49

TABLE D.18. Knowledge of Public Affairs When Opportunities Provided by Class Position Are Equated, for the Late 1950s

	Within Professional Families Chi-Sq. γ		Within Blue-Collar Families Chi-Sq. γ	
Domestic Affairs—Persons				
Name congressman	NS	15	NS	09
Know J. Edgar Hoover (1957)	S	56	S	59
Know head of FBI (1955)	S	71	S	50
Know vice president of U.S.	S	72	S	57
Heard W. Reuther	S	30	S	39
Heard G. Meany	S	15	S	27
Heard D. Beck	S	42	S	31
Heard H. Bridges	S	33	S	39
Heard J. L. Lewis	NS	17	S	25
Heard Petrillo	S	35	S	40
Heard D. McDonald	NS	02	NS	06
Index knowledge of candidates. "high" score	NS	15	NS	01
Domestic Affairs—Events				
Index information: "informed" on 8 issues	S	32	NS	19
Heard about fallout	NS	17	S	33
Heard about president's new budget	S	33	NS	15
Heard about Congress investigating unions	S	29	S	43
Know party election majority	NS	18	S	48
Know party congressional majority before election	NS	24	S	25
Foreign Affairs—Persons				
Know Nehru	S	47	S	41
Know Adenauer	S	47	S	29
Know prime minister of Britain	S	44	S	34

TABLE D.19. Knowledge of Public Affairs When the Opportunities Provided by Class Position Are Equated, for the Early 1960s

	Within Professional Families		Within Blue-Collar Families	
	Chi-Sq.	γ	Chi-Sq.	γ
Domestic Affairs—Persons				
Know Goldwater (3/63)	S	60	S	28
Know Goldwater (8/63)	S	26	S	32
Know Nixon	S	41	S	17
Know Wm. Scranton (3/63)	S	44	S	17
Know Wm. Scranton (8/63)	S	03	S	26
Know Romney (3/63)	S	58	S	48
Know Romney (8/63)	S	17	S	39
Know Milton Eisenhower	S	24	S	28
Know Mark Hatfield	NS	30	S	50
Know Harold Stassen	S	38	S	15
Know Thruston Morton	S	33	S	35
Know Rockefeller (3/63)	S	65	S	58
Know Rockefeller (8/63)	S	42	S	24
Know Clifford Case	NS	15	S	02
Know Johnson home state	NS	18	S	21
Know Goldwater home state	S	44	S	28
Know Kennedy's religion	Control not needed			
Know Kennedy home state	S	37	S	37
Know Nixon's religion	S	05	S	07
Know Nixon home state	S	37	S	44
Know J. Edgar Hoover	S	74	S	37
Know Elmo Roper	S	73	S	33
Know Frank Stanton	S	57	NS	10
Know Sam Lubell	S	81	NS	47
Domestic Affairs—Events				
Heard about civil rights rally	S	40	S	36
Party election majority (fall 1960)	S	16	NS	16
Know party election majority (fall 1964)	S	35	S	44
Know party congressional majority before election (fall 1960)	S	56	S	28
Know party congressional majority before election (fall 1964)	S	30	S	26
Foreign Affairs—Events				
Index knowledge about mainland China	S	35	S	39
Heard about nuclear test ban treaty (3/63)	S	53	S	15
Heard about nuclear test ban treaty (8/63)	NS	17	S	43
Heard about Berlin dispute	S	66	S	27

TABLE D.20. Knowledge of Public Affairs When the Opportunities Provided by Class Position Are Equated, for the Late 1960s

	Within Professional Families		Within Blue-Collar Families	
	Chi-Sq.	γ	Chi-Sq.	γ
Domestic Affairs—Persons				
Know 2 plus Supreme Court justices	S	34	S	42
Know secretary of state	S	48	S	35
Name governor of state (3/71)	S	35	S	33
Know governor (2/67)				
Know school board head	Control not needed			
Know mayor (11/66)	NS	09	S	25
Know mayor (2/67)	Control not needed			
Know congressman	S	13	S	26
Know two senators	NS	16	S	25
Know GOP vice presidential candidate	S	48	S	39
Know Democratic vice presidential candidate	S	33	S	33
Know Charles Percy	S	30	S	37
Know Nelson Rockefeller	S	35	S	39
Know county clerk	S	08	S	01
Know state senator	S	16	S	24
Domestic Affairs—Events				
High score index political information (fall 1966)	NS	35	S	54
High score index political information (fall 1968)	S	55	S	40
Know party with election majority (fall 1968)				
Know party with congressional majority before election (fall 1968)	Control not needed			
Know party with election majority (fall 1970)	NS	33	NS	13
Know party with congressional majority before election (fall 1970)	NS	36	NS	14
High score index political information (fall 1970)	S	63	S	31
Foreign Affairs—Persons				
Know Dean Rusk	S	46	S	45
Know Kosygin	S	48	S	42
Know Nguyen Cao Ky	S	50	S	35
Foreign Affairs—Events				
Know facts about mainland China	S	51	S	38
Heard about Vietnam War	S	59	S	45
Heard about Nationalist China	S	01	S	23
Know Chinese communism	S	43	S	50
Heard about Arab-Israeli conflict (5/67)	S	28	S	20
Heard about Arab-Israeli conflict (9/69)	S	61	S	40

TABLE D.21. Academic Knowledge When Opportunities Provided by Class Position Are Equated, for the Early 1950s

	Within Professional Families		Within Blue-Collar Families	
	Chi-Sq.	γ	Chi-Sq.	γ
History				
Know Columbus	S	45	S	66
Know Napoleon	S	70	S	56
Know Karl Marx	S	40	S	46
Know Gutenberg	S	47	S	50
Humanities				
Know Rubens	S	42	S	47
Know Shakespeare	S	87	S	75
Know Aristotle	S	54	S	69
Know Freud	S	62	S	65
Know Raphael	S	54	S	60
Know Beethoven	S	80	S	69
Know Plato	S	43	S	50
Know author **War and Peace** (2/52)	S	38	NS	29
Know Tolstoy (10/52)	S	41	S	49
Know Bach	S	34	S	43
Name a painter	S	37	S	46
Know author **Huckleberry Finn**	S	55	S	62
Know author **Tale of Two Cities**	S	50	S	63
Geography				
Know ocean between U.S. and U.K.	NS	51	S	43
Locate Formosa	S	29	S	44
Locate Manchuria	S	21	S	45
Locate Iran	NS	32	S	47
Locate Suez Canal	S	39	S	29
Civics				
Know number of senators	S	50	S	37
Know month president elected	NS	33	S	47
Know 3 branches federal government	S	47	S	47
Know term office of president	NS	47	S	50
Know meaning "GOP"	S	27	S	24
Know meaning "isolationism"	NS	14	S	41
Know electoral college	S	69	S	48
Know "filibuster" (1/49)	NS	36	S	47
Know "filibuster" (3/49)	S	52	S	30
Miscellaneous				
Know how many inches in yard	Control not needed			
Know how many 3¢ stamps in 75¢	S	30	S	34

TABLE D.22. Academic Knowledge When the Opportunities Provided by Class Position are Equated, for the Late 1950s

	Within Professional Families		Within Blue-Collar Families	
	Chi-Sq.	γ	Chi-Sq.	γ
History				
Know Bunker Hill war	S	42	S	45
Know Gettysburg war	S	45	S	43
Know Bulge war	S	47	S	49
Know Waterloo war	S	40	S	47
Know Florence Nightingale's profession	S	61	S	54
Know Lindbergh	S	52	S	40
Know city U.N. organized in	S	32	S	39
Know country Waterloo in	S	31	S	42
Geography				
Locate Kremlin	S	57	S	40
Locate Leaning Tower	S	56	S	43
Locate Eiffel Tower	S	60	S	45
Locate Pyramids	S	88	S	56
Locate Parthenon	S	63	S	47
Locate Mt. Vernon	NS	26	S	22
Know largest lake in North America	S	22	S	34
Know highest mountain in world	S	50	S	49
Know ocean Midway Island	S	66	S	46
Know Montana borders Canada	NS	15	S	13
Know Maine borders Canada	S	01	S	02
Know Michigan borders Canada	S	29	S	14
Know Minnesota borders Canada	NS	17	S	13
Know state named for president	NS	27	S	25
Know capital of Spain	S	47	S	40
Know New Delhi Capital of India	S	56	S	48
Humanities				
Know author **Tom Sawyer**	NS	36	S	63
Know author **Macbeth**	S	61	S	77
Know painter Rubens	S	53	S	27
Know Thackeray	S	55	S	41
Know composer **Messiah**	S	49	S	52
Know author **Midsummer Night's Dream**	S	56	S	69
Miscellaneous				
Know planet nearest sun	S	43	NS	21
Know discoverer relativity	S	68	S	65
Know inventor telephone	S	64	S	69
Know discoverer polio vaccine	S	67	S	62
Knowledge "automation" ("high score")	S	37	S	46
Index knowledge cancer:				
Know 4 plus cancer symptoms	S	29	S	42
Know 1 plus cancer symptoms				
Know diabetes not contagious	Control not needed			
Heard about fluoridation	S	63	S	54
Know "pyorrhea"	Control not needed			
Know feet in mile	S	29	S	50
Know pecks in bushel	NS	15	NS	02
Know language of Brazil	S	46	S	37
Know medal for wounded in action	S	48	S	36

TABLE D.23. Academic Knowledge When the Opportunities Provided by Class Position Are Equated, for the 1960s

	Within Professional Families		Within Blue-Collar Families	
	Chi-Sq.	γ	Chi-Sq.	γ
Know cabinet positions	S	45	S	38
Know electoral college	S	64	S	54
Know "filibuster"	S	52	S	51
Know no. terms president serves	NS	32	S	22
Know length of Senate term	S	47	S	26
Know length of term in House	S	33	S	28

Notes

NOTES TO CHAPTER 1: INTRODUCTION

1. Ralph Waldo Emerson, essay on "Education."
2. Christopher Jencks et al., *Inequality: A Reassessment of the Effect of Family and Schooling in America* (New York: Basic Books, 1972), p. 89.
3. Kenneth Feldman and Theodore Newcomb, *The Impact of College on Students*, 2 vols. (San Francisco: Jossey-Bass, 1969), 1: 308. This is not to deny that there are difficulties in drawing large and good samples of students and conducting any follow-up at all or to underrate the importance and heroic scale of recent investigations. For example, Sewell and his associates have been engaged in a long-term program of research in which a statewide sample of about 9,000 Wisconsin high school seniors in 1957 was followed up after seven years. Project Scope is following the careers of about 90,000 students who in 1966 were in the ninth and twelfth grades in four states. For summaries of these follow-ups of school populations, see William Sewell, "Inequality of Opportunity for Higher Education," *American Sociological Review* 36 (1971): 793–809. The International Evaluation of Educational Achievement provides another illustration of recent research that has these same limitations, despite its monumental scope. In 1964, a sample of about 130,000 pupils then enrolled in secondary schools in twelve countries were given achievement tests in mathematics. By now the evaluation has been extended to about a quarter of a million students in twenty-two countries who have been tested in six subject areas. By a sophisticated design and elegant statistical analysis, the influence of home background and a variety of school and student variables on achievement have been examined, but still the study cannot speak to the *enduring* effects. See, for example, Torsten Husen, ed. *International Study of Achievement in Mathematics*, vols. 1, 2 (New York: Wiley, 1967). For an illustration of a college student follow-up, consider the elaborate giant study by the American Council on Education, part of their Cooperative Institutional Research Program, which has already collected data from more than two million individuals. College students have been measured upon entrance and four years later at graduation. The elegance of the analysis and the scale of the inquiry notwithstanding, it is clear that the investigation is limited to a captive population which is not traced beyond the confines of its college environment and into adult life. For a summary, see Alexander W. Astin, "The Measured Effects of Higher Education," *Annals* 404 (November 1972): 1–20.
4. For reviews of such findings, see Jencks et al., *Inequality*; Eli Ginzberg and Douglas Bray, *The Uneducated* (New York: Columbia Univer-

sity Press, 1953); Otis D. Duncan, David L. Featherman, and Beverly Duncan, *Socioeconomic Background and Achievement* (New York: Seminar Press, 1972).

5. *National Assessment of Educational Progress: A Project of the Education Commission of the States* (Washington, D.C.: Government Printing Office, 1970), Report no. 1, p. 5.

6. In 1972, in an otherwise enthusiastic account of the National Assessment stressing the special benefits of the trend measurements contemplated, Henry S. Dyer injects this note: "at this writing the question is still moot whether continuing support and sponsorship can be found so as to prevent the project from becoming just another single shot survey" (Dyer, "Some Thoughts about Future Studies," in *On Equality of Educational Opportunity*, ed. Frederick Mosteller and Daniel P. Moynihan [New York: Knopf, Vintage Books, 1972], pp. 389–90). The same overwhelming sense of uncertainty afflicts one as he contemplates the design of Project Talent. Half a million ninth- and twelfth-grade children across the nation were tested in 1960, and follow-ups were planned for five-, ten-, and twenty-five year intervals. Thus, if the plans are realized, by 1985 we shall know something about the long-term changes that take us up to about age forty-five in the older of the two cohorts studied. That gloom rather than uncertainty may be in order is suggested by the fact that the five-year follow-up in 1965 achieved only a 32% response rate from the sample.

7. Withey et al. focused mainly on college education and its effects over a broad domain of attitudes and behavior, with little special attention to knowledge and none to the duration of the effects. Stember dealt exclusively with prejudice and the effects of education on prejudiced attitudes and beliefs. Glenn's interest in trends over time in the effects of education brings him closest to us, but his inquiry was relatively small in scale and covered the domain of attitudes and behavior, not knowledge. Schramm and Wade mapped the state of public knowledge and its many correlates, including education, rather than attempting to assess the impact of education throughout adult life. All are confined to American data. See Norval Glenn, "The Trend in Differences in Attitudes and Behavior by Educational Level," *Sociology of Education*, summer 1966, pp. 255–75; Wilbur Schramm et al., "Knowledge and the Public Mind: A Preliminary Study of the Distribution and Sources of Science, Health, and Public Affairs Knowledge in the American Public," mimeographed (Stanford: Institute for Communication Research, 1967); Serena Wade and Wilbur Schramm, "The Mass Media as Sources of Public Affairs, Science and Health Knowledge," *Public Opinion Quarterly* 33 (1969): 197–209; Charles H. Stember, *Education and Attitude Change* (New York: Institute of Human Relations Press, 1961); Stephen Withey et al., *A Degree and What Else: Correlates and Consequences of a College Education* (New York: McGraw-Hill, 1973). In the opening paragraph of their 1967 monograph, Schramm and Wade suggest again the gloomy prospect for primary research on the problem: "These secondary analyses . . . were undertaken originally in preparation for a major field study of public knowledge. Now that this study has been postponed for what may prove to be a considerable time, we are making the preliminary results available" (p. 4). For a review of the general method and opportunities of secondary analyses, see Herbert Hyman, *Secondary Analysis of Sample Surveys: Principles, Procedures and Potentialities* (New York: Wiley, 1972).

8. The 1960 census indicated that about 10% of individuals in their eighties lived in institutions. Among individuals seventy-five to eighty, the figure is about 6%, and among individuals in their sixties, it is less than 3%. Around 1960, the rate of blindness, deafness, and paralysis was double or more among individuals aged seventy-five or over, compared with those sixty-five to seventy-four. In the latter group, about 3%, 12%, and 2% of the individuals had these respective impairments. For these and other findings on the aged, see Matilda W. Riley and Anne Foner, *Aging and Society* (New York: Russell Sage Foundation, 1968), 1: 141, 206, passim.

9. In the period under study, the death rate for individuals over seventy-five was twice as high as that of individuals under seventy. See Riley and Foner, *Aging*, passim.

10. From many historical sources, we have actually prepared composite pictures of the schooling and early lives of our sixteen cohorts as essential background for interpreting our findings. Unlike Galton's, they are not, as he put it, "artistic in expression" or "beautifully idealized," and they are too unwieldy to present. But they did provide enough evidence that indeed there are many and wide contrasts represented in our groups. About mass communication, it is easy to present summary figures.

Before 1930, fewer than half of American households had radio. Between 1930 and 1950, ownership mounted to the point where radio was practically universal in American homes. In 1950, fewer than 10% of American households had television; but by 1955, about two-thirds had television. See, for example, Lee Bogart, *The Age of Television* (New York: Ungar, 1958).

11. These figures could have been derived from our own sample survey data but are taken from the Census Bureau estimates for the *white* population, based either on the decennial census or on their very large sample surveys. See *Current Population Reports*, ser. P–20, no. 207 (March 1970); *U.S. Census of Population: 1950*, vol. 4, Special Reports, pt. 5, chap. B (Washington, D.C.: Government Printing Office, 1953).

12. See, for example, the Glenn, Stember, and Withey studies cited earlier.

13. See Appendix C for the full listing of all surveys used and the exact wording of each question employed. Since a few of the 250 tests of knowledge involved an index that was itself a composite of several questions, the original number of questions exceeded 250. Six vocabulary tests were drawn from a survey; individuals over forty-five were not given those tests. Thus the comparisons involving all four cohorts apply only to the other 244 tests. Since the comparisons of vocabulary could be made only for the two younger cohorts, the total number of age-specific comparisons of knowledge of groups contrasted in education was 988 for 1949–71. If we add the four items piggybacked on the 1974 survey, where again comparisons were made for the four age cohorts, the total number of comparisons becomes 1,004. If we also count the comparisons of spelling ability (to be reported in chapter 6, in our discussion of Canadian-American effects), where the mean score on a spelling test is examined for *three* age cohorts, the grand total is 1,007 age-specific comparisons of knowledge among American adults contrasted in education.

14. In effect, a similar procedure was employed in the current National Assessment. Although the total test in any area of knowledge is very lengthy, in order not to burden the respondent excessively it was divided into ten "packages," each containing a much smaller number of items

administered to an equivalent subsample of fewer than a thousand individuals. Thus here, again, the comprehensive profile of knowledge over all items, like ours, is a composite that refers to the category of young adults, which is built up from the answers of many subsamples.

15. A number of additional past surveys rich in knowledge questions were known to us, but despite persistent efforts we could not locate or reconstruct the materials without prohibitive costs. For example, one of the major surveys which Schramm and Wade used had disappeared from the two locations where it might have been. Fortunately, their findings can at least be cited as supplementary evidence.

16. The supplementary analysis of American and Canadian education is based on a multiple-item test of spelling ability, and thus belongs in the domain of academic knowledge. Thus the total number of tests made in this domain over all periods is ninety-three.

17. Readers will recognize the similarity of this to Hovland's classic "effectiveness index." See Carl Hovland et al. "The Baseline for Measurement of Percentage Change," in *Experiments on Mass Communication* (Princeton: Princeton University Press, 1949), pp. 284–92.

18. Feldman and Newcomb, *Impact of College*, p. 309. It should be noted that Feldman and Newcomb do not indicate the full extent of the difficulties of implementing a true experimental design. They treat only the issue of the *initial* equation of the several groups. In experiments of such long duration, a host of factors extraneous to the treatments can destroy the perfection of the original design. Differential mortality and loss of cases that bias the later comparisons are examples. Feldman and Newcomb describe "a next-best design" but again they note "Only one study is known to us that even approximates this second-choice design." In *short-term* studies of students, let us grant for the sake of argument the rather shaky assumption that these have been set up so as to establish the influence of schooling, and let us ignore the limitations of numbers, mode of sampling, and quality of measurements. Nevertheless, all such studies suffer from the terrible indeterminacy already noted. Whatever influence may have been established at a given point may be utterly transitory or be dissipated with the passage of time. And if no influence is established, the defender of the educational system can always retort that the investigator caught the process at too incipient and inchoate a stage. If he only had waited a bit longer or a lot longer, the seeds that had been planted might have matured and flowered.

19. Current research on the short-term effects of *higher* education on *students* (not older adults) is, in fact, based mainly on various kinds of inferential, nonexperimental approaches. This very busy enterprise is characterized by a great deal of elaborate, multivariate statistical analysis, but controversy rages over the question of the best methods for treating or "purifying" the data. Although some large-scale studies are following the clever strategy of "secondary analysis," exploiting the data from routine testing programs at many colleges that are being deposited in special data banks, ironically, no attention seems to have been paid to the data available in adult sample surveys. Much of the research focuses on subtle questions of the influence of particular types of colleges. Particular investigators are generally limited to one or a few colleges (frequently their own institutions), and the total noncollegiate youth population is out of the reach of all of them, since there has never been a point where all have been tested for college entrance. Thus by necessity investigators are limited to studies of different types of college environ-

ments and rarely have any ability to generalize about the effects of various amounts of education. See, for example, Alexander W. Astin and Robert J. Panos, "A National Research Data Bank for Higher Education," *Educational Record* 47 (1966): 5–17; Kenneth A. Feldman, "Studying the Impacts of Colleges on Students," *Sociology of Education* 42 (1969): 207–37; Id., "Some Methods for Assessing College Impacts," *Sociology of Education* 44 (1970): 133–50.

20. It is possible to argue that the rise in the rate of *higher* education among the more recent cohorts simply represents the enrollment of more individuals from the very same select social groups as in earlier times. For example, instead of a certain percent of the upper classes going to college, now double that percent of the upper classes go, accounting completely for the much higher attainment in the population generally or in a given age cohort. Even for those who have gone to college, it is hard thus to account for the change; but certainly it is not tenable that the 50% to 70% of the more recent cohorts who have attained high school, a huge group, could be drawn exclusively from the smallish select strata in the population. Also note that our argument relates to the *rate* of attainment over time and not to the absolute numbers which could be accounted for simply by population growth. For evidence bearing on *college* attainment, see Sewell, "Inequality," especially n. 10. Beverly Duncan's evidence is more relevant. For a national sample of *males*, she finds, by analysis of various cohorts, that the influence of social origins on attainment of education, *below the college level*, has not changed over a considerable time span. However, our data pertain to both sexes and refer to a much longer period over which selective attainment could indeed have diminished. See Duncan, "Trends in Output and Distribution of Schooling," in *Indicators of Social Change*, ed. Eleanor B. Sheldon and Wilbert Moore (New York: Russell Sage Foundation, 1968), pp. 648–53. Studies by the International Evaluation of Educational Achievement provide comparative national evidence supporting our argument. Of eight countries studied in 1964, the United States had the highest proportion, 70%, of the total age cohort enrolled in the last year of "high school" (preuniversity year). An index of social selectivity was computed by reference to the percentages of the total student body at two grade levels drawn from higher-class families. An increase in that percentage as one moves from the thirteen-year-old pupils to the pupils in the last year of secondary school demonstrates the selective attrition of children from the lower classes and yields a high index of selectivity. After examining the relation between the proportion of the total age group being brought up to the preuniversity year (called "retention") and the selectivity index, Husen remarks: "One is justified in making the generalization that the more retentive a school system is, the less selective it is from a social point of view. . . . We must also bear in mind that, as retention approaches 100%, social selectivity must disappear, since almost the whole age group is at school." Of course, if social bias were already extremely *high* at the thirteen-year-old stage, the index would be insensitive and the general conclusion would not be warranted. In fact, in all the countries studied, bias is low at age thirteen, and the U.S. compared to the other seven countries shows the least social bias in the student body enrolled in the *last* year of high school in 1964 (Husen, *International Achievement in Mathematics,* 2:112). To be sure, our argument calls for consideration of one additional complexity, historical changes in the composition of the general population. Even if formerly

disadvantaged groups had improved their educational prospects, if their *numbers* had also declined so radically over the period under scrutiny relative to other groups, the bigger chances they had could be more than offset by their fewer members in the population. Then the net effect of multiplying their vanishing kind by their higher probability of better education could be that the better-educated stratum in the recent period had become *more* "biased" in social composition. Patently, the problem cannot arise for women or Catholics, whose numbers have remained relatively constant. The *occupational* structure of the population, however, has changed radically. There are indeed more professionals than formerly, but, too, there are many more industrial workers. These groups have all grown at the expense of farmers, whose numbers have dwindled markedly. Ironically, in that singular respect, the better-educated stratum within the recent cohorts has a smaller proportion of individuals with farm origins, even though a farmer's child born in the recent period has greatly increased his chances for education. Illustrative data for contrasted cohorts in one 1959 survey reveal the complex pattern. In the cohort aged sixty-one to seventy-two (thus born 1887–98), 51% were children of farmers. Although the probability that such a child graduated from high school (or went on to college) was only thirteen chances in one hundred, 35% of all high school graduates in this cohort were farmers' children. In contrast, in the cohort aged twenty-five to thirty-six (born 1923–34), the proportion from farm origins had dwindled to 25%. By that time, the odds in favor of such a child's graduating from high school had quadrupled—to fifty-four chances in one hundred—but they were only 20% of all high school graduates in the cohort. Among children of blue-collar workers, no such process has occurred. Within the oldest cohort, they were 33% of the total. The odds back then for their graduating from high school were eighteen in a hundred and they accounted for 30% of the high school graduates. In the youngest cohort, the proportion from blue-collar origins had *grown* to 47%; and their chances of graduating from high school had increased to sixty-three in one hundred. They therefore composed 44%, a larger portion of the high school graduates. Although the risk that other types of selectivity account for the superior knowledge of the educated has automatically lessened in the more recent cohorts, the danger that *urban* origins account for the superiority of the educated has automatically increased. But if that were the real explanation of our findings, then the apparent effects of education should be smaller in the earlier cohorts studied, and this, as we shall see, is not the case.

21. Although religion is omitted from a considerable number of surveys, we are, relatively speaking, in far better shape to examine this important variable in secondary analyses of sample surveys than many educational researchers. In normal practice, for various understandable reasons, a student's religion is not a matter of official record; thus evidence about the variable is often lacking. As a dramatic example—the main Coleman report, presumably for policy reasons, did not record the religion of the children, and no such analyses could therefore be made.

22. R. A. Fisher, *The Design of Experiments*, 4th ed. (Edinburgh and London: Oliver and Boyd; 1947), p. 2; italics in the original.

23. William H. Sewell and Robert M. Hauser, "Causes and Consequences of Higher Education: Models of the Status Attainment Process," *American Journal of Agricultural Economics* 54 (1972): 853.

24. Robert L. Thorndike and George H. Gallup, "Verbal Intelligence of the American Adult," *Journal of General Psychology* 30 (1944): 75–85. An adaptation of this test was attached to one of the NORC surveys.

25. Some studies fall between the two stools. They catch neither large, unrestricted samples of adults of mature ages nor children at a young enough age to measure the influence of early intelligence on subsequent attainment. Consequently, the conclusions they report may be questionable or, at best, have very narrow applicability. Such would be the case where the scores on the Armed Forces Qualifications Test have been taken as indicative of intelligence. These are measurements of individuals who have had considerable education, and perforce apply only to males within a narrow age band who have all the characteristics accompanying eligibility for military service. For an example of such studies, see Zvi Griliches and William M. Mason, "Education, Income, and Ability," *Journal of Political Economy* 80, pt. 2 (1972): S74–S103. They are punctilious in stressing that "our ability measure is not ideal because it is obtained after most of the formal schooling has been completed" (p. S76). Consequently, they examine only that increment of education that is subsequent to the recruit's military service and time of testing. The generalizability of the findings is correspondingly limited.

26. "Trends in Schooling," p. 654.

27. "Inequality of Opportunity," p. 799; italics supplied. For a cohort of white *males* born at a slightly *earlier* date, the contribution of intelligence to educational attainment is estimated to be slightly higher, but the amount of variance explained by background and intelligence is of about the same magnitude. See Duncan, "Trends in Schooling," p. 654. Further analyses of these same data supplemented by analyses of other data from a cohort of white *male* veterans aged twenty-five to thirty-four in 1964 and from a sample of white *males* in Detroit are reported in Duncan, Featherman, and Duncan, *Socioeconomic Background and Achievement*, chap. 5.

28. William H. Sewell and Vimal P. Shah, "Parents' Education and Children's Educational Aspirations and Achievements," *American Sociological Review* 33 (1968): 205–6. See also their "Socioeconomic Status, Intelligence, and the Attainment of Higher Education," *Sociology of Education* 40 (1967): 1–23.

29. Karl Alexander and Bruce K. Eckland, "Sex Differences in the Educational Attainment Process," *American Sociological Review* 39 (1974): 668–682.

30. James W. Trent and Leland L. Medsker, *Beyond High School: A Psychosociological Study of 10,000 High School Graduates* (San Francisco: Jossey-Bass, 1968), p. 25.

31. Irving Lorge, "Schooling Makes a Difference," *Teachers College Record* 46 (1944): 489.

32. Ibid., pp. 483–92; Katherine P. Bradway and Clare W. Thompson, "Intelligence at Adulthood: A Twenty-Five Year Follow-up," *Journal of Educational Psychology* 53 (1962): 1–14; Viola E. Benson, "The Intelligence and Later Scholastic Success of Sixth-Grade Pupils," *School and Society* 55 (1942): 163–67; Duncan, Featherman, and Duncan, *Socioeconomic Background and Achievement*, especially p. 83.

33. For a comprehensive summary of the early evidence plus recent nationwide evidence on religious differences in intellectual orientation,

see A. Lewis Rhodes and Charles B. Nam, "The Religious Context of Educational Expectations," *American Sociological Review* 35 (1970): 253–67. The evidence about class differences in such orientations is so voluminous that it defies summarization. For data drawn from many nationwide surveys that would be representative mainly of the earlier cohorts in our study, see H. Hyman, "The Value Systems of Different Classes," in *Class, Status and Power*, ed. Reinhard Bendix and S. M. Lipset (Glencoe, Ill.: Free Press, 1953), pp. 426–42.

34. See, for example, H. M. Blalock, Jr., "Some Implications of Random Measurement Error for Causal Inferences," *American Journal of Sociology* 71 (1965): 37–47.

35. The scarcity is conveyed by Erskine's periodic summaries of poll results, a regular feature in the *Public Opinion Quarterly*. In one of these on "textbook knowledge," her tabulation indicates sixty-four such questions in 1951–62, "virtually all available questions that have ever tested the nation's 'textbook' knowledge." In the period tabulated, the decline was very rapid, only four such questions being noted by her in the last interval entered, 1959–62. See Hazel Gaudet Erskine, "The Polls: Textbook Knowledge," *Public Opinion Quarterly* 27 (1963): 133.

36. For a summary of the special problems of error in surveys of the very aged, see Bernice C. Starr, "Some Problems of Research on Age," in *A Sociology of Age Stratification*, ed. Matilda White Riley, Marilyn Johnson, and Ann Foner (New York: Russell Sage Foundation, 1972), passim.

37. H. Hyman, W. J. Cobb, J. J. Feldman, C. W. Hart, and C. Stember, *Interviewing in Social Research* (Chicago: University of Chicago Press, 1954), p. 161. For a recent study done in the North of changes in the phenomenon and a careful review of the problem, see Howard Schuman and Jean M. Converse, "The Effects of Black and White Interviewers on Black Responses in 1968," *Public Opinion Quarterly* 35 (1971): 44–68.

38. For a description of the SRC designs, see the report from one of the surveys we used in A. Campbell, G. Gurin, and W. Miller, *The Voter Decides* (New York: Row, Peterson, 1954), pp. 227–35. For the descriptions of the two major variations on the basic design used by NORC, see the reports of two of the surveys we used: Sidney Verba and Norman Nie, *Participation in America, Political Democracy and Social Equality* (New York: Harper & Row, 1972), pp. 345–49; John W. C. Johnstone and Ramon J. Rivera, *Volunteers for Learning: A Study of the Educational Pursuits of American Adults* (Chicago: Aldine, 1965), pp. 482–93. For a description applicable to the Gallup designs midway through our period, see Paul Perry, "Election Survey Procedures of the Gallup Poll," *Public Opinion Quarterly* 24 (1960): 531–35. It should be stressed that wherever one of the original surveys included a supplementary, special sample or a given cell was inflated for special analysis, we employed only the core, national sample. At times, the Gallup Poll has used various weighting schemes to improve the representativeness of its samples, the weights being based on education and "times-at-home." Since our design controls education and controls age (often associated with times-at-home) on top of eliminating the very old and the very young, and since weighting usually makes little difference even in aggregate percentages, we have used the raw, unweighted data in most of the surveys. A small number of Gallup surveys, however, were weighted in a way that made it difficult

to reconstruct the raw data. We therefore used the weighted samples in those few instances. While this decision somewhat inflated the reported Ns (particularly for the low-educated groups), it did not systematically affect the percentages on knowledge.

39. For a review of the problem see Norval Glenn, "Problems of Comparability in Trend Studies with Opinion Poll Data," *Public Opinion Quarterly* 34 (1970): 82–94; Norval Glenn and R. Zody, "Cohort Analysis with National Survey Data," *Gerontologist* 10 (1970): 233–40. These papers demonstrate that unadjusted comparisons of age cohorts drawn from earlier and later surveys respectively implicate samples of different social composition. As these analysts point out, if the cohorts are adjusted for the changing educational composition of the samples, the error is contained. By definition, this happens in our case, since our cohort analyses are for groups specified as to education.

40. See the introductory remarks to the census publications cited earlier.

41. See Aage Clausen, "Response Validity: Vote Report," *Public Opinion Quarterly* 32 (1968–69): 596, table 1.

42. Hyman et al., *Interviewing*, p. 247; Joseph Hochstim and Karen Renne, "Reliability of Response in a Socio-Medical Population Study," *Public Opinion Quarterly* 35 (1971): 69–79. For another study where the interval was three years—admitting of the possibility that respondents had obtained additional education—about two-thirds of the respondents gave truly identical answers. But in this study practically all the discrepancies were between reporting some education at a given level and reporting completion of that level. Thus, for the three broad levels used in most of our analyses, the unreliability is almost nil. In this study there seems little evidence of bias; the changes in reports are about equally distributed between reporting more and less education than previously. See Paul Haberman and Jill Sheinberg, "Education Reported in Interviews," *Public Opinion Quarterly* 30 (1966): 295–302; Paul Siegel and Robert Hodge, "A Causal Approach to the Study of Measurement Error," in *Methodology in Social Research*, ed. Hubert M. and A. Blalock (New York: McGraw-Hill, 1968), pp. 30, 37.

43. Don Cahalan, "Correlates of Respondent Accuracy in the Denver Validity Survey," *Public Opinion Quarterly* 32 (1968): 610, 617.

44. Hochstim and Renne, "Reliability of Response."

45. Hyman, *Secondary Analysis*, pp. 99–101, 119.

46. Another such demonstration is reported by Erskine, where self-reported awareness of Dr. Salk's discovery of polio vaccine in two surveys separated by a very brief interval ran 96% and 97% (*Public Opinion Quarterly* 27 [1963]: 498). Another finding suggests the high reliability of self-reports of participation in adult education activities. Two surveys of such activities by independent survey agencies working at *about the same time* yielded estimates of 15% and 12% respectively. See B. Berelson, "In the Presence of Culture," *Public Opinion Quarterly* 28 (1964): 7.

NOTES TO CHAPTER 2: ENDURING EFFECTS ON KNOWLEDGE

1. A *maximum general* estimate of the proportion of the group treated as having had elementary school education when in fact they had had no schooling would be that it is no more than 4%. In the white adult population alive around 1950, from which our samples for the first period

were drawn, that would be the reasonable estimate one could derive from the census sources. From the samples in our own surveys, where it is possible to distinguish the two component groups (drawn from a slightly different universe than that of the census), the estimate of the proportion with no schooling would be slightly lower. Because of the expansion of educational opportunity and attrition of older individuals, in the white population sampled in our surveys for *later* periods, the "no school" component of those treated as having had elementary schooling would be an even smaller proportion. By the same token, the proportion within the younger cohorts is even lower, but among the older cohorts it is slightly higher. In any case, such a small component cannot have much weight in the estimates of knowledge reported in the occasional surveys where they were not eliminated and could hardly begin to account for the large differences observed in the comparisons by educational level. For some modes of comparison, the error even works to make the findings more conservative. For example, when the prevalence of knowledge among young individuals who are treated as having only elementary education is compared to that of old individuals thus treated, any waning with age overstates the difference, since the old are handicapped in the comparison by the incorporation of a slightly higher proportion of totally nonschooled individuals. For the census findings, see the references cited in chap. 1, n. 11.

2. Depending on the period and cohort examined, between 30% and 45% of the "elementary school" group had fewer than eight years of education. As will be shown later on the basis of a dozen tests drawn from surveys which maintained the distinction (see n. 8 below), graduates of elementary school are consistently more knowledgeable than those who had less schooling, but the differences are modest in magnitude. Thus, if the comparisons of the high school and elementary school groups to be presented had been restricted to elementary school *graduates*, the contrast in their knowledge would not have been so sharp. But it is safe to assert that the general conclusions from this one mode of analysis would have remained the same. The inability to distinguish elementary school dropouts from graduates in many of the surveys has varying implications for the conclusions drawn from particular modes of analysis, which will be noted at appropriate points.

3. The *p* values are those for a two-tail test, which may be regarded as a conservative estimate of the significance.

4. Some obscurity and ambiguity are introduced inevitably by the use of our two summary statistics and would have been by any others we might have chosen. Comparisons of age cohorts on the very same item of knowledge present no special problem. However, in comparisons across surveys—for example, when time periods or types of content are compared—the number of cells in the matrix and their corresponding sizes may change because of differences in the fineness of coding and scoring from survey to survey, and the value of gamma or chi-square is correspondingly affected. Small differences observed in comparisons of the statistics may simply represent such artifacts. An inspection of the values obtained from the matrices of different size derived from the full distributions on the variables suggests that the large number of cells used in our computations tend to give a more conservative figure for chi-square and gamma then would be the case if a certain amount of reasonable collapsing of the distribution had been done. On this matter, note the remarks by Goodman and Kruskal in the paper where they introduced

gamma; L. Goodman and W. Kruskal, "Measures of Association for Cross Classifications," *Journal of the American Statistical Association* 49 (1954): 732–764. See also R. Somers, "A New Assymetric Measure of Association for Ordinal Variables," *American Sociological Review* 27 (1962): 809.

5. The reader may also have observed that there are occasional entries of zero in the second set of columns, indicating that the two respective groups are exactly equal in knowledge about the item. To make a fair summary of the number of departures from the usual monotonic pattern, we would need to reckon these zeroes into the accounts. There are only five such entries for each of the two youngest cohorts, and four for the cohort aged forty-nine to sixty. But among the oldest cohort there are twelve such entries, ten of them involving instances where the high school and college group are equally knowledgeable and both are superior to the elementary school group.

6. The word "difficulty" is used broadly and does not imply that any single cause accounts for that difficulty. The item may be difficult because considerable intellect is required to master it, because it is not *inherently* that difficult but is in a sphere that was not emphasized or taught in grade school or taught poorly, because information was not disseminated sufficiently by other institutions, or because it is so trivial or specialized or esoteric that ordinary people have no interest in learning it. When the index is a bigger number, it means that more individuals have answered it correctly. Thus, as the index moves closer to *zero*, it refers to a more difficult item. Of course, in comparing such indexes across surveys from different periods, given the method of derivation, we assume that the composition of the aggregate sample of least-educated individuals is constant. The average level of difficulty of the battery of test items for all content areas and periods is as follows:

	Average Difficulty			
	Early 1950s	Late 1950s	Early 1960s	Late 1960s
Domestic public persons	30	42	34	42
Domestic events	36	54	55	31
Foreign public persons	29	29	—	45
Foreign events	37	—	68	59
Academic: History	38	35	—	—
Humanities	14	8	—	—
Geography	34	40	—	—
Civics	40	—	21	31
Science and miscellaneous	83	45	—	—

For the analysis presented in table 10, areas were omitted if the battery of test items at both time points was very short.

7. This result may appear contradicted by the findings presented in table 9, where the number of reversals of sign when each of the cohorts was examined separately added up to a much larger number, even when only *three* levels of education were compared. One may expect a higher number of reversals when *five* levels of education are compared. However, the contradiction is apparent, not real. In table 9, departures from the monotonic pattern involving more than one reversal for a given test item are entered as many times as they occur, whereas they would be counted only once for the tally in the text. But more obvious is the fact that most of the reversals noted in the table apply only to the oldest co-

hort. Since the decline in percentage points is usually so small in that subgroup, and the oldest cohort so small a component of the aggregate sample, the monotonic pattern observed at the aggregate level remains unaffected.

8. The reader will recall that many of the surveys did not distinguish between graduates of elementary school and those who dropped out before completing eight years of education, Thus, whether the monotonic pattern would apply over the *entire* range of education and, correspondingly, whether the dropouts from elementary school are not qualitatively different from the graduates, cannot be assessed routinely. However, a sufficient number of surveys did enumerate and code educational attainment finely enough to make such tests. Comparisons between the dropouts at several levels of primary school and the graduates on a dozen items from five Gallup Poll surveys establish, almost without exception, that the pattern is monotonic. With each additional increment at this level, there is some gain in knowledge. The findings are as follows:

	Percentage Informed among Elementary School Individuals Whose Education Terminated at		
	0–4 Years	5–7 Years	8 Years
Survey 649 (8/61)	(58)	(169)	(451)
Know electoral college	7%	18%	26%
Survey 669 (3/63)	(99)	(330)	(651)
Know Wm. Scranton	0%	11%	27%
Know Goldwater	2	27	32
Know Romney	3	8	16
Know Rockefeller	17	52	76
Survey 746 (5/67)	(33)	(226)	(390)
Heard of Arab-Israeli conflict	64%	83%	85%
Know Charles Percy	0	23	31
Know Rockefeller	52	63	78
Survey 747 (7/67)	(67)	(196)	(330)
Know Dean Rusk	42%	58%	58%
Know Kosygin	37	44	55
Know Nguyen Cao Ky	9	27	34
Survey 788 (9/69)	(18)	(74)	(134)
Heard of Arab-Israeli Conflict	88%	70%	81%

9. NORC had used ten of the words from the original test. For purposes of economy, we used only six of these ten, choosing them "blindly" at various levels of difficulty, based on the original publications.

10. NORC had included eight occupations in the testing done in the original survey. Again for economy, we chose four blindly but for their contrasting locations in the class structure, to test the hypothesis presented in the text.

NOTES TO CHAPTER 3: THE INFLUENCE OF OTHER VARIABLES

1. For national evidence on changes in religious identity, see Herbert Hyman, *Secondary Analysis of Sample Surveys* (New York: Wiley, 1972), p. 119.

2. For data leading to such estimates, see Abbott L. Ferriss, *Indicators of Trends in American Education* (New York: Russell Sage Foundation, 1969), pp. 21–22.

3. The lack of linearity creates a problem methodologically in applying multivariate correlation procedures for estimating the magnitude of the gross and net effects of education. However, it dramatized for us the phenomenon of differential effects of various amounts of education and led to the substantive studies reported in chapter 5.

4. See, for example, A. O. Haller, "Education and the Occupational Achievement Process," in *Rural Poverty in the United States: A Report by the President's National Advisory Commission on Rural Poverty* (Washington, D.C.: Government Printing Office, 1968), pp. 149–68. The low educational attainment of individuals with rural origins stems to some extent from differences in the racial and socioeconomic composition of rural and urban areas and perhaps even from differences in the sex ratios. Since our overall analysis is confined to whites, and sex and social class origins were controlled, some of the influence of residential origins has already been eliminated without direct control of the variable.

5. Among those with farmer fathers, 8% report growing up in small or large cities. So as not to overload the text and the reader, and to reduce the laboriousness and costs of so many additional tabulations, we shall not present comprehensive evidence that educational effects persist among individuals from a farm milieu, as was demonstrated for those with urban origins in table 20. To illustrate the consistent and large effects within the farmer group, we present the detailed distributions for the four items of academic knowledge in the 1974 piggyback.

Among White Adults Who Grew up with
Farm Fathers, Percentage Informed on:

	(N)	Inventor Telephone	Florence Nightingale's Profession	Bunker Hill War	Location Mt. Vernon
Elementary school	80	53%	33%	13%	51%
Some high school	47	77	49	17	57
Completed high school	72	86	78	28	74
Some college	24	92	79	42	83
Completed college	18	89	100	56	94
Gamma		.54	.60	.48	.40
Chi-Square (p)		<.001	<.001	<.001	<.01	>.001

6. For an analysis of the combined impact of education of respondent and of spouse on adult mass communications behavior (one avenue for gaining knowledge), see C. R. Wright, "Social Structure and Mass Communication Behavior," in *The Idea of Social Structure: Papers in Honor of Robert K. Merton*, ed. L. Coser (New York: Harcourt Brace Jovanovich, 1975).

7. As the reader will recall from chapter 1, the sex composition of a cohort changes as it moves into old age because of the greater longevity of women. Since women, especially those with only modest or little education, are less informed about the filibuster and the Electoral College, some of the gross decline in knowledge observed in table 25 simply re-

flects the attrition of the male members of the cohort rather than the effects that aging would produce on a group constant in its composition. If this demographic component of the gross changes were eliminated by a statistical correction, the net decline owing to "aging" would be even smaller, strengthening the *general* conclusion we have drawn. The other demographic change occurring among *unrestricted* cohorts with aging is an increase in the proportion of whites because of earlier attrition of blacks. But as noted in chapter 1, this cannot affect any of our analyses, which were restricted always to the white adult population.

8. Because these figures are the means of many estimates from different surveys, there is no single base number or cell size for the various educational strata within each cohort. An indication of the range of cell sizes in the different surveys is provided by the following:

	Elementary School Group	High School Graduates	College Graduates
Early 1950s			
25–36	59_81	102–168	33–84
37–48	86–118	58–119	32–68
49–60	109_156	25–95	12–48
Late 1950s			
25–36	19–68	72–167	22–45
37–48	43–106	61–136	27–40
49–60	61–123	23–68	15–22
Early 1960s			
25–36	16–99	76–289	30–113
37–48	58–254	55–341	29–103
49–60	84–415	39–214	26–72
61–72	75–312	16–134	14–36
Late 1960s			
25–36	19–67	64–321	27–109
37–48	35–155	85–267	23–100
49–60	53–266	38–216	10–61
61–72	76–217	21–82	8–33

NOTES TO CHAPTER 4: CONTINUING LEARNING

1. The basic dual purposes of education—cultural transmission and preparation for intellectual development—have been succinctly noted by the late educational scholar I. L. Kandel, *The New Era in Education* (Boston: Houghton Mifflin, 1955). Also see C. R. Wright, "The Dilemma of Education through Mass Communication," *Teachers College Record* 63, no. 7 (April 1962): 517–26.

2. It is rare for a single survey to contain the information needed to explore the full chain of linkage between amount of formal schooling, adult communications behavior, and level of information about a variety of topics, such as have been addressed in previous chapters of this report. Ideally, a longitudinal design would trace these links throughout the life cycle of several cohorts of persons starting at different levels of schooling. Lacking such longitudinal data, however, we can still attempt more limited analysis. Robinson, for example, employed a "two stage" secondary analysis to address the problem. First he searched for the major background characteristics (including education) of individuals which correlated with knowledge about the Far East and combined these characteristics to form six groups of people. But he was unable to study

the media behavior of these groups, because no media usage questions had been asked on the survey. Therefore he used a second national survey, which contained media data, to see how people, classified into six groups similar to those in the first survey, used the media. Obviously there are dangers in such indirect procedures. (See J. Robinson, "Mass Communication and Information Diffusion," in *Current Perspectives in Mass Communication Research*, ed. F. Kline and P. Tichenor [Beverly Hills: Sage, 1972].) Robinson suggests that education is the major factor distinguishing his groups in both information levels and usage of the media.

Schramm and Wade demonstrate that the kind of source of mass communications relied upon by an adult makes a difference in the amount and accuracy of knowledge held about science, health, and certain public affairs. (Serena Wade and Wilbur Schramm, "The Mass Media as Sources of Public Affairs, Science and Health Knowledge," *Public Opinion Quarterly* 33 (1969): 197–209.

Further discussion and analysis of a limited range of data on level of education, media exposure, and political information are also touched upon in C. Wright, "Social Structure and Mass Communications Exposure: New Directions for Audience Analysis," in *The Idea of Social Structure: Papers in Honor of Robert K. Merton*, ed. L. Coser (New York: Harcourt Brace Jovanovich, 1975).

NOTES TO CHAPTER 5: THE RELATIVE EFFECTIVENESS OF SECONDARY AND HIGHER EDUCATION

1. As in the earlier chapters, we restrict our analysis to the white population aged twenty-five to seventy-two. For the analysis in this chapter, our pool of items was augmented by an additional batch of "academic" items from several other national surveys, which were judged insufficiently "rich" in content or were taken at inappropriate points in time for inclusion in the pool of surveys extensively analyzed in chapters 2 and 3. The Roper Center provided us with cross-tabulations of each of these items by education for all white respondents from twenty-five to seventy-two years of age. (These items are shown in Appendix C.) Since the indexes in this chapter are based on the total white sample without regard to age, they represent averages of sorts across a wide variety of American school settings, operating at many different times.

2. We are interested, in other words, in a measure which is related to neither the *height* nor the average *slope* of the curve relating knowledge to education. If we had a continuous measure of education, we could distinguish at least two additional aspects of the curve. If, as we have suggested, the typical deviation from linearity is toward an S-shaped curve, we could attempt to measure both the extent of the deviation— that is, the extent to which the learning is concentrated in a few years of the curriculum rather than "spread out"—and the location of the point of maximum slope—that is, the time at which the learning is concentrated. In fact, we attempted to work with measures of this sort, but the fact that education is usually coded on our questionnaires in rather gross categories ("1–8 years," for instance) makes the precision of such measures more apparent than real, since they must be interpolated from the midpoints of the categories. Falling back on a simple measure of location, however, somewhat obscures these distinctions. An item "located" near the midpoint of the educational process may be there because it is

learned abruptly at about that stage or because it is learned gradually and continuously over the entire course of education. On the other hand, if an item is "located" very early or very late, we may assume that it is also "concentrated" at that location. For this reason, we shall focus on such items in the analysis to follow.

3. This is algebraically equivalent, in fact, to the ratio of the two indexes employed in chapter 2, high school/elementary school to college/elementary school. Another reasonable index could be the point (in school years) at which half of those who are going to "learn" the item between grade school and college graduation have, in fact, learned it. If this index is interpolated from the three points we have been using in our analyses, however, it will order items in the same way as the ratio proposed here.

4. To avoid repeated warnings of the form "if we pretend that these measurements are from the same individuals," etc., and repeated use of quotation marks around the words "learn," "later," "earlier," etc., we shall emphasize the point once more here and then drop it. These data are cross-sectional, from individuals who have terminated their educations at different points. We have discussed the inferential problems this poses, but there is reason to suppose that, if anything, they are of smaller magnitude in this chapter than above. We are looking at the relative ordering of these learnings, which should not be systematically affected by whether each is actually taught at some point but simply discriminates between the individuals who reach that point and those who do not.

5. We have also discussed the impossibility of distinguishing between learnings which are "difficult" and those which are simply "specialized" or not widely taught. If we wish to speak of "specialization" rather than "difficulty," it may be preferable to work with the proportion of college graduates who answer an item correctly—i.e., the proportion who *ever* learn the item. (The two indexes are obviously closely related to one another.) Whichever notion (and corresponding index) we employ, we should expect to find that the more difficult (or more specialized) learnings are acquired later, just as we saw in the two special examples above.

6. Some time ago, one of us lamented the absence of data on issues which are not "hot," since this lack makes it difficult to study this and other important problems. Herbert H. Hyman, "Toward a Theory of Public Opinion," *Public Opinion Quarterly* 21 (1957): 54–60.

7. For a similar model of the emergence of public knowledge, see P. J. Tichenor, G. A. Donohue, and C. N. Olien, "Mass Media Flow and Differential Growth in Knowledge," *Public Opinion Quarterly* 34 (1970): 159–70.

8. Schramm et al. remark on this point, too. See Wilbur Schramm et al., "Knowledge and the Public Mind: A Preliminary Study of the Distribution and Sources of Science, Health, and Public Affairs Knowledge in the American Public," mimeographed (Stanford: Institute for Communication Research, 1967), p. 42.

NOTES TO CHAPTER 6: CONCLUSION

1. Paul Lauter and Florence Howe, *The Conspiracy of the Young* (New York: World Publishing Co., 1970).

2. Christopher Jencks et al., *Inequality: A Reassessment of the Effect of Family and Schooling in America* (New York: Basic Books, 1972), p. 256.

3. Kenneth Feldman and Theodore Newcomb, *The Impact of College on Students*, 2 vols. (San Francisco: Jossey-Bass, 1969), 1:2. Another case in point is provided by Philip Jacob, who, after careful examination of a great many of the early studies on value changes, concluded that college did not produce a "liberalization of student values" but a "socialization," so that "the individual can fit comfortably into the ranks of college alumni." Yet, because of the methodological limitations of the studies and their ambiguity, Barton's *re*examination of the same materials led him to question Jacob's conclusions. Newcomb and Feldman, mainly on the basis of newer studies in the decade that followed, also arrive at different conclusions. See Philip E. Jacob, *Changing Values in College: An Exploratory Study of the Impact of College Teaching* (New York: Harper, 1957); Allen H. Barton, *Studying the Effects of College Education, A Methodological Examination of "Changing Values in College"* (New Haven: Hazen Foundation, 1959).

4. James S. Coleman et al., *Equality of Educational Opportunity* (Washington, D.C.: Government Printing Office, 1966); Jencks et al., *Inequality*.

5. Gregory Bateson, "Social Planning and the Concept of 'Deutero-Learning,'" in *Readings in Social Psychology*, ed. Theodore Newcomb and E. L. Hartley (New York: Holt, 1947), pp. 121–28.

6. Ibid., p. 128.

7. Frederick Mosteller and Daniel Moynihan, eds., *On Equality of Educational Opportunity* (New York: Knopf, Vintage Books, 1972), p. 21.

8. See David E. Wiley, *Another Hour, Another Day: Quantity of Schooling, A Potent Path for Policy* (Chicago: University of Chicago Studies of Educative Processes, Report no. 3, July 1973). In the preface, Wiley proposes "that in any assessment of schooling the primary variable is the quantity of schooling that is received by a pupil." He then reanalyzes the portion of the Coleman data obtained from the sixth-grade pupils in the Detroit schools and finds "tremendous variations in the *amount* of schooling pupils receive" (p. 45, italics supplied), and further establishes that the "quantity of schooling is an important determinant of achievement" (p. 47) in mathematics, reading, and verbal skills. As noted in our text, there is no logical contradiction between the original findings of the Coleman report and our findings. Indeed, *implicit* in the Coleman report were findings most compatible with ours, waiting only for Wiley to make them explicit by thoughtful reformulation of the problem and sophisticated reanalysis. The amount of schooling to which a sixth-grade child is exposed has large *immediate* effects on knowledge, just as the total amount of schooling adults received has large enduring effects. For a short summary of this monograph, see David E. Wiley and Annegret Harnischfeger, "Explosion of a Myth: Quantity of Schooling and Exposure to Instruction, Major Educational Vehicles," *Educational Researcher* 3 (April 1974): 7–12.

9. Mosteller and Moynihan, *On Equality*, p. 44.

10. To be sure, our study among adults admits of the possibility that there were big differences initially among the students from different types of schools that were washed out with time and experience. Many studies conducted on preadults have reported positive findings on the relation between school variables and student achievement. They are thus in contradiction with the Coleman findings and possibly with our own find-

ings—but possibly not, since our measurements postdate schooling by many years. For a summary of such studies, see James W. Guthrie et al., *Schools and Inequality* (Cambridge, Mass.: MIT Press, 1971), especially chap. 4.

11. Jencks et al., *Inequality*, p. 8; italics added.

12. "Perspectives on 'Inequality: A Reassessment of the Effect of Family and Schooling in America,' " *Harvard Educational Review* 43 (1973, no. 1): 38. A survey of a national sample of high school boys in 1966, with three annual follow-ups to observe change, was conducted by the Survey Research Center. It extended Coleman's and Jencks's conclusion in finding no differential between high schools in their effects on values, attitudes, and other noncognitive traits. But its authors stress carefully that the finding could "indicate that our schools . . . are succeeding in making equally rich educational opportunities available to nearly all who desire them. . . . Public schools show a great deal of similarity with one another" (Lloyd D. Johnston and Jerald G. Bachman, "The Functions of Educational Institutions in Adolescent Development," in *Understanding Adolescence*, ed. James F. Adams, 2d ed. [Boston: Allyn & Bacon, 1973], pp. 237–38).

13. Jencks et al., *Inequality*, p. 88.

14. Stephen Withey et al., *A Degree and What Else: Correlates and Consequences of a College Education* (New York: McGraw-Hill, 1973). See chap. 6, by John Robinson, for findings on knowledge and information seeking consistent with ours.

15. Wilbur Schramm et al., "Knowledge and the Public Mind: A Preliminary Study of the Distribution and Sources of Science, Health, and Public Affairs Knowledge in the American Public," mimeographed (Stanford: Institute for Communication Research, 1967), p. 120.

16. In a critical review and reanalysis of the net influence of education on subsequent worldly success over and above the contribution of the socioeconomic background of the parents, Bowles suggests that parents' education and occupation (measured on the usual dimension of *status or rank*) do not adequately represent the contribution of family background. He suggests, for example, that parental income or wealth is only moderately correlated with parental occupation and education. The former aspects of background are therefore not adequately controlled in conventional analyses. Some measures of such missing aspects could be included in future semisecondary analyses, although considerable caution would have to be exercised in treating the offspring's reports as free from error. Of course, the "net worth" of the parents does not have the same relevance to knowledge as it obviously has to the offspring's worldly success, and therefore it would be of less importance to include in secondary analysis of our problem. Bowles goes on to suggest that the usual classification of the rank of an occupation does not tap the aspect of "position of the parents in the hierarchy of work relations," "the degree of independence and control exercised" which, in turn, leads the parents to transmit certain kinds of values and character traits of consequence for the child's success. Surely one could make a good start in following this lead simply by recoding parental occupations in a variety of unconventional and refined ways that would bring us closer to whatever is hypothesized as the potent element of the occupational complex. And more direct measures of the kinds of values the parents urged on children have been readily obtained in a great many surveys and could be piggybacked and incorporated into future semisecondary analyses of the effects

of education. See Samuel Bowles, "Schooling and Inequality from Generation to Generation," *Journal of Political Economy* 80 (no. 3, pt. II, 1972): S219–S251. For a critique of Bowles's critique which argues that the influence of *education* is generally *under*estimated, see Gary Becker, "Comment," ibid., pp. S252–55. For empirical evidence that runs counter to Bowles, see William H. Sewell and Robert M. Hauser, "Causes and Consequences of Higher Education: Models of the Status Attainment Process," *American Journal of Agricultural Economics*, vol. 54 (1972), especially p. 858.

17. The list we have presented does not exhaust the countries that might have been chosen. Sweden, for example, had much to recommend it; Belgium might have been included in our initial list. But there are many considerations that must be entertained jointly in arriving at a good choice for such a comparative design. Compromises are inevitable, and Canada, on balance and despite the limitations of the data, seemed to us the optimal choice for the present.

18. The 1955 survey did not include any measure of social class origins for either country, and there is no way to control this variable in estimating the net effect of education on spelling ability. However, since higher education has been reserved for a much smaller minority in Canada—the opportunity to achieve it is perhaps three to four times greater in the United States—it seems reasonable to infer that the gross effects at the college level in Canada are more likely to include the selective recruitment of a more elite group. Thus the conclusion already drawn, that Canadian education is not more effective in this sphere, seems compelling.

Index